TRADERS PRESS, INC.

P.O. BOX 6206
GREENVILLE, SOUTH CAROLINA 29606

BOOKS AND GIFTS FOR
INVESTORS AND TRADERS

800-927-8222

Martin Pring on Market Momentum

Martin Pring on
Market Momentum

by
Martin J. Pring
International Institute for
Economic Research, Inc.

P.O. Box 624
Gloucester, VA 23061-0624
1-800-221-7514
804-694-0415
Fax 804-694-0028

ISBN 1-55738-508-4

Printed in the United States of America

1   2   3   4   5   6   7   8   9   0

Production work by Shepherd, Inc. Book production manager was Mary Jess.

Printed and bound by Braun-Brumfield, Inc.

Dust jacket designed by Lisa Pring.

To my wife Lisa

Contents

INTRODUCTION

Over the years many general books on technical analysis, such as John Murphy's *Technical Analysis of the Futures Markets* or my *Technical Analysis Explained,* have covered the subject of momentum in one or two fleeting chapters. Because these books address a wide range of concepts and approaches, they leave insufficient room to explore the subject in the depth that it requires. This book, which is completely devoted to momentum, has been written from the perspective of filling that vacuum.

To my knowledge, this is the first book to be completely devoted to this subject. This is an important point because momentum is arguably the most widely used but least understood concept employed by traders. I have written *Market Momentum* to delve into the topic a little deeper with the hope of helping you to get a better grasp of the subject. A supplementary objective is to broaden your horizon by describing in-depth a number of different indicators. By and large, the book is a compendium of indicators that have been developed and used over the years. Some new "wrinkles" for some of these concepts are offered for consideration, as well as a few new indicators of my own.

The book will have a special appeal to the growing number of traders and investors who use computer software charting packages. This group includes individuals as well as the huge number of traders at major financial institutions around the world. For this reason many of the examples will be global in nature and not limited to U.S. markets. Since the principles of technical analysis can be applied to *any* freely traded market, the wide scope should not hinder U.S.-based traders and investors who may limit their activities to local markets.

An introductory knowledge of technical analysis is assumed, so *Market Momentum* is primarily targeted at those who have already gained some experience; namely, those traders and investors who have made mistakes and want to learn how to avoid making them again. The book departs from most financial publications, which promise instant and easy wealth. If you are looking for such a Holy Grail, don't read any further. I cannot help you; nor can anyone else. If, on the other hand, you have already developed a curiosity and fascination with charts and want to expand your knowledge, please read on.

This book does not have all of the answers to your questions about momentum. As a matter of fact, it may well raise more questions. However, it is guaranteed to place you farther up the learning curve. I say "farther up," because the more you study technical analysis, the more you will find there is to learn. You may *think* that you are at the end of the curve, but there is no end. As with all art forms, technical analysis is a never-ending learning process.

In the "old" days before personal computers, calculating most momentum indicators was a slow and monotonous process. As a result, few traders bothered to use these indicators. Now, with the touch of a button it is possible to calculate, plot, and manipulate even the most complicated formulas. There are two schools of thought. The first is the traditional one which argues in favor of manual calculations because the trader can get a better "feel" for the data. The second school believes that this labor-intensive method is not important and that the use of the computer gives the trader a far wider range of indicators with which to do the analysis. Deciding between the two will depend a great deal on the individual. Some people have an affinity for making their own calculations and plotting their own data, while others prefer to use the computer so that their time is freed to consider a wider range of markets. It is probably best to choose the method that makes you feel more comfortable.

Whatever method is adopted, its overriding principle should be to keep things as simple and uncomplicated as possible. The reliability of indicators should continually be questioned, and careful thought should supersede blind application. This by no means rules out using the computer; indeed, I favor that approach because it allows us to quickly and easily test the huge array of indicators that have been developed. The most important thing is not to let the fun and ease of using a computer keep you from thinking and questioning.

Generally, most successful traders limit themselves to the use of just a few favored indicators, perhaps five or six at the most. Typically, they choose these oscillators after much investigation and research. One of the objectives of this book is to introduce you to as many indicators as possible. Having learned about the available selection, you must then decide which to select for your own technical arsenal. From time to time, I will point out what I believe are the weaknesses inherent in some of the indicators, but you shouldn't take my word for it. Test them for yourself. In addition, I suggest that you carry out the same tests on the indicators that I review favorably.

As used here, the term "momentum" refers to the velocity of a price trend. This indicator measures whether a rising trend is accelerating or decelerating or whether prices are declining at a faster or slower pace. There is one indicator included in many charting packages, and it's literally called "momentum." I believe it is a misnomer because "momentum" is really a generic term that embraces a range of specific indicators that attempts to measure this velocity factor. Momentum is represented in graphic form as a fluctuating line that is continually oscillating from one extreme to the other. All momentum indicators oscillate, so it is reasonable to call them "oscillators" as an alternative descriptive title. I mention this because many books refer to certain types of momentum indicators as "oscillators" and others as "momentum indicators." To me they are synonyms, and they are used as such in this book.

In today's fast-paced global marketplace, there are many vehicles that can be traded: currencies, commodities, bonds, stocks, stock market indexes, and precious metals—just to name a few. The same principles apply for trading all of them. The two exceptions are open interest, which is an aspect of futures data, and opening prices, which are not available for stocks. Throughout the book I use the term "security" when referring in general to these vehicles. This usage avoids constant repetition of the individual items.

The first two chapters describe the principles of momentum interpretation. It is my belief that each momentum indicator is subject to these same principles of interpretation; therefore, it is better to deal with them at the outset than to be forced to repeat them when describing the specific indicators themselves. Each indicator has its own idiosyncracies, and each emphasizes specific characteristics of these momentum principles. These characteristics are described in later chapters.

It is a fact that prices in any freely traded market are determined more by the *attitude* of traders to the emerging fundamentals than by the fundamentals themselves. This means that markets (i.e., price trends) are essentially driven by psychological forces. We know from our own personal experience in the markets that our emotions dart from one extreme to another—from greed to fear, from hope to despair, and so forth. This reality is what causes momentum indicators to fluctuate from overbought to oversold extremes. In a sense, momentum reflects crowd psychology and measures the intensity of the general mood of market participants. In this respect, the chart opposite measures market sentiment and shows how it compares in some ways to a rate-of-change indicator, a type of momentum oscillator that I describe in the book. There are some subtle differences between the two series from time to time, but by and large they move in tandem. This shows that momentum is really another way of looking at market sentiment. I do not mean to imply that we should totally disregard indicators of market sentiment, for there are times when they can show us a totally different dimension of what is actually happening in the market.

I regard technical analysis as the *art* of identifying trend reversals at a relatively early stage and riding that reverse trend until the *weight* of the evidence proves satisfactorily that the trend has reversed. Many indicators work well over most periods under study, but no one indicator works perfectly at all times. The best approach for identifying trends is to use several *scientifically* derived indicators and then to sift through the signals they provide. If the weight of the evidence confirms that a trend is underway, it is time to make your move.

Also a personal note: I have used the term "he" throughout this book to be non-gender in its meaning. It just makes both the writing and reading of the text much easier.

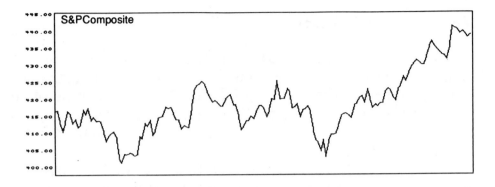

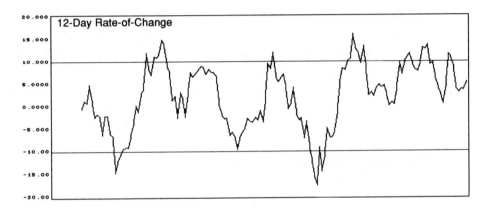

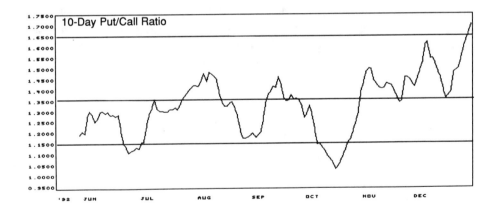

ACKNOWLEDGEMENTS

There are many people who I would like to thank for their help in preparing this book. Several friends took time out from their busy schedules to read parts of the manuscript. Special thanks therefore go to Tom Aspray, Alex Elder, Thom Hartle and John Murphy, as well as John Conroy who helped to "translate" the manuscript into readable English.

In the past, I have always written books for major publishers which has made life relatively easy. Self-publishing is very rewarding but does not come without its headaches. In this respect our North American distribution agents, Probus Publishing, spearheaded by Michael Jeffers and Kevin Cummins were extremely helpful and encouraging. Ed Dobson of Traders Press also deserves special mention for his encouragement and substantial marketing support. No book can be published without care and attention from the production house. In this case thanks go to Stephen Shepherd and Mary Jess of Shepherd Inc. for helping to meet our publishing deadlines.

I would also like to thank Brenda Singer of the International Institute for providing tremendous support and encouragement when things didn't quite go according to plan. The biggest debt of all goes to my wife Lisa who enthusiastically and without *one* complaint spent many long hours checking and correcting manuscripts, charts, and page proofs.

chapter 1

PRINCIPLES OF MOMENTUM INTERPRETATION– PART I

- **A Few Words on Time Frames**
- **Principles of Momentum Interpretation**
- **Overbought and Oversold**
- **Divergences**
- **Significance of a Divergence**
- **The Divergence Trap**
- **Complex Divergences**

Momentum measures the velocity of a price move. It is a generic term. Just as the word "fruit" encompasses apples, oranges, grapes, bananas, and so forth, "momentum" embraces a host of individual indicators such as rate-of-change (ROC), relative strength indicator (RSI), moving average convergence divergence (MACD), and stochastics. Each indicator has different attributes, but the principles for interpretation apply to all of them.

For a better understanding, let's examine the analogy further. Two common characteristics of fruit, for example, are that it is sweet and is almost always grown during the warmest season. Some kinds of fruit are sweeter than others, some require very hot temperatures, and still others require a long growing season and so on. Momentum indicators also share common characteristics, but the indicators themselves, like the different kinds of fruit, differ individually in their interpretive properties. Some are better suited to specific rules than others. We shall learn later, for instance, that the rate-of-change indicator lends itself to trendline construction. So does the stochastic indicator, but that is not how it is normally interpreted. This chapter and the next address these common principles of interpretation. After we have examined the individual indicators themselves, we can consider their underlying concepts, their construction and the peculiarities of interpreting these helpful investment tools.

A Few Words on Time Frames

In technical analysis we are concerned with identifying trend reversals at a relatively early stage and assume that the new trend will continue riding that trend until *it* reverses. The operating assumption is always that the prevailing trend is in force until the *weight of the evidence* proves otherwise. By this I mean that more than one momentum indicator must point to a trend reversal; one by itself is insufficient evidence. All indicators, however valid, can and do fail from time to time. Therefore, we must take a consensus approach and use several indicators to determine the direction of a trend. When a majority of them are in agreement, we can be more confident that the trend has indeed reversed. It is this weight of the evidence provided by momentum indicators that primarily concerns us here.

There are many types of trends, but the most widely followed are short, intermediate, and long. These last approximately 3–6 weeks, 6–39 weeks, and 1–2 years, respectively. When attempting to analyze a trend, it is crucially important to keep in mind the type of trend that you are trying to measure. Turning an oil tanker around is a much more formidable task than changing the direction of a sports car. Markets operate in a similar fashion. The reversal of a short-term trend takes less time and involves a substantially smaller change in collective psychology than the reversal of a long-term trend. This also means that a signal from a momentum indicator with a long time span has far greater significance than a buy or sell alert from one with a 5- or 10-day span. Investing and trading decisions should be made with this perspective in mind.

Most of the material later in this chapter will focus on short, and to a lesser extent, intermediate trends (i.e., trends lasting 3–6 and 6–39 weeks, respectively). Nevertheless, it is still of paramount importance for any trader to gain some understanding of the current position of the long-term trend. Just as the unwary swimmer finds it difficult to swim against the tide, the short-term trader will certainly encounter problems if he is swimming against the main trend. Time and again we find that trend-spotting systems often will lead traders to make money-losing decisions based on erroneous signals. These are short and intermediate-term price trends that are swimming against the tide of the primary trend.

It is not always possible, of course, to ascertain the direction of the main trend, especially in its initial stages. Even so, it is very important, even for short-term traders, to try and understand the direction and duration of the main or primary trend. If you know that the trend is down, and if you are also aware of the fact that moving against it is usually unprofitable, you will be wary of taking long positions even though the short-term momentum indicators show that the momentum is favorable. To do so only invites failure, no matter how attractive the opportunity *may* seem at the time.

The momentum indicator is normally plotted as an oscillator underneath the security that is being monitored, making convenient comparisons easy. Occasionally, two or more indicators will be plotted along with the price. This practice offers a comparison of different momentum approaches or different time spans. The objective is always to determine whether the weight of the evidence shows a trend in reversal. The more evidence that points in a particular direction—be it up or down—the greater the odds that the momentum has shifted.

Principles of Momentum Interpretation

The remainder of this chapter and all of the next chapter discusses the various techniques of momentum interpretation. These methods can be divided approximately into two broad categories. The first category deals with overbought and oversold conditions and divergences. I will call these "momentum characteristics." The second category deals with interpretive principles that measure reversals in the momentum trend itself, the assumption being that when momentum changes direction prices will follow sooner or later.

Trend-determining techniques such as trendline violations, moving average crossovers, and the like can be applied to momentum as well as to price. The important difference is that a trend reversal in momentum is just that—a reversal in momentum. Momentum typically reverses along with price, often with a small time lag. However, just because oscillators change direction doesn't always mean that prices will also. Normally, a reversal in the momentum trend is evidence of a price-trend reversal signal. In effect, this momentum signal acts as a supplementary "witness" in our weight-of-the evidence approach to determine the validity of a trend reversal. I will have more to say on this a little later, but for now take special note of this fact: *Actual buy and sell signals can come only from a reversal in trend of the actual price, not from a reversal in the momentum series.*

Overbought and Oversold

All momentum series have the characteristics of an oscillator as they move from one extreme to another. Figure 1.1 illustrates this point. These extremes are known as "overbought" and "oversold levels". In my seminars I often equate these zones with a leash attached to an unruly dog taking a walk. The animal continually strains at the leash, moving from one side of the sidewalk to the other. One moment he roams to the curb on his extreme left, and

Figure 1.1

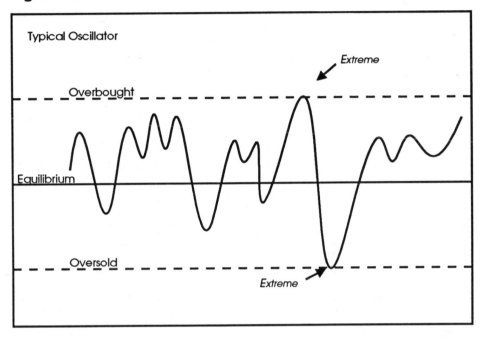

the next he scampers back toward the lawns on his right as far as the leash will allow him. Market momentum works in a similar manner.

Some indicators, such as the RSI, are calculated in such a way that they have finite extremes above or below which the momentum cannot go. In these cases there is an established "default" level for the overbought and oversold lines. For the most commonly used 14-day time span, these lines are drawn at 70 for overbought and 30 for oversold. Conversely, other indicators, such as the "rate-of-change," have no such theoretical boundaries, at least on the upside. This means that we must judge for ourselves where to establish the levels for overbought and oversold. Chapter 3 describes how to use the ROC indicator. For now, let us simply say that these lines should be drawn so that the space between them includes the bulk of the trading activity. In this case, try to think of the oscillator as a rubber leash that from time to time will be stretched beyond its normal length. Drawing lines to represent the extremes is not particularly helpful. What we must do is find the metaphorical equivalent of the end of the leash; that is, the points that include most of the rallies and reactions in the market under study.

The character and magnitude of an oscillator swing depends on three factors. These are: (1) the nature of the formula relating to the indicator's construction, (2) the volatility of the security being monitored, and (3) the time span being used. It is not usually possible, for example, to compare the oscillator of a docile utility stock with that of a volatile mining stock. The latter's volatility stems from the fact that the earnings of mining companies are much more difficult to predict than those of the somewhat staid utilities. The greater uncertainty that results allows for a wide variance in views and attitudes toward such companies. Even when earnings can be predicted, mining company profits tend to fluctuate wildly in comparison with those of utilities. A final contributor to the stability of utility prices is the fact that investors in these issues are, in general, far more conservative than people who invest in mining securities. They will be looking for safety and yield, whereas actual and potential owners of mining stocks are more concerned with a quick capital gain. Since the perception of what constitutes a sharp price move will be different for a conservative investor than for a trader or speculator, momentum levels between widely differing securities cannot be meaningfully contrasted. The best way to determine momentum in this case is to compare the current reading to an historical range.

Time spans are also important in determining the magnitude of a swing in momentum series. For instance, it is conceivable that the price of a stock could increase by 30% during the course of a year. Thus a 12-month rate-of-change may easily rally to the range of 30% or higher. However, it is highly unlikely, except in the case of a takeover or other unusual event, for the price to rally 30% in the course of five-day period. While an oscillator based on a short-term time span is subject to *more* oscillations than one constructed from a long-term one, the *magnitude* of these fluctuations will be much smaller.

The technical interpretation of overbought and oversold lines is that they represent an intelligent point for anticipating a trend reversal. An overbought condition is where you should consider taking profits or reducing your exposure. For example, if you are holding three gold contracts and the price rallies to where it generates an overbought reading, you might wish to take some partial profits. Even though the trend may continue, or the price has failed to cross below its moving average, or it violates a trendline, the overbought reading by itself indicates that *the odds* of a reversal have increased. If the *risks* of a top have grown, then it makes sense to reduce your exposure. If press stories concerning the bullish nature of the security are beginning to emerge, and your emotions are telling you to buy more, use these signs as further confirming evidence that it is a good time to begin to *decrease* rather than *increase* your exposure.

On the other hand, if you believe that the main trend is down and you have been waiting for a short-term bounce as a time to sell, an overbought reading is as good a time as any. For the same reason, it would normally be a grave mistake to even consider making a purchase when an oscillator signals an overbought condition. The problem with this interpretation is that this is precisely the time when most people have the urge to buy, because rising prices attract optimism, positive news stories, and bullish sentiment.

The opposite is true for an oversold condition. Few people want to buy after prices have been falling and the news is inevitably discouraging. Unfortunately, this is the time when we need to control our shaking hands, pick up the phone, and call our friendly broker. This is also the moment when we should overcome (at all costs) the temptation to take a short position. In fact, the correct action is to cover part of any outstanding short positions. At the time, you may think that it is possible to make more money by holding on to your investment, but, believe me, taking some partial profits will put you in a far more objective frame of mind when that inevitable rally gets underway. Figure 1.2 shows that when the momentum indicator moves through its overbought or oversold level and then re-crosses it on its way back to the equilibrium level that this often represents a good buying or selling signal.

The importance of an overbought/oversold reading will depend on the time frame under consideration. For example, if the period used in constructing the indicator is five days, the implications from extreme readings will be nowhere near as profound as those from a momentum indicator spanning twelve months.

Oscillators that move in the direction of prevailing market trends tend to move to a greater extreme and stay there longer than those that move against the trend. In figure 1.3, we see that the main trend is up. Note how the overbought and oversold extremes are positioned equidistant from the equilibrium level shown by the solid line. Rallies in the indicator have a tendency to move well into overbought territory and remain there for a longer time than do reactions. Reactions are almost always reversed at the oversold

Figure 1.2

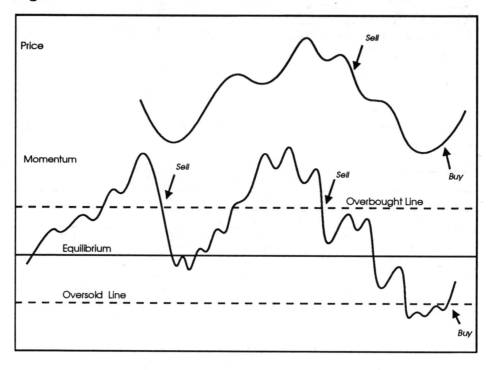

Figure 1.3

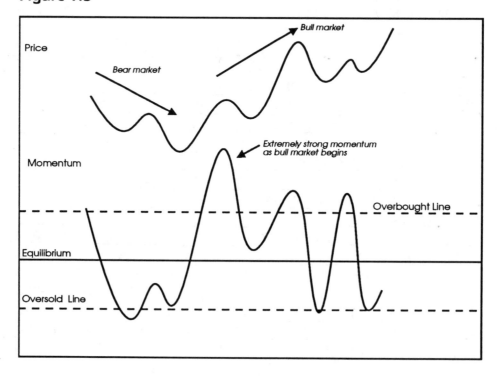

line or sometimes even before the oscillator reaches that point. This trait itself is a primary characteristic of a bull market.

You may also notice that the initial thrust off the final market low accompanies what I call a "mega-overbought condition." A mega-overbought condition is a sign of a very young and vibrant bull market. The fact that an oscillator is able to generate such a condition can be used with additional evidence of a trend reversal to indicate that the bulls are running once more. In effect, such action signals that the state of equilibrium between buyers and sellers has unequivocally shifted in favor of buyers. This is about the only instance when an *investor* can justify opening a long position if a particular market is saturated with buyers. Even so, the only rationale for opening long in this case is that the investor has a long-term time horizon. Whenever an oscillator experiences a mega-overbought condition, higher prices almost always follow at some point down the road.

In the case of oversold extremes, the same condition also applies in reverse. In other words, a characteristic of a bear market is an oscillator that tends to (1) move beyond the accepted norm, (2) remain in an oversold state for an extended period, or (3) do both. Another sign of a bear market occurs when a price decline following a new bull-market high pushes a momentum indicator to an extreme low that is well beyond anything seen in the previous six months or so. This implies that sellers now have the upper hand. The fact that it is possible for the momentum indicator to plunge so sharply and so deeply is by itself a sign that the character of the market has changed. This is illustrated in figure 1.4. An actual marketplace example is shown in chart 3.2.

Divergences

When price and momentum are moving in the same direction, they are said to be "in gear." There is nothing important to be learned from this state of affairs except that the trend is healthy. However, when momentum does not confirm the price, beware: The prevailing trend may be about to reverse. In the description of overbought and oversold conditions we assumed that the oscillator peaks and troughs at roughly the same time as the price. This is not often the case, however. An equally likely possibility is that the momentum indicator will turn *ahead* of the price. Think of a pen thrown into the

Figure 1.4

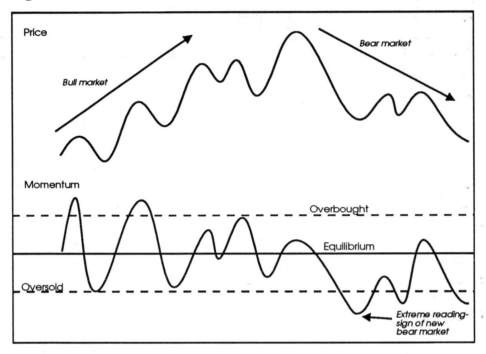

air. The pen reaches its point of maximum velocity the instant it leaves the hand. It continues to rise—but at a slower and slower rate—until it is overcome by the force of gravity. Only then does it begin to fall back toward the ground. The same effect occurs figuratively in the marketplace, where the price action is the pen and the momentum indicator depicts the velocity of its rise in a graphic way. Figure 1.5 looks at momentum in a slightly different way. It shows the price appreciating in every period,—first in increasing amounts, later in smaller increments. This example shows quite clearly not only how the price continues to rise but how the *speed or velocity of the advance decelerates before the final peak.* All that a momentum indicator is trying to do, is measure this acceleration and deceleration factor and present it in a graphic format.

Figure 1.6 shows how this works in practice. Point A marks the point of maximum velocity, but the price continues to rally at a slower and slower pace until point C. This conflict between momentum and price is known as a "divergence," since the oscillator is out of sync with the price. It is also called a "negative divergence,"

Figure 1.5

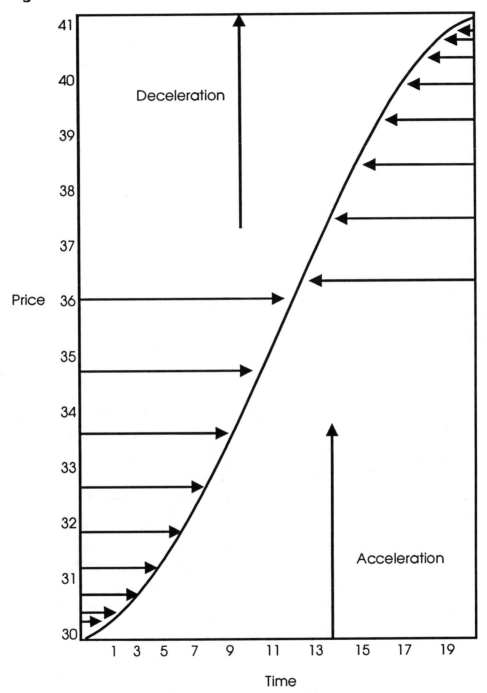

Figure 1.6

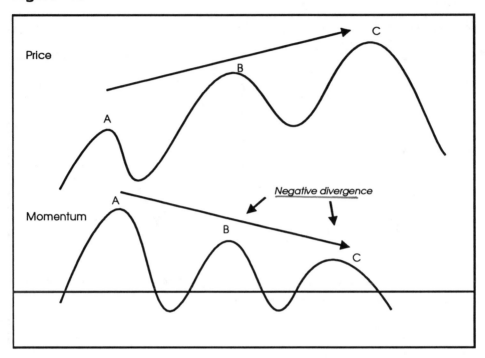

because rising prices are supported by weaker and weaker under-lying momentum. The deteriorating momentum represents an early warning sign of some underlying weakness in the price trend.

In one respect markets are like houses: They take longer to build than they do to tear down. Markets spend most of their time advancing rather than declining. This means that *the lead charac-teristics of momentum indicators are usually more pronounced at market peaks than at troughs.* Even so, divergences also occur at market bottoms where they are called "positive," because momen-tum hits bottom before price does. This phenomenon can be likened to a car in neutral gear being pushed over a hill. As the vehicle progresses down the slope, it gradually picks up speed, or momentum. Then, as the gradient levels toward the bottom of the hill, the car slows down. Even though the speed is decreasing, the car continues to move before it finally slows to a halt. In this example the speed of the car should be thought of as market momentum and its position as the price. Positive divergences, as shown in figure 1.7, tell us that even though a price is declining it is declining at a slower and slower rate. In this instance, the

Figure 1.7

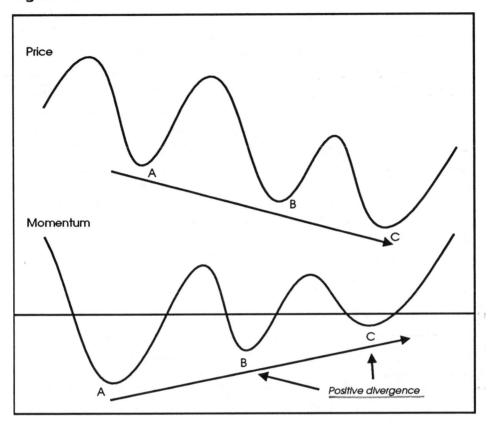

technical position is said to be "improving" or getting "stronger". Indeed, if you think a market is in the process of reaching its bottom and you do *not* see a divergence, you may want to reconsider your analysis, because most market bottoms are preceded by at least one positive divergence.

It is very important to note that although they indicate either a deteriorating or an improving market condition, *divergences in and of themselves do not signal that the prevailing trend has reversed.* That signal can come only from some kind of trend-reversal sign generated by the price itself. This cue could take the form of a price-pattern completion, a moving-average crossover, or some other signal. When this occurs technicians say that the divergence has been "confirmed" by the price.

Interpreting negative-momentum divergences can be compared to watching a moving car that has a mechanical problem.

The car has just begun to make a clanking noise. Nevertheless, the driver is still able to propel the car faster and faster because the problem is in its early stages. To an observer from afar who cannot hear the noise, it appears that the car is in great shape.

Similarly, in the case of a negative-momentum divergence a market observer can see that the price is moving higher and higher. To him it would seem that the trend is perfectly healthy. Indeed, the fact that prices are advancing gives a misplaced sense of confidence. Yet, if he could see that the underlying momentum is deteriorating, he would be far more inclined to sell. By the same token, the driver of the car, aware from the din under the hood that some serious trouble was developing, would be inclined to visit the repair shop or risk a breakdown. The lesson is this: If we accept the premise that a malfunctioning car is likely to require more attention the longer an engine problem is ignored, then we should agree that the greater the number of divergences an indicator shows the more serious the consequences of a reversal in trend when it inevitably takes place.

Another sign of a mature trend occurs when the momentum index moves strongly in one direction but the price fails to follow through with any degree of gusto. This indicates that the price is tired of moving in the direction of the prevailing trend; for despite the strong momentum, thrust prices are unable to respond. This is an unusual but nevertheless powerful phenomenon. Figures 1.8 and 1.9 indicate this phenomenum for both market tops and bottoms respectively.

Significance of a Divergence

Divergences are significant for three reasons: their number, the time span separating them, and the closeness of the momentum reading to the equilibrium level at the final turning point in price. Let's consider each one in turn.

Generally, the more divergences that occur, the greater their significance. In the case of a market peak, a large number of negative divergences indicates a trend that is undergoing a very long and serious weakening process. We might think of this situation as analogous to a sick person who needs to undergo surgery but keeps postponing the operation. Timely medical atten-

Figure 1.8

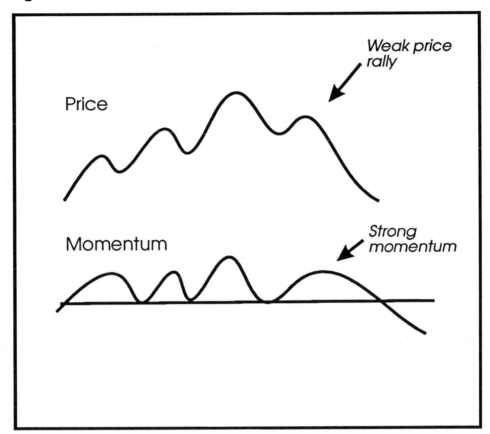

tion could soon remedy the problem, but the continual postpone-
ments only aggravate the condition. Hence, a cure becomes much
more difficult to attain, and the suffering increases commensurately.

The same can be said of negative divergences. The initial
divergence indicates a need for corrective action in the market, but
the failure of the price to respond indicates that fewer and fewer
informed investors are purchasing the security as more and more
uninformed buyers move in. This additional "distribution" means
that the corrective process, when it finally does begin, is likely to be
that much more severe. The same principle applies to positive
divergences at market bottoms. The more plentiful they are, the
stronger the technical position.

The time period separating the divergence is also important.
Usually, the greater the time span between the peak in momentum

Figure 1.9

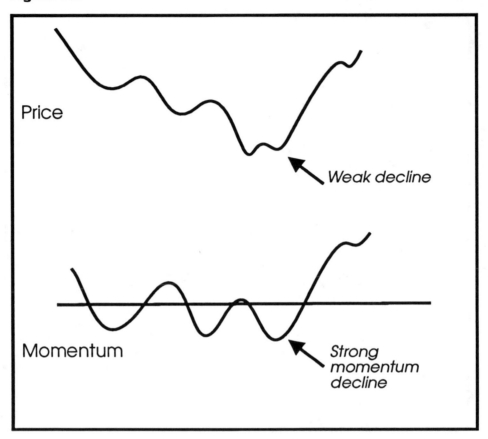

Price

Weak decline

Momentum

Strong momentum decline

and the peak in price, the greater the significance. By the same token, it is important to use a little common sense by relating the series of divergences to the prevailing trend.

In figure 1.10, for instance, the actual peak in momentum appears at point A1, but that momentum peak reflects the rally that occurred between points A and B. The divergences are important from the point of view of the prevailing trend (i.e., the rallies between C and D are B1, B2, and B3). This returns to the idea discussed earlier of determining whether the trend you are analyzing is short, intermediate, or long-term. For the purpose of this example, we might make the assumption that the momentum indicator reflects the short-term trend. Consequently, the A-B and C-D price movements are really intermediate up trends. The thick line represents an intermediate down trend. This means that it is not really valid *from the point of view of divergence analysis* to

Figure 1.10

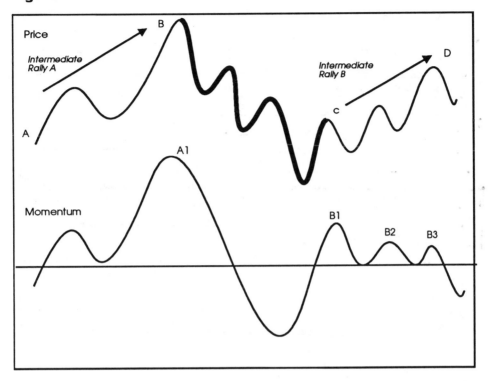

compare peaks in the momentum of two short-term trends with two different intermediate trends.

The type of trend being monitored raises the final point concerning the length of time separating divergences. If a trader is analyzing short-term price movements he would expect the divergences to take place over the course of a week or so at most. On the other hand, an investor is primarily concerned with the primary trend, so he would look for divergences associated with a momentum graph constructed from an intermediate time frame. In this case three divergences in an intermediate oscillator are obviously more significant than three divergences in a short-term momentum series.

It should be clear, that the length of the time span separating divergences is a function of the trend itself. In other words, when there are two, three, or four divergences within one short-term trend, their primary significance rests in their relation to the next short-term trend. Their secondary importance relates to the type of trend under consideration. For example, divergences between intermediate trends have significance for the next primary trend, whereas divergences in short-term momentum are important for the next intermediate trend and so on.

Our final point concerning the importance of divergences concerns the level at which the last divergence takes place. At market peaks, rallies in a momentum indicator that are barely able to move above the zero level are often followed by a very sharp decline, as shown in figure 1.11. This is one of the few instances in technical analysis when a clue hints at the character of the next move. I must stress that such instances are not *always* followed by a sharp drop. Remember: Technical analysis is far from perfect. However, in most cases when weak momentum of this nature *is confirmed by a trend-break in the price*, be on your guard for a larger-than-normal sell-off.

The same principle, only in reverse, holds for market bottoms. This occurs when the price hits a new low following a number of positive divergences. In this case, though, the latest decline barely takes the momentum indicator below the equilibrium point. When the action has been confirmed by a positive break in the price trend, an explosive advance usually follows, see figure 1.12.

Figure 1.11

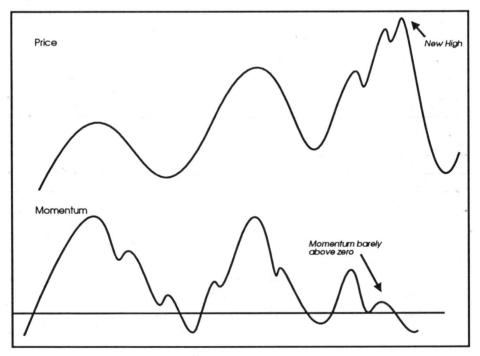

Figure 1.12

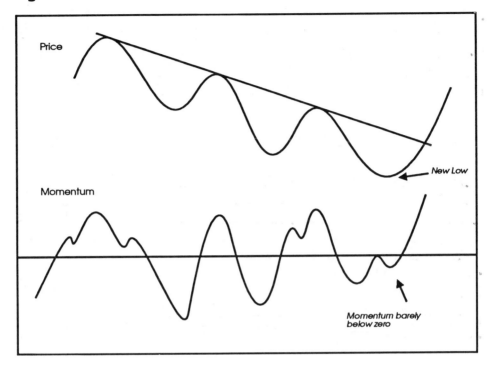

In summing up the significance of divergences, we could use the following meteorological analogy. A woman leaves her house in the morning. As she steps outside she looks up to see a sky filled with dark clouds. The woman naturally concludes that there is a good chance of rain and takes an umbrella or raincoat with her as an insurance policy against getting soaked.

The same scenario applies to money management. If you see a number of negative divergences clouding the market, it makes sense to bring along some "insurance." This protection could take the forms of modest profit-taking, tightening stops, or hedging your position.

Of course, it is quite possible for a high-pressure front to arrive and blow the clouds away. The woman believes rain is in the offing, but she does not actually know this to be a fact until she holds out her hand, actually feels the drops begin to fall, and runs for cover or puts up her umbrella. That's why it is of paramount importance to wait for an actual reversal in the price trend to confirm that the underlying momentum is weak.

Taking the analogy a step further, it is generally accepted that the darker the clouds, the heavier the rain shower if it does materialize. The same is true for the relationship between price and momentum. The completion of any given trendline price pattern signals a reversal in trend. However, the more divergences that precede this break, when combined with the other principles of momentum significance discussed, the *more* emphasis is placed on the significance and intensity of the break.

The Divergence Trap

Most of the time divergences proceed in a fairly orderly way. By this I mean that they get progressively lower or higher depending on the direction of the trend. Then, just as you expect the price to drop as at point A in figure 1.13, a final rally develops out of the blue. Normally, this advance will push the momentum indicator back above at least one of the two previous peaks, causing the wary trader to surrender his bearish sentiment. Typically, this latest rally will prove to be a "divergence trap" after which the price will *then* fall in the manner previously expected. This final burst will probably

Figure 1.13

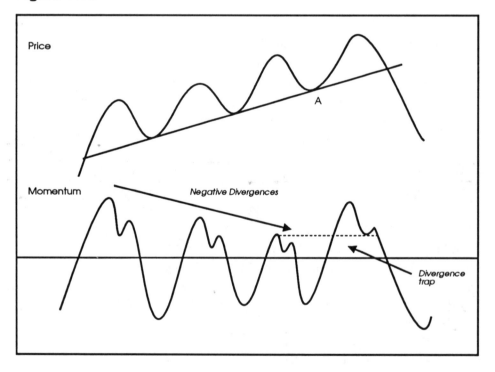

result from some unanticipated news event that causes short covering. When the short-covering ends, there is very little to support the price and down it goes. Figure 1.14 shows this same phenomenon for a market in the process of bottoming.

Complex Divergences

Price trends are determined by the interaction of many different time cycles. Most momentum indicators, however, reflect only one cycle, since they are constructed using a specific time span. One way to solve this problem is to overlay two different momentum indicators constructed from two different time spans and compare them. Normally, both series will move in a broadly similar direction. A divergence in the indicator signals an impending trend reversal.

Figure 1.15 shows two oscillators. Most of the time they are moving in the same direction, which tells us very little. On the other hand, when the shorter of the two reaches a peak and then falls toward the zero level while the series with the longer time span

Figure 1.14

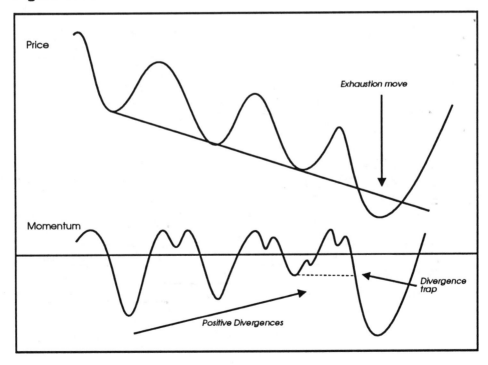

Figure 1.15

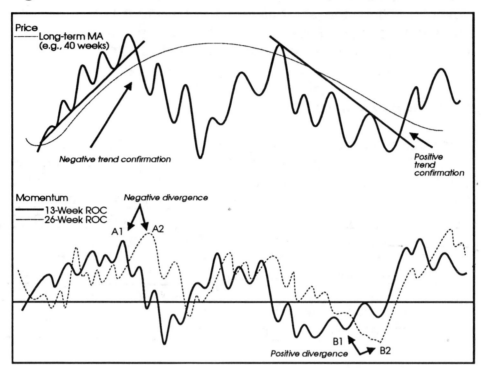

continues to rally to a new high, this indicates that the two cycles reflected by the oscillators are "out of gear" with each other. Remember the analogy of the car with the engine problem? The concept of complex divergences works in a similar way.

There are several factors to consider in analyzing complex divergences.

1. It is important to compare two time spans that are separated by a long interval. In this sense the term "long interval" is a relative one. By definition, what is lengthy for a short-term trend will be brief for a long-term trend. For example, it makes sense to compare two oscillators based on a 10- and 20-day time span for a short-term trend because the indicators are separated by a substantial time span. As a result, they will reflect two totally different time cycles. If we compare a 10-day

with a 12-day span, this would not be the case because the two are so close that they would reflect price trends caused by more or less the same cycle. A 10- and 12-week comparison would also be counterproductive. Even though the two indicators are separated by ten days by definition, they would be trying to monitor intermediate-term price movements where a time difference of two weeks is immaterial. In this respect chart 1.1 shows how the two series are far too similar to give us any meaningful complex divergences. Compare this chart though with chart 1.2, which shows a 12 and 30-day ROC where their paths can move very differently. Note the complex divergence in February 1992.

2. The peak in the longer-term indicator must be substantial in relation to the shorter one. For example, if you are comparing a 13-week oscillator with one constructed from a 26-week time span, the latter should achieve a new high lasting at least six months or longer.

Chart 1.1   Treasury Bonds 3-Month Perpetual Contract and a 10-Day vs. a 12-Day Rate-of-Change

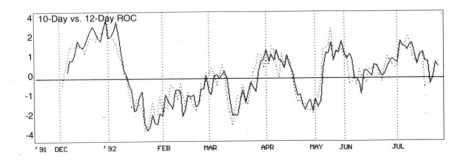

Chart 1.2   Toronto Stock Exchange Index and a
                12-Day vs. a 30-Day Rate-of-Change

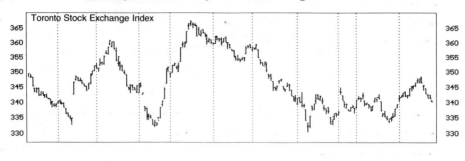

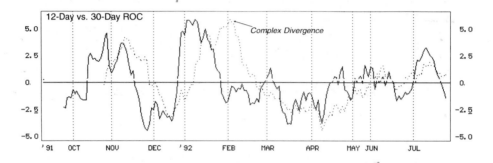

3. The oscillator with the shorter time span must be at the equilibrium level or close to it when its longer-term counterpart is peaking.

4. Complex divergences also occur at market bottoms, but in this case all the conditions are reversed. In other words, the indicator with the longer time span should be registering a bottom of relatively long duration as its shorter-term counterpart is rallying close to the equilibrium level.

5. Perhaps most important of all, complex divergences *must* be confirmed by a reversal in price. In figure 1.16, a complex divergence appears at point A exactly as described above, but the price continues to rally. In this instance, the divergence is telling us that a large price movement is underway, but in this case it is in the *same* direction as the previous one. Note that in this situation no indication of a reversal in the price trend itself was given.

Figure 1.16

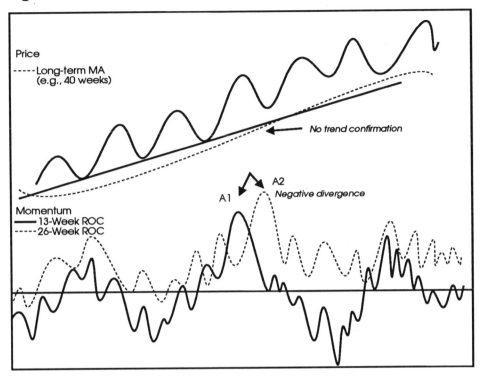

Summary

1. Momentum is a generic term that comprises a number of different indicators. It measures the rate at which prices rise and fall, often giving advance warning of latent strength and weakness in a specific price trend.
2. The principles of interpretation apply to all types of momentum indicators to some degree or another.
3. Momentum interpretation can be broken down into three primary areas: overbought/oversold, divergences, and momentum trend analysis.
4. Extreme readings and momentum divergences do not in and of themselves represent actual buy and sell signals. These can come only from a trend-reversal in the price itself. Momentum characteristics do, however, emphasize the significance of price signals when they are given.

chapter 2

PRINCIPLES OF MOMENTUM INTERPRETATION– PART II

- **Some General Thoughts**
- **Trendlines**
- **The Significance of a Trendline**
    Measuring Objectives
- **Price Patterns**
- **Peak and Trough Analysis**
- **Advance Breakdowns**
  and Breakouts
- **Moving Averages and**
  Momentum Indicators
- **Double Moving Average**
  Crossover
- **Moving Average Directional**
  Change
- **Overbought/Oversold**
  Crossovers
- **Equilibrium Crossover Signals**
- **Derivatives of Moving Averages**

Some General Thoughts

Momentum, like price, moves in trends. This means that the techniques used for analyzing price trends can be used for appraising momentum trends. Despite this fact, we must still keep in mind that a trend reversal in momentum is usually, *but not always*, associated with a similar reversal in the price. Occasionally, an analysis of an oscillator trend will accurately tell us that momentum has reversed, and a reversal in price may indeed follow. However, the lag between the signal of a reversal in momentum and the actual turning point in price may be so great that trading decisions based on this signal will be unprofitable.

In this chapter we will consider some techniques for analyzing trend reversals that can help us to better understand the momentum process.

Trendlines

Trendlines are perhaps the most easily invoked tool of technical analysis. After all, it is a relatively simple matter to pull out a ruler and draw a line connecting a series of peaks or troughs. Despite its simplicity, the effectiveness of this approach never ceases to amaze me. Figure 2.1 represents a momentum series where it is possible to construct a trendline joining several momentum bottoms. The figure shows that when the trendline is violated, the uptrend in momentum is reversed. Of course, this tells us only about momentum and nothing about the trend in price. For this we must try to isolate some kind of trend reversal as well. I have found that one of the most effective techniques for this is to try and match a violation of the trendline in momentum with a similar violation in price. When both are penetrated, the market usually reverses trend or, at the very least, consolidates for a while. In effect, the momentum signal represents additional confirmation in our "weight of the evidence" theory of trend reversals discussed earlier.

When trendlines are violated one of two things normally happens. Either the price trend reverses, or it halts temporarily before resuming. In momentum analysis a reversal in the momentum trend is more likely than a consolidation. The nature of a momentum trend accounts for this likelihood. Whether the direction of the

Figure 2.1

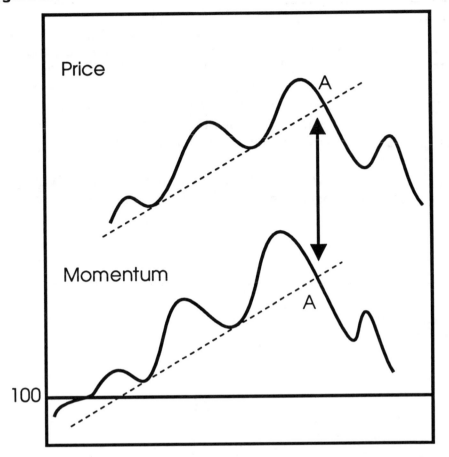

market's momentum is up or down, the trend requires increasingly faster velocity in order to continue. By definition it is far more difficult to maintain rising or falling velocity than rising or falling price. (Remember the example of the pen thrown in the air in chapter 1.) It is normally a wiser choice to assume that a trendline violation in momentum signifies a reversal rather than a consolidation in the trend of momentum.

The Significance of a Trendline

Any trendline obtains its significance from a combination of three factors: its length, the number of times it has been touched or approached by the price (or in this case the oscillator), and its angle of ascent or descent. Let's examine each of these factors in turn.

If we make the assumption that a trendline is a graphic way of portraying the underlying trend, then it follows naturally that the longer the period used when constructing the line, the more significant the trend. Since reversals of long trends have greater significance than reversals of short trends, the same must hold true for the length of the lines reflected by these trends. For the purposes of this discussion it is assumed that the line remains inviolate.

Figure 2.2 shows that a trendline really represents a support and resistance point, depending on whether the line is rising or

Figure 2.2

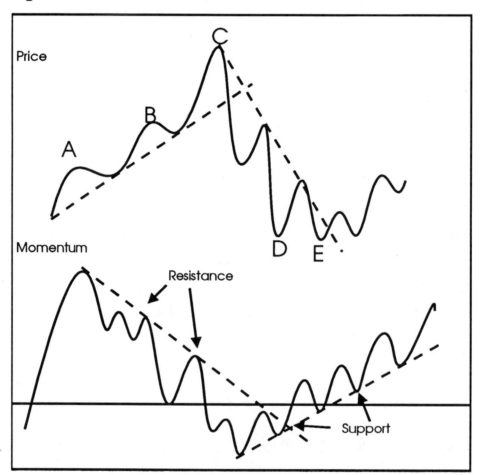

falling. The more a line has been touched or approached, the greater the significance of that line as a support or resistance point, hence, the greater the implication of its violation. A line that has been touched or approached only twice has nowhere near the importance of one that has made contact with an oscillator (or the price) four or five times. We tend to think of support and resistance as horizontal levels, but trendline analysis points to the fact that support and resistance can alter their levels with the passage of time. A good trendline reflects this phenomenon.

Finally, the angle of ascent or descent is important in assessing the significance of a line. In figure 2.3, the dotted line AB represents a very steep slope. A trend in price that rises sharply is less sustainable than one which rises in a gentle fashion. This means that trendlines constructed with a sharp angle of ascent or descent carry less weight than ones drawn with a smaller angle. Just think of a runner racing to victory in the 100 meters. He can keep up this speed for a short period but could never maintain such a pace for a long distance race. Markets act in the same way. They can sprint for short periods, but then they have to rest. A signal based on this quick dash will be less significant than one showing a price trend

Figure 2.3

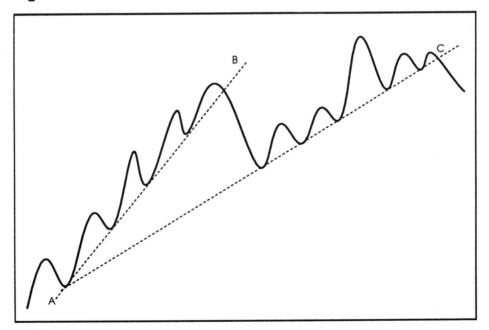

that has advanced slowly over a much longer period. We can conclude that if there is any time when it is wiser to assume that the violation of a line will be followed by a consolidation as opposed to a reversal in trend it is when an unusually steep line is penetrated. In this instance the dotted line AC in figure 2.3 has much more significance, since it has a much lower angle of ascent.

Most people disregard a trendline once it has been violated. I believe this to be a mistake, since an extended trendline has as much significance as it did prior to the violation. In figure 2.4, we can see that after trendline AB was penetrated the momentum indicator fell. It subsequently rallied and found resistance in the area of the extended line. If the line was important prior to the violation, it will be equally as important after it. The trendline's role merely shifted from one of support to one of resistance. It works the same way in the real world. For example, if you jump on a floor and

Figure 2.4

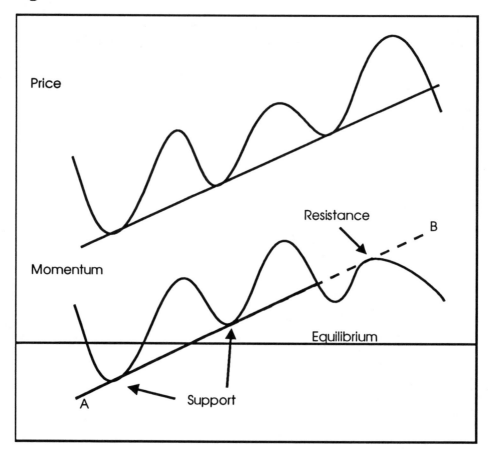

the floor gives way, you will fall through to the level below. From your new position the ceiling has become a barrier. In other words, it was support; now it's resistance.

When a momentum series experiences a rally such as the one shown in figure 2.4, most traders naturally assume that the penetration was a whipsaw. However, if they had taken the trouble to extend the line, they would have discovered that the return point was an excellent place for anticipating a price decline. Figure 2.5 depicts the same type of situation, but in this case the line shows a reversal from a downtrend to an uptrend.

Obviously, these rules are general in nature. They need to be applied with both eyes open and with a dose of common sense. It is not impossible for a severe market decline to follow the penetration of a short, sharp, momentum trendline that has been touched twice. Nor is it impossible for an explosive rally to develop from a similar set of conditions. However, by and large you will find that the penetration of lines that contain the elements of the three factors discussed will generally be followed by a commensurately significant move in momentum and price.

Figure 2.5

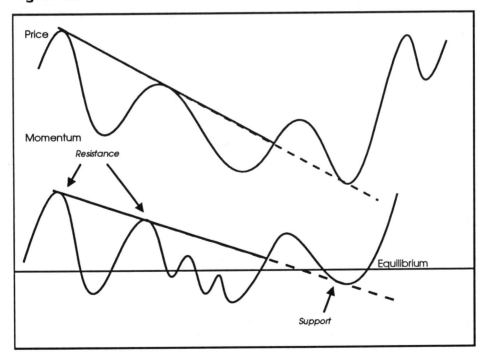

Measuring Objectives

In some instances when dealing with trendline violations in price, it is possible to come up with measuring objectives. This concept can also be applied to momentum analysis. For instance, it is a normal practice to measure the maximum distance between the trendline and the price (Point AA1 in figure 2.6) and extend it downwards at the point of penetration (Point AA2). (The process would be reversed for a down trendline as in figure 2.7.)

Figure 2.8 shows this same approach applied to an oscillator. Of course, the measuring objective only has implications for the oscillator, but quite often momentum and price reverse simultaneously. Moreover, these measuring objectives sometimes repeat several times and also serve as important pivotal points, as shown in figure 2.9. In all these examples the measuring objective should be used as a *possible* turning point or an additional piece of testimony in our weight-of-the-evidence concept. Since the reliability of this technique is somewhat limited it should *never* be used in isolation as a basis for making a forecast.

Generally, the more significant the momentum trendline, the stronger the possibility that it will be followed by an important reversal in price. If the trendline for price is just as impressive, then the odds of a major reversal relative to the time span under consideration will be that much greater.

Figure 2.6

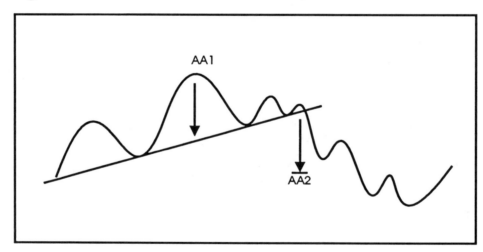

Figure 2.7

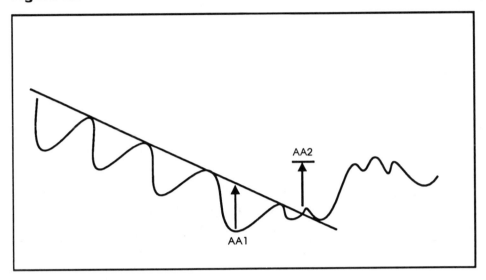

Figure 2.8

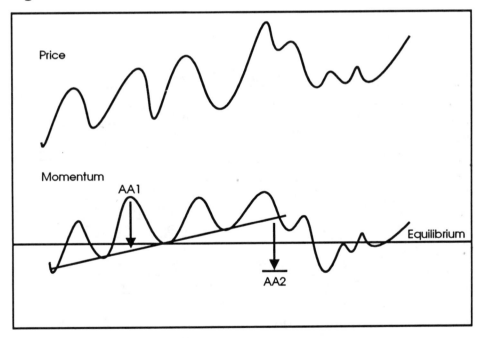

Figure 2.9

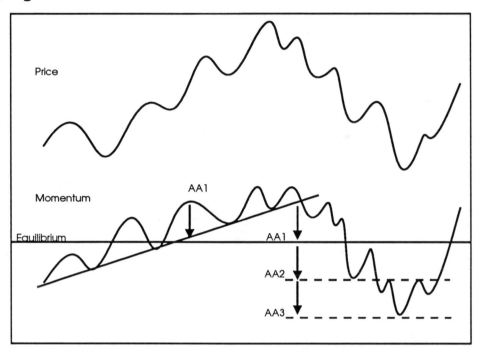

Price Patterns

One of the basic price-reversal techniques used in technical analysis is price formations, or price patterns. These same techniques also can be applied to momentum analysis. Price formations do not occur very often in oscillators, but when they do it's time to sit up and pay attention, because the formations carry great portent for future price activity. I want to stress once again that the momentum reversal is just that, a reversal in momentum, not in price. However, when a reversal is confirmed by a price break, it almost always has important consequences for the market under consideration.

Price patterns in momentum indicators take the standard forms: rectangles, head-and-shoulders, triple tops, triangles, and so forth. The same principles used in price analysis also apply. For example, any formation gains its significance from its size and depth. However, since trends in momentum are, generally speaking, less sustainable than trends in price, momentum configurations are not generally as large, and they are certainly far less plentiful. Figures 2.10 and 2.11 show several possibilities for both rising and falling markets.

These figures also connect the breakout point of the momentum pattern with the trend reversal signal in the price. It is very important to understand that there is usually a lag between the point when the price formation in the momentum indicator is completed and the actual reversal in the price. The momentum series nearly always gives an *advance* warning that the underlying technical picture is improving or deteriorating.

One very important principle applies more to momentum formations than formations that develop in a price series: A pattern must have something to reverse. Consider, the situation in figure 2.12 where a breakout from a reverse head-and-shoulders pattern occurs close to an overbought line. Based on the material discussed in chapter 1, this is a point at which we should be thinking more about selling than buying, yet this particular configuration is indicating a "buy." In this case a good rule to follow is this: A "buy"

Figure 2.10

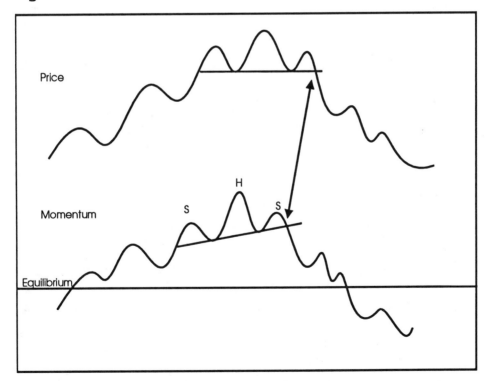

Figure 2.11

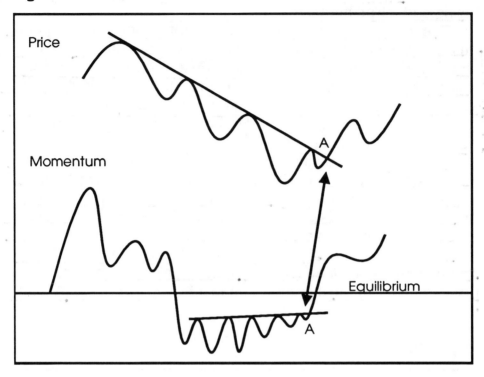

Figure 2.12

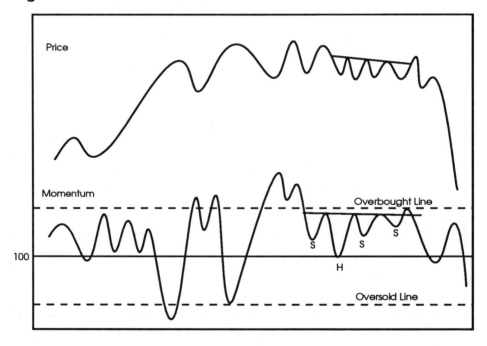

or "sell" signal is less reliable the closer it occurs to an extreme in a momentum indicator.

In effect, the rule is telling us to use a little common sense, and not to blindly assume that every price-pattern breakout will result in a reliable move. As a general guideline, I tend to ignore upside price breakouts in momentum that occur much above the equilibrium line and downside breakouts that develop much below it. In conclusion, price patterns are a fairly rare occurrence in oscillator series. Provided they are not formed near an overbought or oversold zone, it certainly pays to respect them.

Peak and Trough Analysis

The central building block of technical analysis is the concept that a rising trend consists of a series of rising peaks and troughs and a falling one of declining peaks and troughs, as represented in figure 2.13. When the prevailing trend of rising tops and bottoms is broken and the price experiences a lower peak and lower trough, it is assumed that a new downward trend is underway, and vice versa. The significance of this new trend will depend directly on the nature of the rallies and reactions. If they are of an intra-day variety,

Figure 2.13

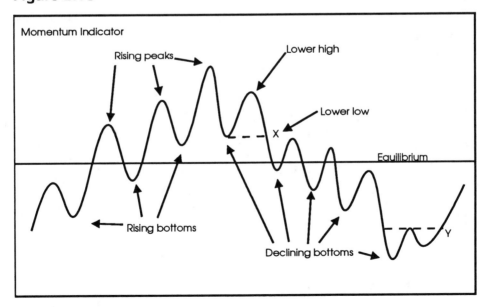

the reversal will be very short-term in duration. On the other hand, if the peaks and troughs are associated with rallies and reactions lasting six weeks or more, then it will be of a primary-trend in nature.

Peak and trough analysis also can be applied to momentum indicators. In figure 2.13 we see a series that is at first in an uptrend because each succeeding peak is higher than its predecessor. Then a rally develops, which for the first time fails to exceed its predecessor. During the next reaction the indicator falls below the previous bottom at Point X; the series of rising peaks and troughs has now reversed. This downtrend remains in force until the fluctuations signal rising peaks and troughs again at Point Y. This simple technique signifies only that the trend in momentum may have reversed. It is not a signal that the price trend itself has changed direction, although in most instances it will. I should add that although this is a legitimate technique for both price and momentum analysis, it appears to be more reliable for the former. In most instances trendline analysis is the most reliable method for identifying momentum trend reversals.

Some traders do not wait for a reversal in *both* rising peaks *and* troughs before concluding that the trend has reversed. Instead, they treat the break to a new low, at point X in figure 2.14, as the indication that the trend has changed direction. The same would be

Figure 2.14

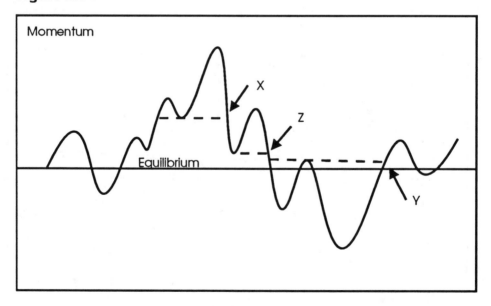

true in reverse at point Y. My view is that this represents half a signal because at X, the rising peaks are still in force, only the troughs have been broken. However, if there is other evidence to back up this half-signal, it is perfectly legitimate to use it. My preference, all things being equal, is to wait for the trend of both peaks and troughs to reverse (point Z), since oscillators in their raw, or unsettled, state tend to be far more random in nature than movements in the price. Because of this it makes more sense to rely on trend-reversal signals that are more reliable.

Advance Breakdowns and Breakouts

Occasionally, an indication of an impending trend reversal in price occurs when the momentum indicator breaks a series of rising peaks and troughs, but the price indicator does not. In figure 2.15 we can see that the oscillator breaks below its previous bottom at Point A, but the price does not. What often happens in such instances is that the next rally in price proves to be the final one for that specific trend. I term these momentum failures "advance breakdowns," because they represent very subtle warnings that the trend in momentum has reversed. Figure 2.16 depicts a reversal from a downtrend to an uptrend signalled by an "advance breakout." The principle is identical, only the direction is reversed.

Moving Averages and Momentum Indicators

Because raw momentum indicators are often quite jagged and seemingly random affairs, the practice of smoothing them with moving averages has evolved. This makes it easier to get a better sense of the underlying momentum trend.

There are several ways to determine a moving average. The most obvious is to calculate some form of moving average of the oscillator, using the crossover points as indications of where the momentum trend has reversed, as in figure 2.17. This method is not generally successful, because the momentum series is so jagged that it generates more whipsaws than reliable signals. This happens because purely random factors have greater influence on short time spans than they do on longer ones. Therefore, this flaw

Figure 2.15

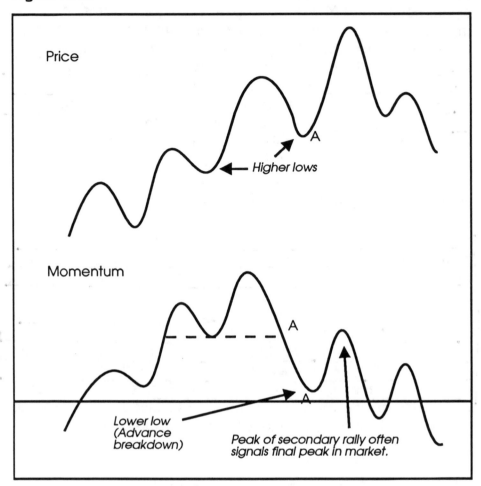

typically recedes in importance as the time span of the raw
momentum series increases. For example, an oscillator based on
a 5-day time span is more likely to be affected by rumors and
manipulation by floor traders than one calculated over on a 30-day
period. Such biases are nonexistent if the period under consideration is a year or more. This is not to imply that long-term time spans
are perfectly free from irregular fluctuations, merely that they are
less likely to be subject to them.

A secondary influence will be the type of security being monitored. Take pork bellies, they are notoriously volatile, much more
so than, say, three-month Treasury Bill contracts. As a result, we
may well find that it is possible to discern some kind of trend using
a moving-average crossover over a 30-day time span for the

Figure 2.16

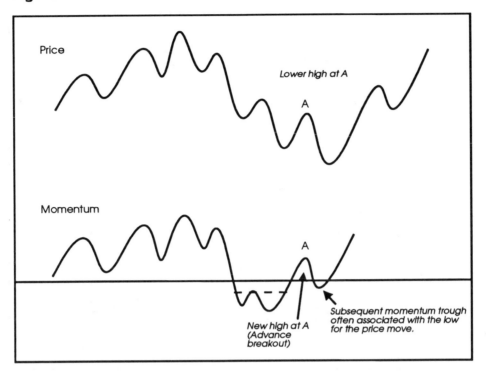

Treasury Bill prices than we can for pork bellies during the same time period. Once again we see that technical analysis requires the application of a little common sense and experimentation.

The position of the momentum indicator at the time of the crossover is also an important contributing factor to the reliability of the signal. The farther from the equilibrium line an indicator is, the more difficult it will be to maintain that particular trend. Consequently, the more extreme the momentum reading at the time of the crossover, the more reliable that crossover is likely to be. In figure 2.18 we see four crossovers, all from an overbought or oversold extreme. Note that the last one failed. This example was used deliberately to indicate that every rule in technical analysis is broken from time to time. It again emphasizes the need and indeed, the requirement to consider the position of several indicators in a weight-of-the-evidence approach that emphasizes consensus.

The reliability of crossovers also can be improved by increasing the time span of the moving average, but even here problems arise. This is because the choice of a moving average is always a trade-off between sensitivity and reliability. Consequently, while a longer

Figure 2.17

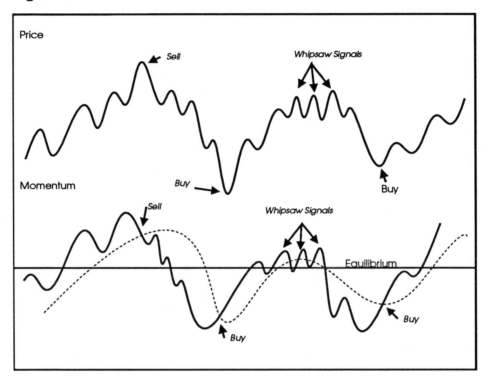

time span always means that buy and sell signals are more reliable, in the case of raw oscillator data where volatility reigns supreme, it is doubtful that enough whipsaws can be filtered out to make the trade-off profitable.

My view is that moving averages should be used in a specific and not in a general way. By this I mean that you must examine the relationship between momentum and the price of the security being monitored along with the time span being used in determining the moving average. As long as the movements in the raw momentum data are not too jagged, as in a 12-month rate-of-change analysis of most stock and bond markets, it is possible to use the moving-average approach. On the other hand, it is unlikely that you will be able to find anything that works successfully in the day-to-day combat of the futures pits. Other concepts are, I believe, more practical and reliable for short-term trading.

There are four ways to use moving averages to greater advantage in momentum analysis. They are: (1) double moving average

Figure 2.18

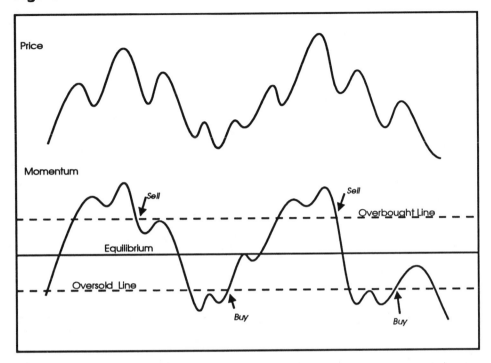

crossovers, (2) a change in direction of a moving average, (3) a predetermined benchmark crossover, and (4) the construction of a moving-average derivative. Let's examine each of them.

Double Moving Average Crossover

This approach deals with the problem of misleading moving-average crossover signals, described earlier in this chapter, by calming the raw oscillator data with a short-term moving average. Signals are generated when the short-term average crosses above and below its long-term counterpart. This concept is shown in figure 2.19. As you can see, the large number of whipsaws that would have occured around the time of the second sell signal are filtered out, yet the system does not lose much in the way of timeliness. This method forms the basis of the trend deviation and Moving Average Convergence Divergence (MACD) indicators that are discussed in chapter 4.

Figure 2.19

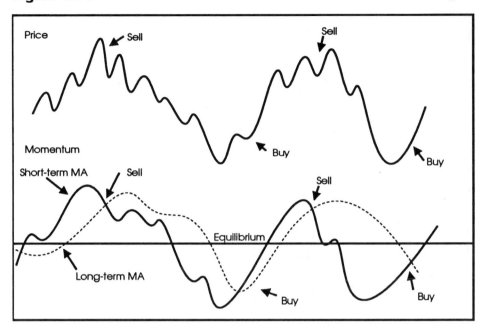

Moving Average Directional Change

We have established that moving-average crossovers of raw oscillators are often quite useless due to their numerous whipsaw signals. However, if the moving average itself is considered, it is apparent that a *change* in its direction offers a promising approach for providing reliable and timely signals for momentum-trend reversals. (see figure 2.20.) There are two points here worth expanding. First, the *quality* of the signal will depend on the relative distance of the turning point from the equilibrium level. The further the distance, other things being equal, the more significant the signal. Second, in many instances a moving average will still be unable to remove all of the volatility. Consequently, several false or "late" signals will be triggered. On the one hand, this is a disadvantage, because we were looking for a method that gives us a few reliable but relatively timely signals. On the other hand, it is an advantage because it is often possible to observe divergences between the smoothed momentum and the price series. In effect, the smoothing gives us a bird's-eye view of specific rallies and reactions in momentum. In this way it is easier to spot trends showing improving or deteriorating momentum. In some cases it is

Figure 2.20

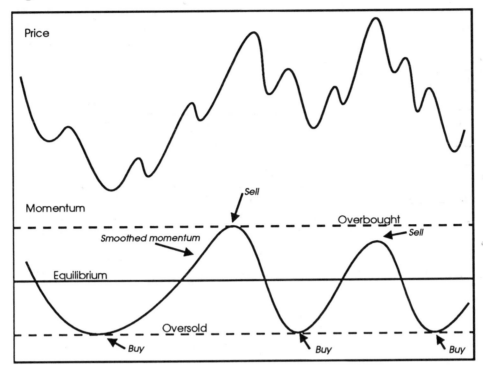

even possible to construct trendlines joining a series of peaks or troughs in the moving average. When violated, these lines will generally carry greater significance than those constructed from the raw data over a similar time frame.

If the smoothed momentum series fails to give reliable signals from a change in direction and the object of the exercise is to make it do so, then the solution is either to expand the time frame or smooth the average with an additional exponent. I will explore the possibilities of using specific spans for specific trends in later chapters.

Overbought/Oversold Crossovers

There are other ways in which long-term moving averages can signal reversals in the momentum trend. One approach is to establish overbought and oversold levels. As discussed in the previous chapter, this is typically done on a trial-and-error basis with the specific security being monitored. The buy-and-sell indications are given when the average moves through one of the extremes and then recrosses it on its return journey to the equilibrium level. These points are indicated by the arrows in figure 2.21.

The main drawback of this method is that very often price fluctuations in the security in question are of insufficient magnitude to enable the momentum indicator to reach an extreme. In such instances a buy signal is generated, but there is no countervailing sell signal, and vice versa. This means that this type of approach is not appropriate for a mechanical trading system unless subsidiary rules are developed to account for such situations. Nevertheless, it can be of invaluable help in picking out reliable buy-and-sell points in a more general way. Pay attention to these signals when they occur and use the indicator in the weight-of-the-evidence approach. Do not necessarily wait for a countervailing signal to take you out of the market because it may very well fail to materialize.

Figure 2.21

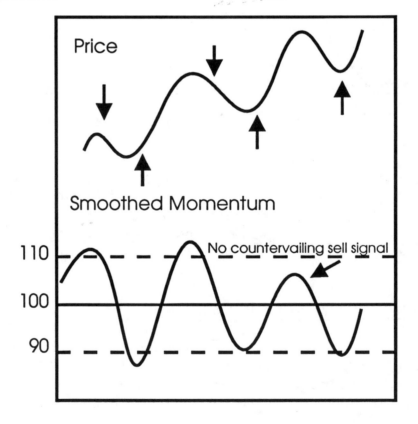

Equilibrium Crossover Signals

Another signal-generating possibility comes from an equilibrium crossover as shown in figure 2.22. Buy alerts are given when the indicator moves above zero and sell signals when it moves below zero. This method avoids the problem of countervailing signals from the overbought/oversold crossover technique, but unless the selection of a moving average is made very carefully there is a chance that most of the signals could be quite late. It is also possible to use this technique for unsmoothed oscillator data but unless the time span is chosen very carefully, you will find that there are a substantial number of whipsaws.

Figure 2.22

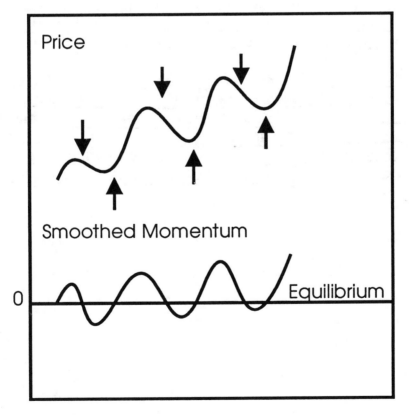

Derivatives of Moving Averages

This process involves a "double smoothing," which is a moving average of a moving average. It is even possible to take the process a step further by smoothing the result for a third time. There is no end to the possibilities, but also remember there is no Holy Grail. It is usually best to keep things as simple as possible. Interpreting indicators based on these types of calculations is the same as interpreting them for a simple moving average. Signals can be generated by changes in direction, moving-average crossovers, overbought/oversold crossovers, zero crossovers, and so on. Research is the key. Examine several markets over a long period of time—2–3 years for daily data, 10–20 years for weekly figures, and 20–30 years for monthly statistics—to make sure that the method you have chosen works in practice.

Summary

1. Trend-determining techniques, normally used to ascertain price trends, can be applied to momentum indicators. These include trendlines, price patterns, moving averages, as well as peak-and-trough analysis.
2. Trend reversals in momentum are usually followed by a trend reversal in the price, but normally with a lag between the two.
3. Always make sure that trend reversals in momentum are confirmed by price action.
4. Since raw momentum figures can be quite jagged, it is usually a good idea to incorporate some form of smoothing into the analysis.

chapter 3

RATE-OF-CHANGE

- **Introduction**
- **Construction**
- **Overbought and Oversold Levels**
- **Choice of Time Spans**
- **Short-Term Trends**
- **Intermediate-Term Trends**
- **Long-Term Trends**
- **Trendline Construction**
- **Price Patterns**
- **Divergences**
- **Complex Divergences**
- **Moving Averages of ROC Indicators**

Introduction

Rate-of-change (ROC) is probably the easiest momentum indicator to construct. Do not let this fact lead you to believe that ROC is inaccurate, because this indicator is definitely one of the most effective. Many people believe that a mathematically simple formula is inferior to a complex one because of its simplicity. The facts, however, disprove this belief.

We often use complexity as a crutch to substitute for simple reasoning. This inclination is certainly evident in the practice of technical analysis, where a belief exists that if an indicator is constructed from a long and complex formula, it is somehow more likely to signal the precise turning points that we all crave. Unfortunately, this is a myth. There are no indicators that can consistently and mechanically generate profitable buy and sell signals. Do not toss aside an indicator just because it is simple. Reject it only when it consistently fails.

Construction

Rate-of-change compares today's price with yesterday's. For example, a 10-day ROC is calculated by comparing the price today with the price of 10 days ago. Tomorrow's price would be compared with that of 9 days ago, while the price the day after tomorrow would be compared with the price of 8 days ago, and so forth. The result is then plotted as a continuous series that oscillates above and below the equilibrium level. Table 3.1 shows how this calculation would be done for a 10-day rate-of-change.

Scaling for the ROC takes one of two forms. In figure 3.1 the equilibrium line is plotted at zero. Positive periods appear as +1, +2, etc., while negative periods are represented as minus numbers. The alternative, shown in figure 3.2, is for the equilibrium level to be plotted as 100 and positive and negative numbers to appear as percentages. Readings in excess of 100 indicate a rising trend, and those below it indicate a negative one. From an interpretive point of view it is immaterial which method of scaling is used because the general movements are identical. I prefer to use positive and negative numbers rather than the percentage method, since this gives a better sense of bullish and bearish tendencies. In any

Table 3.1

Date	Price (A)	Price 10 days ago (B)	ROC (A ÷ B) × 100
Jan 1st	80		
2nd	81		
3	83		
4	80		
5	78		
8	82		
9	84		
10	87		
11	91		
12	95		
15	94	80	117.5
16	90	81	112.5
17	89	83	107.2
18	86	80	107.5
19	84	78	107.6
22	82	82	100.0
23	81	84	96.4
24	86	87	91.9

Figure 3.1

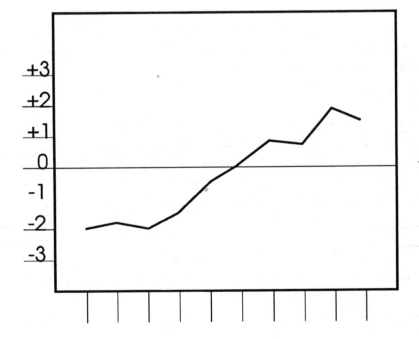

Figure 3.2

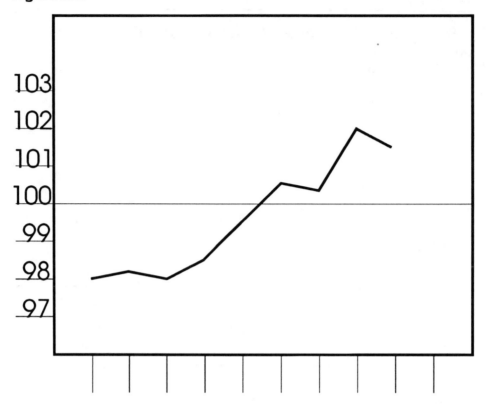

event, the scaling will probably be decided by the type of computer software you use. The comparison in the ROC calculation can be done either by subtraction or division. In several charting software packages this method of ROC calculation is called the "momentum" indicator.

In this case the formula is M = V − Vn, where V is the latest closing price and Vn, the closing price *n* periods ago. If the two prices are identical, the momentum oscillator would be plotted right at the equilibrium, or zero line. If the latest price were greater than the price *n* periods ago, then the oscillator would be in positive territory (i.e., above the equilibrium line). If the latest price were smaller than the price *n* periods ago, then the oscillator would be plotted below the equilibrium line.

My personal preference is to use the division method, because the division calculation gives you a sense of proportion. It is a known fact that price trends in markets are as much a function of psychology as is any other element, and market psychology *tends to move in proportions.* Garfield Drew, a well-known writer and technician, once said that "stocks don't sell for what they are worth, they sell for what people *think* they are worth." There is considerable merit to this observation, as anyone who has experienced irrational price movements will testify. I emphasize the word "irrational" because most of us think that the markets are irrational when they move in the opposite direction to our position or where we think they 'ought' to go. More specifically, though, the term here reflects the fact that investment and trading ideas often take the form of fads, fashions, or phobias that later prove to be illogical.

In any event, the idea that prices are determined by the attitude of traders to the emerging fundamentals means that markets are subject to collective mood swings from fear to greed. Going one step further, we could say that these emotions are subject to proportional swings that can be monitored by the ROC indicator.

This is precisely why the division calculation is superior to the subtraction method. The division method permits a realistic comparison between different securities as well as the same security during different time periods. For example, if you were to compare the performance between a $10 and $100 stock using the subtraction method, the ROC would give you distorted results. This is because a $2 move in the lower-priced stock represents a 20% movement, whereas it reflects only a 2% price change in the more expensive equity. A rally in the former security would generate an extreme overbought reading on a 10-day basis, but it would create hardly a ripple in the $100 equity.

The same principle applies when we compare the performance of a security over two different time periods when the value of the security has changed considerably between periods. Let's look at the technical characteristics of Wal Mart stock over a 20-year time span between 1972 and 1992. This stock appreciated well over tenfold in price during this period. Consequently, comparing a $1 move in these two periods using the subtraction approach would be quite meaningless. This is a case where the division method is far superior, since proportional price moves are represented by an equal rise or fall in the oscillator, regardless of the level of the actual price.

For short-term traders who rarely look at charts covering anything more than, say, a 100-day time period, the subtraction method is unlikely to give any significant distortions. Therefore, using either the subtraction or division method of calculating the

ROC indicator will produce results that are more or less identical. However, if you are comparing two or more stocks or two periods for the same security in which the price is significantly different, then I recommend using the division method.

Overbought and Oversold Levels

The ROC indicator lends itself handsomely to overbought and oversold interpretation. The problem is that there are no hard-and-fast rules about where the lines should be drawn, since the magnitude of the oscillations will vary according to the volatility of the underlying security and the time span being considered. Generally, the longer the time span, the greater the higher and lower readings, or extreme, in the oscillator.

For this reason overbought and oversold lines are constructed on the basis of judgement. Wherever possible it is important to place them *equidistant* from the equilibrium level. This is because fear and greed tend to move in proportion and should be represented graphically to reflect this fact. In instances where the security being monitored is in a linear trend, this is not always possible. A "linear trend" is defined as a trend whose corrections are mild or almost nonexistent. Chart 3.1, shows the 1980's bull market for the Nikkei.

Note how relatively easy it was to construct an overbought line at the +20% level. However, plotting an oversold line at the proportional equivalent of −20% would have served no useful purpose, since the oscillator failed to decline to that point during the whole period. It would have been better to place the oversold line at −10%, where reversals would have at least given us some indication of when a correction ended.

Chart 3.2 shows the same market, only for a different period. Negative long-term momentum characteristics would have offered some indication that the main trend was in the process of reversing. But the decline in the 13-week ROC in early 1990—which read well below its "normal" oversold readings of the 1980's—would have confirmed that something was happening totally beyond the normal experience of the bull market. This type of extremely weak momentum was discussed in chapter 1. Note that after 1990 it is now possible to construct a meaningful oversold line at −20%.

Chart 3.1   Nikkei Weekly and a 13-Week Rate-of-Change

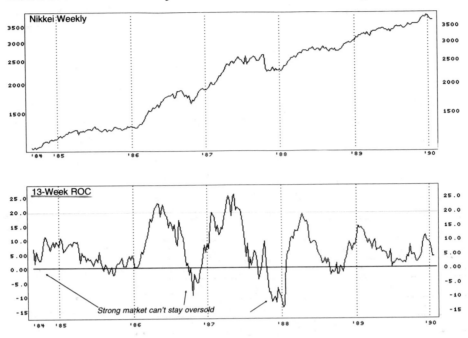

Chart 3.2   Nikkei Weekly and a 13-Week Rate-of-Change

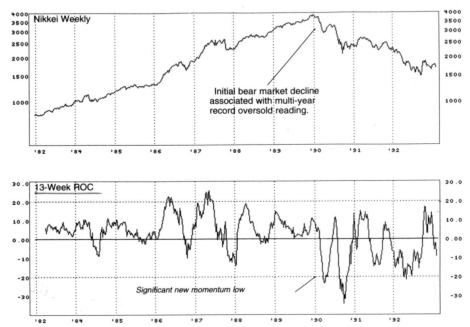

Remember the analogy of the dog on the leash in chapter 1? Ideally, we want the plotting of the overbought/oversold extremes to correspond to the limited lengths that the dog can wander when he comes to the end of his leash. Unfortunately, the ROC oscillator acts like a rubber leash, allowing the extremes too much flexibility, so it is necessary to be a little creative. Conceptually, the lines should be drawn at such a level that they encompass as many large rallies and reactions as possible, yet do not include so many fluctuations that they dilute the meaning of the terms "overbought" and "oversold." This is very much a trial-and-error process based on your own judgement and common sense.

It is impossible in a book of this kind to give you precise pointers on how to accomplish this, but let's at least take a look at a couple of examples. In chart 3.3 I have drawn in an overbought level at about 50%. Since this is constructed at a point that includes only the unusually large 1987 summer rally, it is unlikely to be reached again except in the most unusual circumstances. It would, therefore, make more sense to ignore this freak condition and draw the overbought/oversold lines at about +/–20%. Now, most reversals in the indicator occur as they reach the line which is exactly what

Chart 3.3   Silver Weekly and a 12-Week Rate-of-Change

we want. In chart 3.4, on the other hand, the lines are constructed at the +/−10% level, which clearly includes almost every twist and turn. While the oversold line 'works' pretty well the overbought line is relatively useless in signaling trend reversal points.

Finally, in chart 3.5 the lines have been drawn at levels that represent a realistic compromise. In practice, you will discover that a substantial number of these overbought/oversold lines will turn out to be a compromise. But as long as they reflect most of the turning points in price, they will be of invaluable help.

Choice of Time Spans

This section has been subdivided into the three types of trends: short, intermediate, and long. While several ROC time spans are suggested, it should be understood that there is no one span that applies perfectly to all occasions. It is always possible to find a length that works for a precise period in time for a specific security. However, this success would reflect a specific situation that oc-

Chart 3.4   Commerzbank Index Weekly and a
                10-Week Rate-of-Change

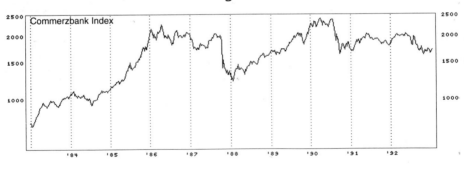

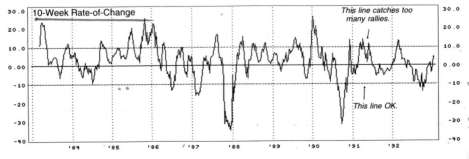

Chart 3.5   Commerzbank Index Weekly and a 10-Week Rate-of-Change
with Adjusted Overbought/Oversold Lines

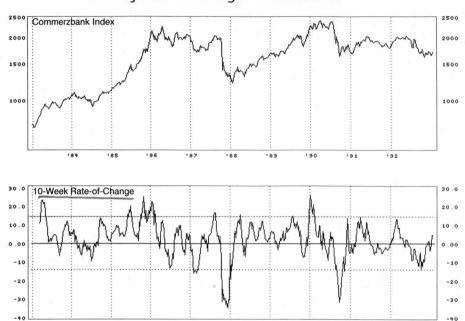

curred in the past and would be of doubtful practicality for predicting
the future. On the other hand, it is not possible to find a time span
that is satisfactory in all markets at all times. This means that we
need to confine ourselves to those periods that work well most of
the time in the majority of markets. The concept of compromise
once again comes to the fore. The following suggestions, then, are
made with that proviso.

Short-Term Trends

Excluding hourly intraday trends, short-term market movements
typically extend 3–6 weeks but can be as short as 5 days and be
as long as 45 days. Since this covers a fairly wide range, there are
several possible time frames that can be chosen. The most popular
are spans of 5, 10, 12, 14, 25, 28, and 30 days. The 5-day ROC is
used to monitor extremely short-term price movements lasting
between 7 and 10-days. The 12-day span is used for trends
extending between 15- and 25-days. In this respect, I prefer a 10-

day span because it encompasses two weeks of normal trading data. The 25, 28 and 30-day span is used for short-term trends in excess of 25 days. Many analysts claim that the lunar cycle of 28 days has a strong psychological effect on the markets, which perhaps accounts for the fact that these three spans seem to work so well. We know, for example, that hospitals report that more accident-prone people appear in their emergency rooms during the full-moon period of the month than at any other time, so is it not unreasonable to believe that the lunar cycle also has some influence on the psychology that determines price trends in markets. The only problem is that the lunar cycle includes weekends and holidays (28 days) whereas momentum indicators are based on *trading* days i.e., about 20 per cycle.

Even so, this is only one of a number of cycles that are simultaneously affecting prices at any one time. Consequently, analysis *should not* be limited to oscillators based on *one* time span but should include other periods in order to obtain a more complete picture of what is happening. For example, a trader may be using a 5-day ROC as shown in the second panel in chart 3.6. Because of its brief time span, this indicator easily moves between the overbought and oversold extremes. However, just because the cycle reflected by the 5-day ROC is oversold the price will not immediately react to the downside. Much of the price action will depend on the position of additional short-term cycles. This is why it is often a good idea to monitor several different ROC indicators simultaneously.

Chart 3.6 further demonstrates this point. In mid-June the 5-day ROC was oversold. Based on the other market turning points, when this series was moving back toward zero from an overbought or oversold zone, it would have been reasonable to anticipate a rally. One did not materialize, however, because the 30-day series was still overbought and clearly putting substantial downside influence on the price. This was not the case at the August bottom when *both* series were showing an oversold reading.

Another reason why it makes good sense to compare several ROC time spans is that some series may be giving extremely strong signals of an impending trend reversal while others may not. In chapter 2, I pointed out that price patterns are a fairly rare momentum phenomenon. When they do appear in the charts though, their trend reversal implications are quite significant. If the

Chart 3.6   CRB Index and Two Momentum Indicators

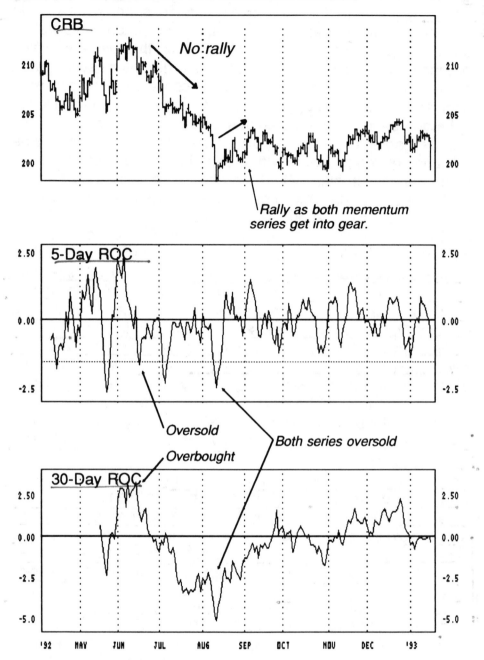

analysis is limited to just one oscillator measuring one time span, the overall picture may be missing a key element. However, if several time frames are considered it may well turn out that one of the oscillators is in the process of completing a price formation, a quadruple divergence, or a very significant trendline break. Whatever the signal, if it is a significant one, it will give us a more explicit indication that the prevailing trend may be about to reverse.

We can take this even one step further. The odds that the price is about to reverse its trend decrease significantly if two, or even three different time spans are simultaneously giving strong signals that a reversal in the momentum trend is imminent. An example is shown in chart 3.7. Note the important top in the mark at the beginning of 1992.

Intermediate-Term Trends

Technical lore has it that intermediate trends range in length from as short as three weeks to as long as six months, sometimes a little longer. I like to use ROC time spans that reflect calendar quarters or fractions thereof. This involves spans of 6, 13, and 26 weeks. The intermediate time frame can also be expanded to include a 39-week ROC, but this length of time is better utilized to monitor long-term trends that are below average duration. The same is true of the 30-day short-term ROC and the 6-week intermediate ROC (i.e., when expressed in 5-day trading weeks, both reflect an identical time span). Calendar quarters are useful, I believe, because they reflect the seasonality of the year and therefore the dominant cycles that influence intermediate trends.

The same concept of comparing several ROC indicators of varying time spans discussed previously can be applied to intermediate analysis. In this respect, chart 3.8 shows the relationship between the 6, 13, and 26-week ROC indicators for the S&P Composite between 1981 and 1983. Note how all three are in gear at the major 1982 low.

Long-Term Trends

Most people understand the long-term trend to mean a primary bull or bear market. This implies a cycle that extends for approximately four years from trough to trough. In fact, the 4-year cycle, which has

Chart 3.7 Deutsche Mark Daily and Three Momentum Indicators

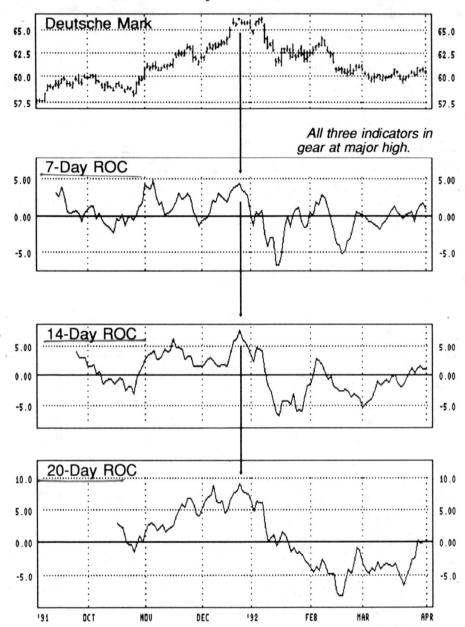

Chart 3.8 S&P Weekly and Three Momentum Indicators

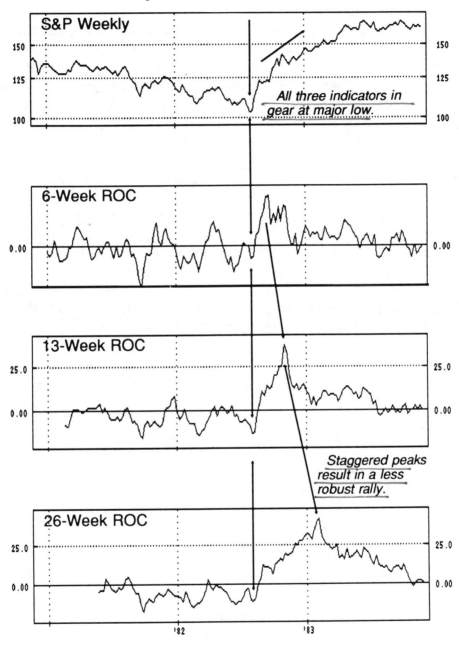

S&P Weekly

All three indicators in gear at major low.

6-Week ROC

13-Week ROC

Staggered peaks result in a less robust rally.

26-Week ROC

been modeled on the U.S. business cycle since the early part of the 19th Century, is 41 months.

The most commonly used long-term time frame is a 12-month ROC. The annualized rate-of-change is a useful measure because it eliminates all seasonal variations. For very seasonal markets, such as heating oil or agricultural commodities, seasonal factors can have a very important influence. Since the year also comprises 52 weeks, it too can be used in ROC calculations.

I have found that the 39-week (9-month) time span is often a very useful interval to follow. Some analysts have argued that this is an important emotional period because it is the length of the natural cycle in a woman's pregnancy. That, after all, is the *first* cycle that any of us experience. In many instances, I have found that this 9-month period brings out momentum characteristics that are superior to those highlighted by a 26 or 52-week ROC. Chart 3.9 featuring the weekly gold price is a fine example. Commonly used long-term ROC spans also include 18 and 24 months. Multiples of annualized rates-of-change in the form of 36 and 48-month spans occasionally supplement the analysis.

Chart 3.9   Gold Weekly and a 39-Week (9-Month) Rate-of-Change

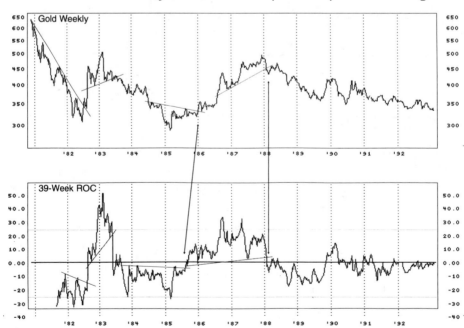

The idea of monitoring several indicators based on different time spans is just as relevant to long-term trends as it is short and intermediate trends.

Trendline Construction

ROC indicators lend themselves to trendline construction as much as any other momentum indicator. The principles discussed in chapter 2 are, therefore, quite relevant. One note of caution arises from the fact that ROC indicators are on our rubber leash, where they occasionally move to unusual extremes that are well beyond the normal overbought or oversold levels. This means that it is often quite easy to construct a very steep trendline joining two or three reversal points. Since the lines have a very sharp angle and the extreme connecting point (point A in figure 3.3) is somewhat random in nature, some degree of caution should be exercised in the interpretation of such violations. Often it is better to construct a shorter line, such as CD, at a less extreme angle of descent, provided it has been touched or approached on at least two

Figure 3.3

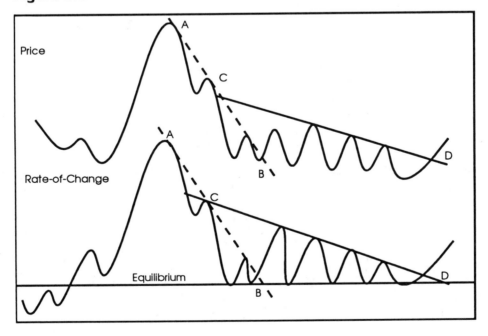

occasions. These same principles would hold in reverse following an unusually severe selling climax.

Chart 3.10 shows how the joint penetration of an ROC and price trendline often gives valuable buy and sell signals. Always remember that a price trendline violation often occurs well after the momentum violation. More reliable signals seem to develop when the trendline for either price or momentum is violated simultaneously with the completion of a price formation.

Price Patterns

With the possible exception of the RSI, price formations probably occur more in ROC oscillators than in any other indicator. Examples of this phenomenon in action are shown in chart 3.11. Always remember to look at the level where the breakout occurs. A completion pattern that develops near an overbought level in a rising trend is far less likely to work than if it takes place at an oversold or even neutral level. The opposite is true for a reversal in a declining market.

Chart 3.10   GTE Corporation and a 39-Week Rate-of-Change

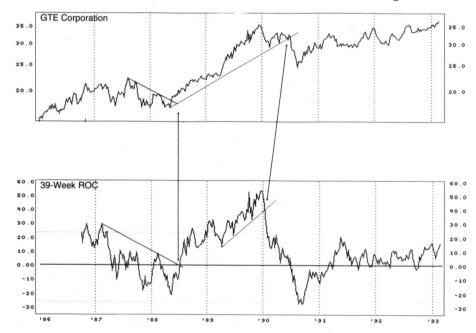

Chart 3.11   Swiss Franc and a 12-Day Rate-of-Change

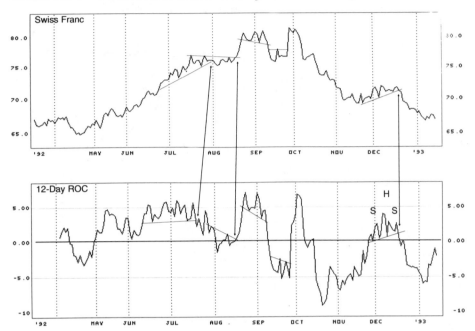

The principle of "commonality" can also have an important effect on price patterns. The commonality principle states that the more a specific characteristic can be observed, the greater the significance when the trend reverses. For example, if the ROC indicator of one stock in an industry group was tracing out a head-and-shoulders formation, this would imply either that the company itself was heading for trouble or that the whole industry was in for bad times. On the other hand, if the majority of the stocks in the industry were showing the same signs, there would be little doubt that this particular sector was due for a correction.

We could take it one step further and state that if a huge number of equities in the stock universe were experiencing "toppy" momentum then the stock market itself would be vulnerable. In fact, this happened on an international scale in the 1986–87 period just before the crash. Almost all markets around the world experienced some kind of intermediate momentum top or trendline break prior to the actual break. Several are shown in charts 3.12 and 3.13. Needless to say, a significant decline in prices followed this near "agreement."

Chart 3.12   S&P Weekly with a 26-Week Rate-of-Change and the
Commerzbank Index Weekly with a 39-Week
Rate-of-Change

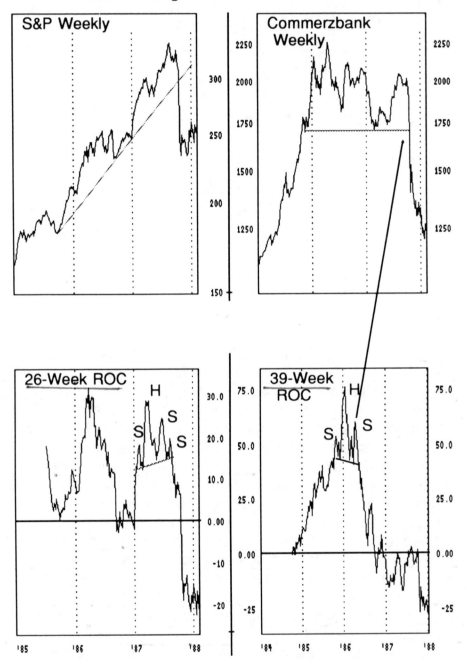

Chart 3.13   Nikkei Weekly with a 39-Week Rate-of-Change and
the Financial Times All-Ordinary with a 65-Week
Rate-of-Change

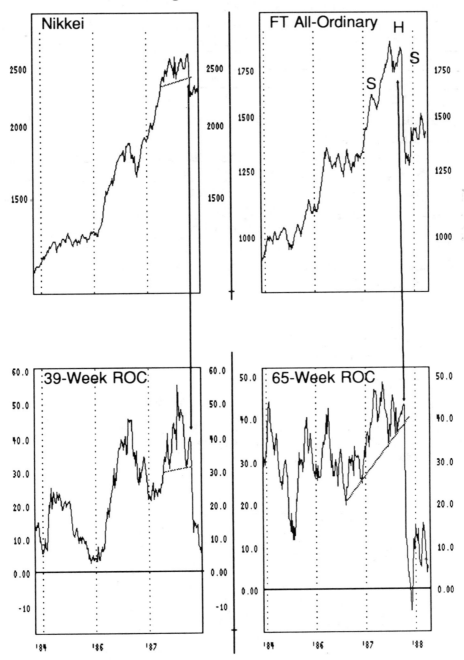

Divergences

Divergences represent an integral part of ROC analysis; the examples in this chapter are testimony enough. However, it is important to note that the ROC indicator is often an excellent vehicle for portraying an oscillator that warns of an impending sharp reversal in trend. This occurs when the price makes a new high or new low for the move, but the oscillator—after one negative or positive divergence—is barely able to rally above or slip below the equilibrium point.

Technical analysis rarely gives us clues to the character or steepness of an impending move, but divergences do just that. For this reason, it is well worthwhile to watch for them, because when they materialize and are also confirmed by a trend break in the price series, expect an unusually powerful move to follow. Examples are shown in chart 3.14 at Points A, B, and C and chart 3.15 at X and Y. Note that Y represents the right shoulder of a head-and-shoulders top.

Chart 3.14   ECU Bonds and 3-Month Perpetual Contract and a 12-Day Rate-of-Change

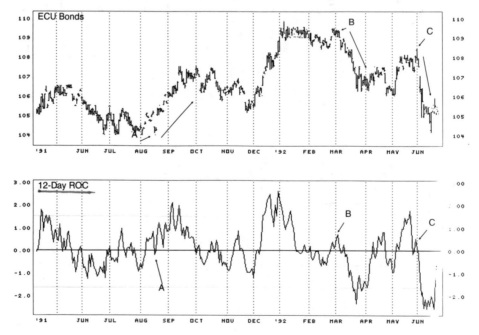

Chart 3.15   Australian Dollar and a 12-Day Rate-of-Change

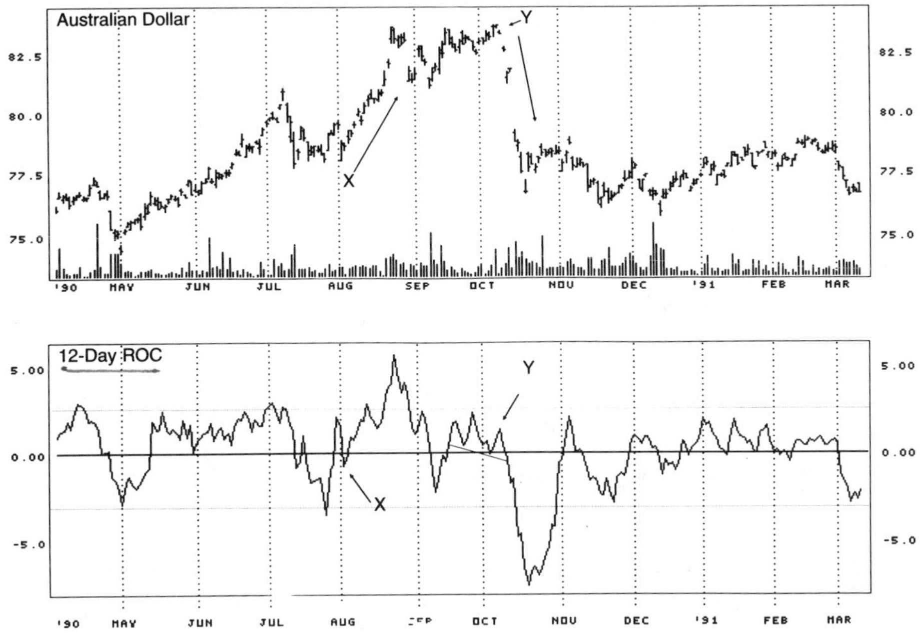

Complex Divergences

Complex divergences work quite well with the rate-of-change concept. In this respect, chart 3.16 illustrates how a 10 and 20-day time span can be integrated for the timing of short-term price movements. It is important to make sure that the time spans for the two oscillators are sufficiently far enough apart to reflect two different cycles and that when a complex divergence appears, it is also confirmed by some kind of reversal in the price trend.

Moving Averages of ROC Indicators

The ROC lends itself very easily to the smoothing process. Even though we will be devoting a whole chapter to this concept in the form of the KST System, a few comments are relevant at this point. As mentioned in chapter 2, the volatility common to short-term time spans makes these oscillators subject to a significant amount of whipsaw crossovers. A better approach is to use the moving

Chart 3.16   Deutsche Mark and Two Momentum Indicators

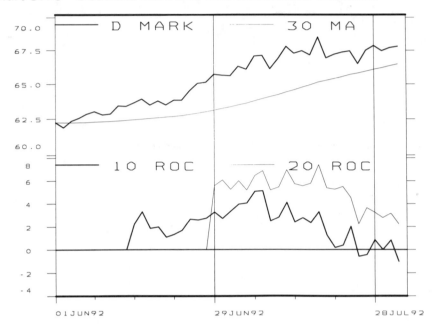

average itself as a signaling device. In chart 3.17, changes in direction of the 12-month moving average of a 12-month ROC are used as the signaling points. These are indicated by the arrows. In chart 3.18 a 12-day moving average of a 12-day ROC and an 8-day moving average of both the Moving Average and ROC are featured. Signals are generated when the shorter-term average crosses above or below the longer-term one. Chart 3.19, on the other hand, features a longer-term time frame. Signals are generated when the oscillator, having moved into overbought or oversold territory, then moves back through the barrier lines on its way back towards the equilibrium level. The oscillator is a 12-month ROC Smoothed with a 6-month moving average. One of the drawbacks of this approach is that it can fail to signal countervailing signals. Thus the mid-1980 buy signal was not offset by a sell signal and so forth.

A variation of this approach involves an additional smoothing. The advantage of the double-smoothing is that it filters out several false or temporary changes in the direction of the unsmoothed version. The disadvantage is that the signals appear at a later date and can occur well after the signal you are waiting for. This drawback becomes a major disadvantage if this approach is being

Chart 3.17   Comit Index Monthly and a 12-Month Moving
Average of a 12-Month Rate-of-Change

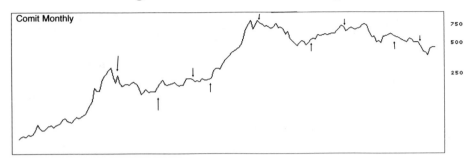

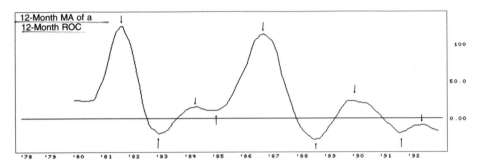

Chart 3.18   S&P 500 and a 12-Day Moving Average of a
12-Day Rate-of-Change with an 8-Day EMA

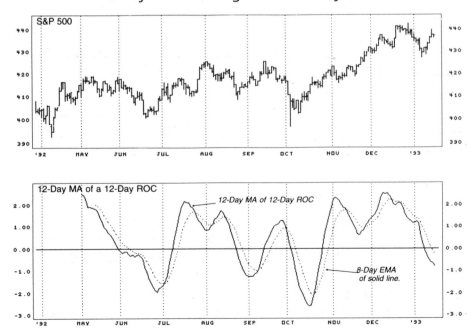

Chart 3.19 AAA Bonds and a 12-Month Moving Average
                 of a 12-Month Rate-of-Change

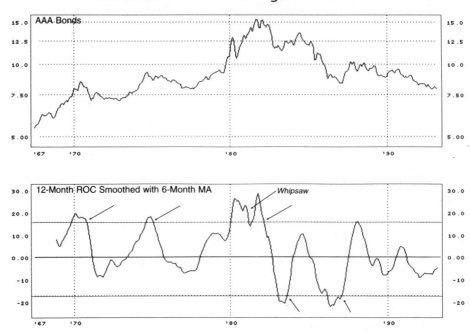

used as part of a mechanical trading system in conjunction with a
signal confirming a reversal in the price trend. On the other hand,
if the chosen combination offers reliable but sometimes untimely
signals, just use the timely ones for the purpose of making a trade
or an investment. This method will not, by definition, be able to offer
a suitable exit point, since you will not know whether the
countervailing signal will be timely or late. However, if we work on
the assumption that the timely entry point will be followed by a
worthwhile price move, it should be a fairly simple matter to use
some other method to signal a good time to take profits.

This idea of "smoothing" an ROC indicator at least once opens
up a whole series of possible variations. These include choosing
time spans for specific rate-of-change indicators, picking various
time spans for the smoothing, and, of course, deciding whether to
smooth once, twice, three times, and so forth. Obviously, the
potential combinations are innumerable. I would add, though, that
it is a wise philosophy to keep things as simple as possible. Most
people believe that they will not be successful unless they try out
as many possibilities and combinations as they can. In the days

when the calculations were done with pen and paper these possibilities were limited, but in this age of powerful personal computers, it is very easy to toy with a thousand variations looking for the perfection that I guarantee you does not exist. In my view, the better approach is the simple and thoughtful one: Spend your time and effort on studying and analysis.

Summary

1. Rate-of-change is a simple concept that measures the acceleration or deceleration of a price trend over time.
2. It can be calculated for any period and is subject to all of the principles of interpretation described in chapters 1 and 2.
3. It lends itself well to trendline construction and price-pattern recognition.
4. The principal disadvantage of the ROC indicator is that it does not provide pre-defined levels that can be used for the construction of overbought and oversold lines.

chapter 4

THE RSI INDICATOR

- **Introduction**
- **RSI Calculation**
- **Pros and Cons of the RSI**
- **Interpreting the RSI**
- **Equilibrium Crossovers**
- **Comparing RSI Time Spans**

Introduction

The RSI indicator, commonly known as the "Relative Strength Indicator," was introduced by Welles Wilder in his 1978 book *New Concepts in Technical Trading*.[1] RSI indicates momentum only. It should never be confused with the principle of (Comparative) Relative Strength, where *one* series is divided by another. Relative strength is most commonly used to compare the performance of a stock with a market average. Figure 4.1 shows that it is plotted as a continuous line. A rising line indicates that the stock is outperforming the market; a falling line signifies an underperforming stock. The RSI, on the other hand, is a front-weighted, price-velocity ratio for a specific security. In effect, it is a momentum indicator that *compares* the price of a security relative to itself and is, therefore, "relative" to its past performance.

Figure 4.1

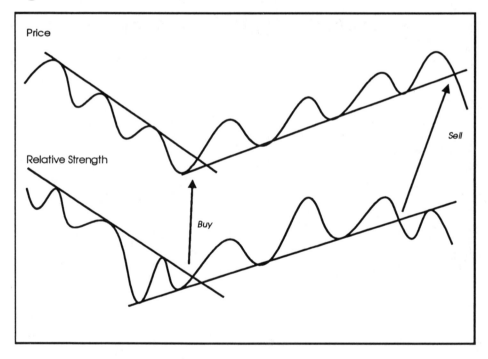

[1] Wilder, Wells, *New Concepts in Technical Trading*. Greensboro, NC: Trend Research, 1978.

RSI Calculation

The formula for the RSI is as follows:

$$RSI = 100 - \left[\frac{100}{1+RS}\right]$$

RS equals the average of the closes of the up days divided by the average of the closes of the down days. In the standard calculation originally presented by Wilder, the time span for the total was set at 14. Thus, RS would be the average of the closes of the up days over a 14-day period divided by the average of the down days over a 14-day span. This 14-day period represents half the lunar cycle, or 28 days, although the time span can be set for any period. Wilder selected this particular time span because he considered the 28-day cycle as the most prevalent one for short-term markets. This is difficult to rationalize though, since the indicator is calculated on the basis of *trading* not calendar days and there are only about 20 trading days in a month. Since the introduction of the RSI, traders have experimented with a number of alternative time spans, thus creating the very popular 9- and 22-day periods.

Today, most traders and investors use a software package such as MetaStock or Computrack to automatically plot market indicators. But for those who prefer to use pen and paper here is the method of calculation for a 14-day RSI:

1. Add the closing values for the up days and divide the total by 14.
2. Repeat this process for the down days.
3. Divide the resulting up-day average by the down-day average. This quotient is the "RS" in the formula.
4. Add one to the quotient obtained from step three (i.e., add 1 to the RS).
5. Divide 100 by the sum resulting from step four.
6. Subtract the result of step five from 100.
7. Repeat steps 1–6 the next day, adding the data for day 15 and dropping the data for day 1. This process can be continued ad infinitum. (For a short cut to this manual method of computing the RSI, refer to Wilder's book pp 66-67.)

Pros and Cons of the RSI

The RSI has several advantages over a simple ROC calculation. They do not make this method a better momentum indicator, because the ROC has some benefits that the RSI lacks. Nevertheless, the RSI offers many advantages:

1. It is less volatile than the ROC. Consider the example of a 10-day rate-of-change as shown in table 4.1. As the table shows, the price of the particular stock falls sharply from 102 to 80 between Day 11 and Day 12. The ROC calculation calls for the value on Day 12 to be divided by the stock's price on Day 3. Because the closing price is identical on both days, the calculation results in a reading of 100. This is an increase over the previous day's reading of 79, but, as we see, the stock's price is declining. Of course, a lot will depend on the specific day of comparison. In most instances this problem will not arise because the ROC will not usually give such a distorted picture.

    Because the RSI takes the average of the up and down days, its results are less affected by a sharp dip or rise on a specific day. As a result, this method tends to be a more stable momentum indicator than the ROC calculation.

Table 4.1 Calculation of a 10-Day ROC

Price	ROC	
Day 1	100	
Day 2	101	
Day 3	80	
Day 4	80	
Day 5	95	
Day 6	97	
Day 7	96	
Day 8	95	
Day 9	98	
Day 10	100	
Day 11	102	
Day 12	80	79
Day 13	80	100

2. In chapter 1 we discussed the analogy of a dog on a leash and its relationship to overbought and oversold levels. We also saw in chapter 3 that one of the problems with the ROC is that it is possible for this indicator to move to unusual extremes, making it act like a rubber leash. Some securities perform this way and are more volatile than others. In other words, the leashes vary in their elasticity. This means that it is often not possible to compare the volatility of two different securities because their oscillators are plotted on different scales. To quote Wilder: "There must be some common denominator to apply to all commodities so the amplitude of the oscillator is relative and meaningful."[2]

The RSI avoids this drawback, because its absolute levels are set at 100 and 0, although in practice these extremes are rarely attained. With the RSI it is possible to gauge whether one security is more volatile than another by comparing their up and down movements. A more important benefit that flows from this characteristic is that it is much easier to establish universal standards for the overbought and oversold benchmarks. Using the 14-day default, these levels are traditionally set at 30 for oversold and 70 for overbought as in figure 4.2 and chart 4.1.

It is important to note that the magnitude of the oscillations of the RSI relative to the time span are inverse to that of most other momentum series. To illustrate, over a long time span the rate-of-change indicator is subject to wider fluctuations than the relative strength indicator. The opposite is true for the RSI. Charts 4.2 and 4.3 show this for a 9-day and a 65-day RSI and ROC. Note how the overbought and oversold lines for the 65-day ROC are placed at twice the distance from the zero level (5.0) than for the 9-day series (2.5). In the case of the RSI these lines are plotted closer to the 50 (equilibrium point) for the longer span (i.e., 57.5 and 42.5 vs 80 and 20 respectively). The nature of the oscillations of the ROC and RSI do not change materially with different time spans. This can be seen by comparing the broad movements of both 65-day series.

In *New Commodity Trading Systems*, Perry Kaufman questions the 14-day time span selection. He points out that a maximum divergence occurs when the moving average is exactly half the

[2] Ibid.

Figure 4.2

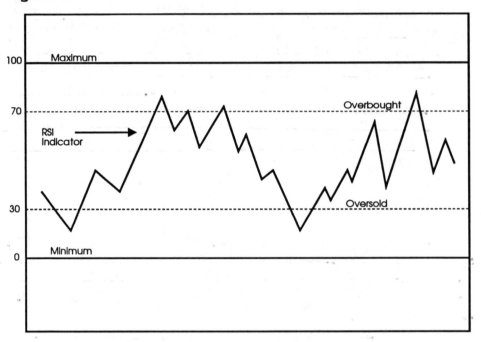

Chart 4.1   Treasury Bonds 3-Month Perpetual Contract and 14-Day RSI

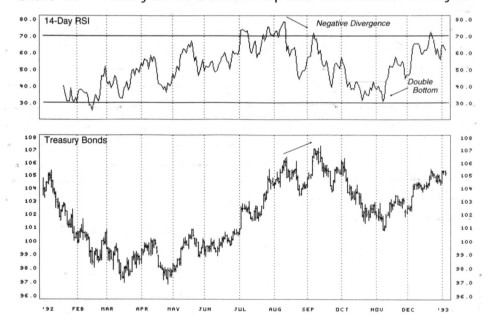

Chart 4.2   Treasury Bonds 3-Month Perpetual
Contract and the RSI Indicator

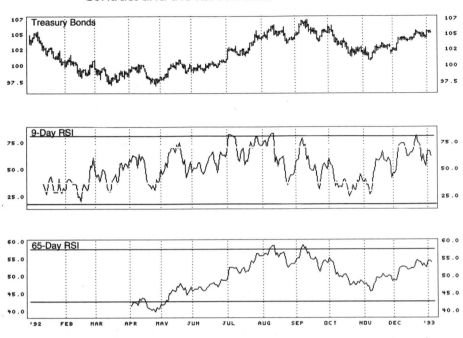

Chart 4.3   Treasury Bonds 3-Month Perpetual
Contract and 2 ROC Indicators

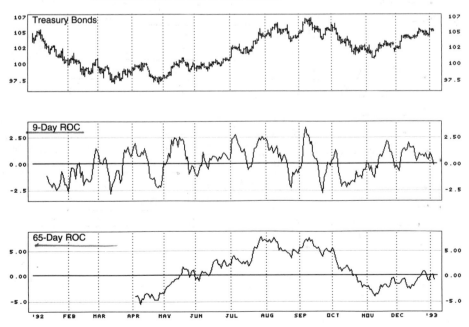

time span of the dominant cycle.[3] In other words, if you accept the
assumption that the primary trend of the stock market revolves
around the 4-year business cycle, a moving average of a 24-month
period will give you the greatest divergence between the high and
low points of the cycle. In the case of the 28-day cycle, 14 days is
the correct choice, but it is important to understand that there are
many other cycles other than the lunar cycle. Working on this
assumption, this would mean that a 14-hour RSI would be inappropriate if the dominant cycle was something other than 28-hours.
The same would be true for weekly and monthly data.

Interpreting the RSI

Many of the basic principles of momentum interpretation described
in chapters 1–2 and expanded somewhat in chapter 3 apply to the
RSI. To avoid repetition, those readers who have skimmed through
those sections should review that material. I will cover just a few of
the points that are most germane to the RSI.

Wilder lists five basic interpretations of the RSI. They are as
follows:

1. Tops and Bottoms. Tops occur when the indicator moves
   above 70, bottoms when it falls below 30. This, of course, is
   another way of expressing the overbought and oversold
   characteristics described earlier. Since momentum typically
   turns ahead of the price, these "tops" and "bottoms" often give
   advance warning of a strengthening or deterioration in the
   underlying technical structure.
       It is important to remember that the longer the time span in
   the RSI calculation, the shallower the swing in momentum. Of
   course, the opposite is also true. Consequently, the 70/30
   combination is inappropriate when the time span is either
   shorter or longer than the standard 14-day period. Chart 4.4
   demonstrates a 5-day RSI where an 80/20 combination gives
   a much better feel for the overbought/oversold extreme than

[3] Kaufman, Perry, *New Commodity Trading Systems*. New York : John Wiley,
1987.

Chart 4.4   Swiss Franc and 5-Day RSI

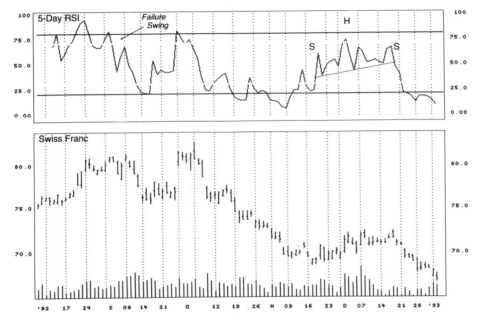

the 70/30 default value. This is because shorter time spans result in wider RSI oscillations. In chart 4.5, on the other hand, a 30-day span returns an RSI where the extremes of 80 and 20 are rarely achieved. Even though the 80 level was reached in late 1991, a more appropriate point for the overbought/oversold lines appears to be 65 and 35.

When referring to the type of data under consideration the terms "long" and "short" are relative. For example, a 60-day RSI would represent an extremely long span for daily data, but for monthly numbers, a 60-day period (i.e., two months) would be very short. Therefore, some consideration should be given to this factor when choosing an RSI time span. Ideally, you want to choose an interval where the peaks and troughs of the RSI more or less occur simultaneously with tops and bottoms in the actual price. Alternatively, you might wish to select a shorter time span, which allows for the accumulation of divergences. In the real world, where the duration of any given price-trend classification fluctuates over short, intermediate, or long terms, it is not possible to come up with the perfect span for either instance. Chart 4.6 shows that tops and bottoms do

Chart 4.5   Japanese Yen and 30-Day RSI

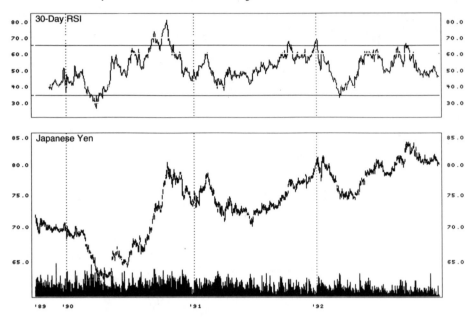

Chart 4.6   Japanese Yen and 14-Day RSI

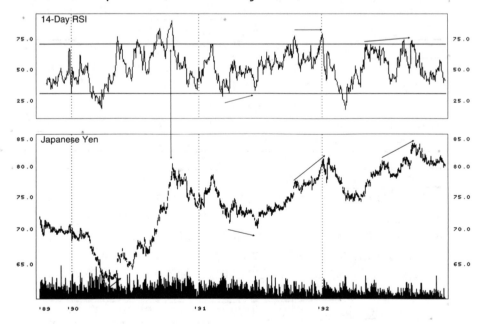

not generally signal important reversal points. The late-1990
peak is one exception, but generally the 14-day RSI used here
is more suitable for the analysis of a divergence or a near-
divergence. On the other hand, chart 4.7 uses the same data
but expands the time span to a 60-day period. Now we can see
that the peaks and troughs in the RSI more or less correspond
to those of the yen. Even here, the record is not perfect, since
the early 1991 bottom is associated with a positive divergence. Even so, a comparison of these two time spans
indicates that one is more suited to divergence analysis than
the other.

2. Chart Formations. The RSI is one of the few indicators that can
   be used to chart pattern construction. Such configurations do
   not appear to form as often as in the ROC indicator, but they
   nevertheless represent a useful addition to the RSI analysis.
   In *New Concepts in Technical Trading*, Wilder points out that
   the RSI is subject to "head-and-shoulders tops or bottoms,
   pennants or triangles often show up on the index."[4] Charts 4.8

Chart 4.7 Japanese Yen and 60-Day RSI

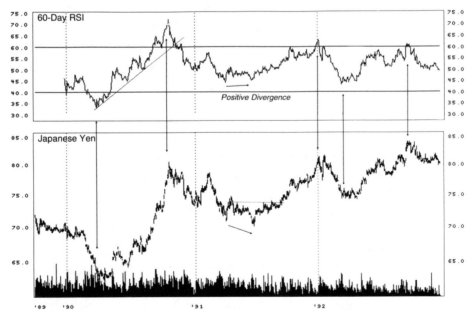

---

[4] Ibid.

Chart 4.8   British Pound and 14-Day RSI

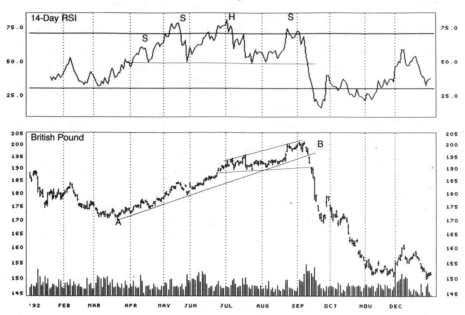

and 4.9 show some classic examples. Chart 4.8 shows a 14-day RSI for pound sterling. Note how the September 1992 peak was associated with a giant head-and-shoulders top in the RSI. Once the neckline at 50 was penetrated and the (AB) trendline in the currency was violated, there was only one possible outcome, especially since the price had simultaneously completed a broadening formation with a flat top. These patterns form when a horizontal line of support diverges from an ascending trendline which "roughly" connects two or more ascending peaks. It is, in effect, a head-and-shoulders top where the technical position is so weak that the price does not have enough time to form the right shoulder.

Chart 4.9 also shows a broadening formation with a flat bottom but this time for the RSI. These are very dangerous configurations, and in the rare case when they put in an appearance they should be treated with great respect. Price movements that follow are usually very significant and long lasting. A head-and-shoulders top in both the RSI and the Dollar Index are also a feature of this chart.

Chart 4.9   Dollar Index Weekly and 26-Week RSI

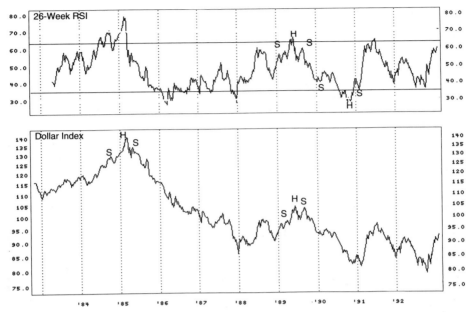

3. Failure Swings. Wilder's "failure swing" is illustrated in figure
   4.3. This swing occurs at both tops and bottoms. It is, in effect,
   a variation of the peak-and-trough analysis described in
   chapter 2. The accepted wisdom is that failure swings are
   most significant after the RSI has moved through an overbought or oversold level (i.e., a level above 70 for a rally or
   below 30 in the case of a decline for the standard 14-day
   span). Once the peak reaches 70 or higher, a reaction sets in.
   A failure swing occurs when the next rally fails to surpass its
   predecessor and the second reaction pushes the RSI below
   the previous low. The second, or failing rally can take the form
   of one large movement or several small ones. The key to
   determining whether a failure swing has been signaled lies in
   the fact that the second rally does not exceed the first. Failure
   swings also occur at bottoms where the exact opposite set of
   conditions appear. This would involve a decline below the
   oversold level, a subsequent rally, a successful "test" of the
   previous low, and finally a rally that takes the index above the
   previous high. Generally, the more extreme the reading at the

Figure 4.3

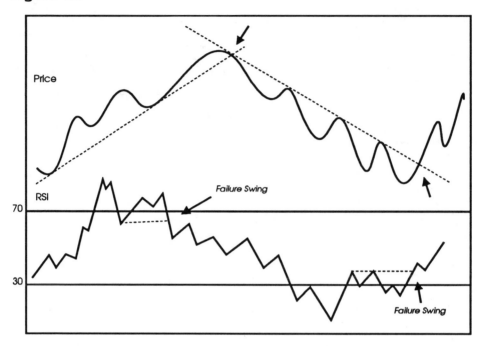

time of the failure swing, the greater its significance. Chart 4.10 shows an actual example of a 9-day RSI for the German Dax Index. The first failure swing is signaled at point D, and the second at H. Note that two tops denoted by A and C are really the head and the right shoulder of a head-and-shoulders top. On the other hand, H marks the breakout from a double-bottom formation in the RSI. This failure-swing principle implies, that it is a perfectly correct assumption that peak-and-trough analysis can be applied justifiably to RSI interpretation. Chart 4.10 also shows how the late 1991-early 1992 rally experiences a series of four ascending peaks in the RSI. These were reversed at point D at the time of the failure swing. The second failure swing at point H also signaled that the series of declining peaks and troughs in the RSI between June and July had been reversed.

While the concepts of peak-and-trough analysis and failure swings can be quite useful, in many instances they are not as reliable as we might like. For this reason, I believe that they should be used in conjunction with other RSI techniques, such as trendlines and price patterns. When more than one of these

Chart 4.10   German DAX and 9-Day RSI

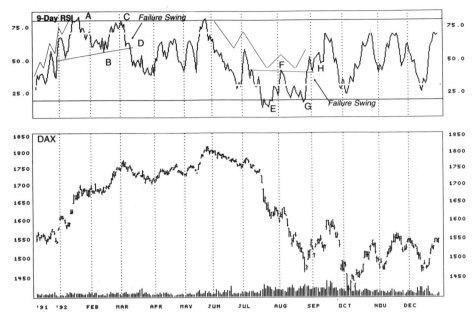

phenomena are present, the signals are likely to be significantly more reliable.

4. Support and Resistance. We touched on this concept in
   chapter 2 as it applied to trendlines. However, horizontal
   support and resistance areas can also be applied to momentum. It is more apparent in the RSI than in the ROC indicator
   because the 0–100 parameters of the RSI means that the
   same points are crossed and recrossed a greater number of
   times than in the case of an ROC with a similar time span.
   Wilder emphasizes that the support and resistance lines
   constructed from the Index often correspond to trendlines
   drawn on the price series. In *New Concepts* he does not
   differentiate between support and resistance levels that are
   actual numbers such as 50/35, for example, and support and
   resistance that is reflected in trendlines or moving averages.
   "Support and resistance" as described here refers to actual
   horizontal levels.

   An example of this is shown in chart 4.11. I have drawn the
   lines to correspond to the approximate 20, and 50 levels.
   Smaller lines have also been placed at various other points
   where the Index finds support or resistance. You can also see

Chart 4.11   Comex Gold and 14-Day RSI

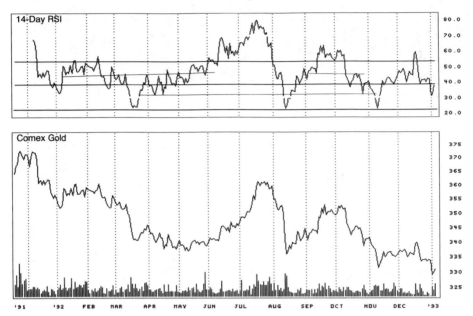

that the 30 and 70 levels can act as pivotal points on occasion. Clearly, it is one thing to know that these benchmarks exist but quite another to put them to practical use, since their repeated appearance is often quite random in nature. For this reason I do not consider support-and-resistance characteristics to be particularly helpful in charting momentum.

5. Divergence. One of the most useful functions of the RSI is to point out divergences between the price and momentum. This subject was discussed at length in chapter 1 and examples occur in most of the charts in this chapter. In particular we might consider the August-September bottom in the British stock market featured in chart 4.12. The actual low in late August was preceded by an RSI that had begun to walk uphill. Even more impressive was the fact that each time the Index touched the 2375 area, the RSI continued to record increasingly higher numbers. These points have been flagged on the chart as X1 through X4. This characteristic does not represent an actual divergence between price and momentum, but it does reflect the concept that the longer the trend of an improving momentum is after a sharp setback, the more bullish the technical position becomes.

Chart 4.12 Financial Times Stock Exchange 100 and 14-Day RSI

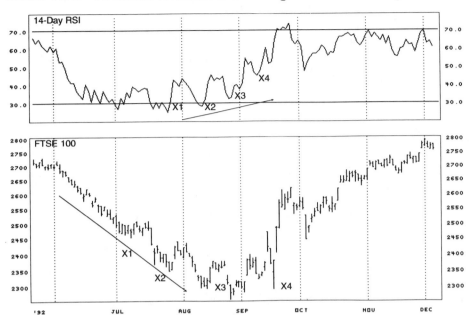

By the same token, it is important to note that if this trend of improving momentum falters, the consequences are equally as bearish as they were *potentially* bullish. I like to compare this situation to that of a spring being wound. If the spring is wound up tightly and then allowed to unwind in a powerful but controlled way, the result is highly favorable. On the other hand, if the spring snaps while being wound, the effect is highly destructive. Chart 4.13 gives a good demonstration. The RSI was gradually walking uphill between December 1991 and March of 1992, yet the Nikkei was marking time. Finally, the trendline for both the RSI and Index were violated. This indicated that the technical structure had completely broken down.

6. Trendlines. As discussed above, Wilder extends the idea of trendline construction for the RSI under the banner of support and resistance. It is true that support and resistance are reflected in trendlines, but this is a concept that technicians generally reserve for actual levels. For example, between 1966 and 1983 the Dow 1,000 level proved to be a major psychological barrier of resistance. Experience in the marketplace demonstrates that the concept of RSI trendline con-

Chart 4.13   Nikkei Stocks Index and 14-Day RSI

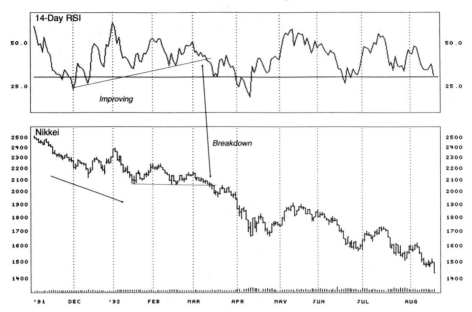

struction is an unquestionably valid approach to plotting momentum. Arguably, it is the most important of all.

We can see some trendlines in operation in charts 4.13 and 4.14. In chart 4.14 the violation of line AB signified that the downward trend in momentum was probably being reversed. As we can see, this turned out to be the case. However, this did *not* signal the actual price low. The low was signaled only after the price had *violated* a trendline. This episode stresses the reason why momentum must be confirmed by price. Note the two head-and-shoulders tops that occurred in July and December 1990 for both momentum and price. Additional examples of trendlines in action are presented in chart 4.15 for the weekly Gold Fix and a 39-week RSI.

7. RSI and Moving Averages. It is possible to extend the idea of moving-average crossovers to the RSI. However, even though this indicator is more docile than the ROC in the sense that it is less erratic, it is still not smooth enough to avoid a significant number of whipsaws. Furthermore, since the RSI is confined within the parameters of 0 to 100, trends are less sustainable than those calculated using the ROC indicator. Hence, a

Chart 4.14   S&P 500 and 14-Day RSI

Chart 4.15   Gold and 39-Week RSI

moving average serves to smooth the RSI calculations, making it a more reliable alternative to the ROC. The raw data is then discarded and the moving average is used to trigger buy-and-sell alerts. In chart 4.16, the 14-day RSI of the gold price has been smoothed with a 10-day simple moving average. Signals are given when the average reverses direction from an extreme zone and crosses back on its way towards the 50 level, or level of equilibrium. At first glance this approach looks to be almost perfect, but if the relationship is examined a little more closely, we discover that some of the signals, such as those of early 1990, result in a consolidation rather than a rally. The buy signal in early 1992, on the other hand, was a little too early, and so forth.

In this example the overbought and oversold zones have been tightened to a 65/35 combination. Despite the fact that the time span for the RSI is 14-days, the smoothing effect from the moving average results in smaller swings, so naturally the overbought/oversold zones need to be closer to the equilibrium point.

Chart 4.17 shows a 9-day RSI smoothed by an 8-day moving average for the Australian dollar. The buy and sell alerts based on

Chart 4.16   Comex Gold and 10-Day Moving Average of RSI

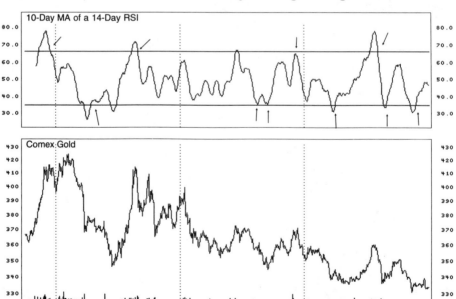

Chart 4.17   Australian Dollar and Smoothed RSI

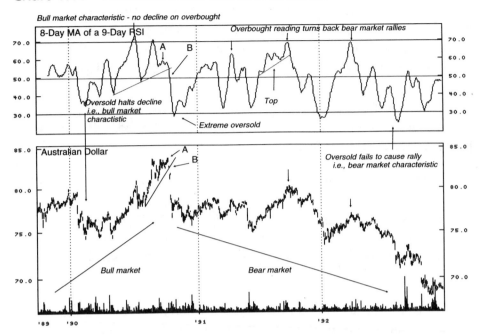

the overbought/oversold crossover principle also appear to work reasonably well. However, a study of the chart also brings out some other very useful ideas. First, even though this is a short-term indicator, it reflects the concepts of bull- and bear-market characteristics discussed in chapter 1. Note how the early 1990 reaction was associated only with a moderately oversold condition, yet this was sufficient to stem the decline in the Australian currency.

Contrast this *bull-market* movement with the late 1991 decline. In this instance, a deep oversold condition, far greater than anything seen in the recent past, failed to trigger a meaningful rally. This condition was even more obvious in the two mid-1992 oversold readings and is characteristic of *bear-market* activity.

The chart highlights another notable point: The first overbought rally in the summer of 1990 did not result in a sell-off of any magnitude. Such action indicates a *bull* market and is in stark contrast to the three rallies that penetrated the 70 area in 1991 and 1992. This extreme sensitivity to an overbought condition is again characteristic of a *bear* market.

Finally, the turning point between bull and bear was signaled loud and clear in the fall of 1990. As you can see, the rally at point

A was just barely able to push the RSI above the 50, or equilibrium, level. When this was followed by a trendbreak at point B in both the indicator and price, this particular calculation indicated that the currency would experience a very sharp setback, which it did.

The above points are important enough to reiterate:

1. Overbought or oversold conditions in a bull or bear market do not customarily generate meaningful reactions unless preceded by divergences.
2. In bull or bear markets meaningful rallies are usually signaled once an overbought or oversold condition has been generated.
3. One of the first signs of a new bull (bear) market occurs when a short-term oscillator moves to the type of extreme overbought (oversold) condition that has not been seen since the previous bear (bull) market.

There are countless other ways in which the RSI could be used in conjunction with moving averages on the lines discussed in the previous two chapters. The possibilities are limited only by the imagination of the user.

Equilibrium Crossovers

In the *Encyclopedia of Technical Indicators*, Colby and Meyers tested various overbought/oversold combinations.[5] They based their research on weekly periods using several decades of stock market data, but they were unable to find any combination of time span and overbought/oversold level that resulted in significant profits. Given what we have learned about the characteristics of bull and bear market momentum, these results are not surprising. Technical analysis is an art, not a science. That means it is very important to consider the *manner* in which an indicator moves into an overbought or oversold zone rather than treat the signal as a mechanical device requiring no interpretation.

Indeed, Colby and Meyers found that the best results came from a simple equilibrium (50) crossover: Buy when above 50, sell

[5] Colby, Robert and Meyers, Thomas, *Encyclopedia of Technical Indicators*, Homewood II: Dow Jones-Irwin, 1988.

when below. The best time spans were clustered on either side of the 20 weeks, with the 21-week span providing the highest profit of all. Of the 75 trades 21 of them, or 28%, produced a profit.

Comparing RSI Time Spans

The greater volatility of shorter-term RSI indicators over the ROC has been previously noted. So, too, has the fact that the overbought and oversold levels should be adjusted to fit the time span. In this respect the shorter the span, the larger the swing and the more extreme the level. A third point to remember is that time spans are always relative to the chosen data format (i.e., day, week, month and so on). In other words, a 5-day RSI is likely to be just as volatile as a 5-week or 5-month RSI, even though in terms of actual time passed their spans are far different.

Comparison of different spans can also be useful from two aspects. The first deals with perspective. For example, a 14-day RSI gives you little inclination as to the direction or maturity of the main trend. On the other hand, a 12-month RSI, such as the one shown in chart 4.18, often can warn of an imminent turning point.

Chart 4.18   S&P Composite Monthly and 12-Month RSI

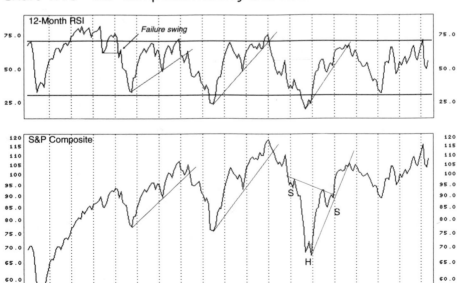

This, in turn, puts signals from a shorter-term series into perspec-tive. Short-term traders entering a long position in the market are better able to do so when both the short- and long-term RSIs are in an oversold condition. As discussed earlier, if a trader is going to make a mistake it is much easier to do so when going against the primary trend. Monitoring the action of a long-term RSI will not provide all the answers by any means, but it will certainly help to warn a trader that the prevailing trend is very mature and that perhaps the odds are against a short-term position. I will have more to say on this idea of relating primary to short-term trends when discussing the KST system in chapter 8.

The second point of time-span comparisons revolves around the fact that at any juncture there are a number of different cycles simultaneously operating on the price. If we just consider a 5-day RSI, we completely overlook any information that might be gleaned from other time spans. In some cases it might be possible to spot a price pattern in one period that does not show up in another. Trendlines and divergences are additional characteristics that may appear more prominently in some series than in others. This point was discussed in greater detail in chapter 3, but it applies equally to the RSI and the ROC.

Summary

1. The RSI fluctuates between the extreme levels of 0 and 100.
2. The magnitude of the RSIs movements vary inversely with the time span. The shorter the period the more extreme the oscillation; the longer the period the more moderate the oscillation.
3. The RSI can be calculated for any period, but the accepted standard is 14-days. 9- and 22-day intervals are also widely used.
4. The establishment of overbought and oversold benchmarks varies with the time span used in constructing the RSI. The default value for a 14-day period is 70 and 30.
5. The RSI can be interpreted using most of the principles discussed in the first two chapters.

chapter 5

TREND DEVIATION AND THE MACD INDICATOR

- **Introduction**
- **Trend Deviation and a Moving Average**
  - **Moving Averages**
  - **Interpretation**
- **The MACD Indicator**

Introduction

In this chapter, I will explain the various ways to construct trend-deviation indicators and describe the advantages and disadvantages of these indicators. I will also cover principles of interpretation. The final section is devoted to the Moving Average Convergent Divergent (MACD) method, one of the most popular momentum indicators in the technical arsenal.

So far the discussion has been limited to indicators that are constructed from a comparison of the current price to a previous one. Another possibility is to relate the current price to some form of trend measurement. This concept works on the assumption that while prices move in trends, they do not move in a straight line. Rather, they fluctuate around that trend. These fluctuations form the basis for trend-deviation momentum oscillators. The *types* of trends and the *way* that the price relates to them gives rise to the variety of methods for calculating these oscillators. When a rate-of-change momentum indicator is compared to a trend-deviation series, the results are more or less the same as long as the time frames are identical. There are, of course, some subtle differences. That is why it is often a useful idea to compare indicators based on these different construction methods.

Trend Deviation and a Moving Average

The simplest form of calculating a trend deviation involves the relationship between the current price and a moving average. The oscillator is constructed by comparing the latest price by the average. This comparison is shown in figure 5.1.

Calculating a trend-deviation oscillator can be done using either subtraction or division. The merits of each method were discussed in chapter 3, which covered the rate-of-change indicator. Since the principles of interpretation for both the ROC and trend-deviation methods are essentially the same, they will both give the same conclusion. For very short-term trends there is very little difference, but for longer-term price movements the division calculation is much preferred because it is better reflecting any proportionate price movements. Table 5.1 shows how the calculation would be done for a deviation from a 15-day simple moving average.

Figure 5.1

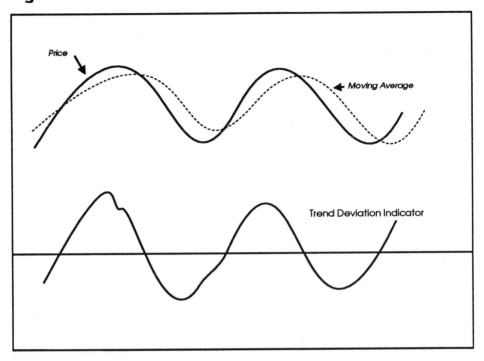

Table 5.1 Simple 15-Day Moving Average Deviation

Date	Price	15-Day Moving Average	Price + Moving Average × 100
March 1	25	20	125%
2	26	21	123.8%
3	28	22	127.3%
4	26	23	1.13%
5	24	24	100%
8	21	24	87.5%
9	18	23	78.3%

Quite simply, when the price and the average are identical, the oscillator is plotted at zero. When it is above the average, the momentum series is in positive territory, and vice versa. Zero or equilibrium crossovers, therefore, indicate when the price crosses above and below its moving average. This approach has an advantage over the ROC method because zero crossovers, by definition, also offer a *price trend reversal signal*. In effect, simple trend deviation oscillators represent b*oth* momentum and trend reversal signals in one indicator.

The principles of momentum interpretation, outlined in the first two chapters, by and large apply to oscillators constructed from the trend-deviation method. We shall delve a little deeper into this matter later. First, though, let's take a look at the implications of the length and type of moving averages used in the construction of these indicators. I would like to start with a few words on moving averages.

Moving Averages

A "moving average" is a technique that helps to smooth out or eliminate random day-to-day fluctuations in price. In effect, it is the technician's way of trying to graphically come up with a mechanism that can represent the underlying trend. It is important to remember, though, that there is no such thing as a perfect moving average. In his 1930's book *Profits in the Stock Market,* H.M. Gartley said this about the moving average:

> "If stock market cycles were absolutely regular, as to both time and amplitude, it would be possible to select a moving average which, when plotted on the charts, would be an absolute straight line. But as the likeliness of successive stock market cycles is only coincident, and rarely are there two cyclical movements in stock prices which even closely resemble each other, there is practically never a case where a moving average, when applied to a trend in stock prices, forms a straight line.
>
> "However, the selection of moving averages of certain duration frequently results in a line which is far more straight than the actual price fluctuations upon which the moving average is based."[1]

Gartley is referring to stock prices, but the comments apply to any freely traded market. The simple average is just a continuous-mean average of a set of data over a specific period. A 10-day moving average for today is the average of the current and previous

[1] Gartley, H. M., *Profits in the Stock Market*, Lambert-Gann Publishing.

9-days of data (closing prices are almost always used). Tomorrow's average will include tomorrow's closing price, but the price nine days ago from today will be dropped in order to keep the span to 10 days. The process is continued each day as demonstrated in table 5.2. The simple moving average treats each day's data equally, but other moving-average calculations give greater emphasis to the more recent data.

There are many ways to do this, but the most popular are the "weighted" and "exponential" methods. In its simplest form the weighted average places gradually greater emphasis on the more recent data. In this way, the latest period carries the greatest weight. For example, in a 10-day weighted moving-average calculation we might give the first day a weight of 1, the second a weight of 2, and so on all the way up to the current day which would be weighted by a factor of 10. This idea is shown in table 5.3. The advantage of the weighted moving average is that it reverses direction faster than a simple moving average. The disadvantage, apart from the drudgery of the calculation, is that it reverses direction many more times than the simple average. As a result of this sensitivity, it is subject to many more whipsaws. In technical analysis there is no way to escape the need to balance timeliness and sensitivity. This comparison, of course, assumes that the time frames are identical. A weighted moving average with a substan-

Table 5.2   Simple 10-Day Moving Average Calculation

Date	Price	10-Day Total	10-Day Average
Jan 2	121		
3	124		
4	123		
5	128		
8	130		
9	132		
10	129		
11	127		
12	125		
15	124	1,263	126.3
16	126	1,268	126.8
17	128	1,272	127.2
18	130	1,279	127.9

Table 5.3   10-Day Weighted Moving Average Calculation

Date	Col.1 Price	Col. 2 10× Col. 1	Col. 3 9× Col. 1 1 wk. ago	Col. 4 8× Col. 1 2 wks. ago	Col. 5 7× Col. 1 3 wks. ago	Col. 6 6× Col. 1 4 wks. ago	Col. 7 5× Col. 1 5 wks. ago	Col. 8 4× Col. 1 6 wks. ago	Col. 9 3× Col. 1 7 wks. ago	Col. 10 2× Col. 1 8 wks. ago	Col. 11 1× Col. 1 9 wks. ago	Col. 12 Total Col. 2-11	Col. 12 + Sum of the Total Weights
Jan 2	121	1210										1210	
3	124	1240	1089									2329	
4	123	1230	1116	968								3314	
5	128	1280	1107	992	847							4226	
8	130	1300	1152	984	868	726						5030	
9	132	1320	1170	1024	861	744	605					5724	
10	129	1290	1188	1040	896	738	620	484				6256	
11	127	1270	1161	1056	910	768	615	496	363			6639	
12	125	1250	1143	1032	924	780	640	492	372	242		6875	
15	124	1240	1125	1016	903	792	650	512	369	248	121	6976	126.8
16	126	1260	1116	1000	889	774	660	520	384	246	124	6946	126.8
17	128	1280	1134	992	875	762	645	528	390	256	123	6985	127.0

tially longer time span will always be less sensitive than a simple moving average using a shorter time frame.

The third popular method of moving-average calculation is the "exponential average," commonly referred to as an EMA. The EMA is really a shortcut to obtaining a form of a weighted moving average. It utilizes a smoothing constant (the alpha sign) that approximates the number of periods (days, weeks or months) for a simple moving average. The difference between today's closing price and yesterday's moving average is multiplied by the exponent or constant according to the following formula: EMA (today) = EMA (yesterday) + alpha sign (today-EMA yesterday).

The first step involves the calculation of a simple moving average. Table 5.4 is for a 10-week EMA. The result is then placed in column 2 for the next day, which in this table is Jan. 2. It is then compared with the closing price for the difference (i.e., 121 – 120 = 1.0) recorded in column 3. The next stage is to multiply the result by the exponent, which for 10 periods is .2. The exponent will vary based on the period under consideration. It will be the same whether the period is 10 days, weeks, months, or even years. Exponents for some selected periods are shown in table 5.5. The exponentially treated difference is then added (or subtracted for a negative number) to the EMA for the previous period and the calculation repeated ad infinitum.

Exponents for periods other than those shown in table 5.5 can be calculated by dividing 2 by the desired time span. For example, a 5-day EMA will be twice as sensitive as a 10-day EMA. Therefore,

Table 5.4

Date	Col.1 Price	Col. 2 EMA for Previous Week	Col. 3 Difference (Col. 1 ± Col. 2)	Col. 4 Exponent	Col. 5 Col. 3 × Col. 4 ±	Col. 6 Col. 2 + Col. 5 EMA
Jan 2	121	120	+1.0	0.2	+.2	120.2
3	124	120.2	+3.8	0.2	+.8	121.0
4	123	121.0	+2.0	0.2	+.4	121.4
5	128	121.4	+6.6	0.2	+1.3	122.7

Table 5.5

Number of Weeks	Exponent
5	0.4
10	0.2
15	0.13
20	0.1
40	0.05
80	0.25

the exponent 2 divided by 5 (0.4) will be twice as great, since 2 divided by 10 gives an exponent of 0.2.

Fortunately, most of us do not need to worry about making tedious calculations because the computer now does it for us.

Interpretation

We discovered in chapter 3 that the magnitude of an ROC oscillation is, other things being equal, a function of the time span under consideration. In other words, the longer the span, the greater the swing and vice versa. A similar principle applies to trend-deviation oscillators. The big difference here is that the time span is a function of the length of the moving average. In this case, the longer the average, the greater the fluctuation. Since the weighted and EMA averages are more sensitive than a simple moving average, this also means that the magnitude of the oscillations associated with them will be less than a comparable time span. Moreover, their greater sensitivity also results in greater timeliness gained, of course, at the expense of more whipsaw signals.

Chart 5.1 shows a simple moving average deviation for a 12-day time frame in the lower panel and a weighted one in the lower box. The subtle differences in scale and volatility are evident. Most futures traders seem to prefer the EMA as opposed to the simple moving-average deviation. I have never seen any evidence that suggests that one is more accurate than the other. This is probably true because a substantial part of the sensitivity benefit offered by the EMA approach is offset by the numerous whipsaws it gives off. Of course, it is always possible to smooth the exponential average twice (i.e., use two exponents) but this too becomes counterproductive, since reliability is gained at the expense of less timely signals.

My belief is that the EMA is more popular because it offers "faster" signals in the highly leveraged, short-term-oriented futures arena. The more complicated math used in its construction also has some appeal. Working on the theory that there is no Holy Grail and that simple is superior to complex, I have tended to use simple moving averages in my work much more than exponentially based indicators. Indeed, in their book *The Encyclopedia of Technical Market Indicators*, Robert Colby and Thomas A. Meyers point out that in the 19 years leading up to 1980 there was really no significant difference between simple, weighted, and EMA crossovers when tested for a range of time spans (1-75 weeks) using weekly data. During that period the best weighted average crossover (69 weeks) turned in the best points profit, 118 points in the S & P Composite. This result compared with 112 and 111 for a 42-week EMA and a 45-week simple moving average, respectively.

However, when other measures such as risk/reward per trade and simple average return are considered, there was little meaningful difference among the three approaches. We must also bear in mind that even though it makes sense to search for a time span or method of construction that avoids inferior results, it is doubtful whether the time spent on ultra fine tuning or debating the advantages of simple-versus-exponential calculations will result in significantly greater profits. Always use indicators you feel comfortable with and have confidence in. If you lack confidence in your indicators, you will have no staying power when the markets turn against you.

Chart 5.1   12-Day Trend Deviation Single vs. Weighted and
Eurodollar Three-Month Perpetual Contract

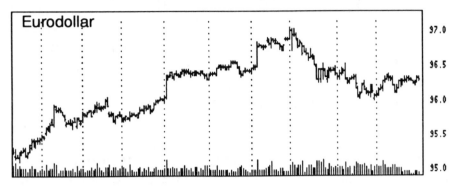

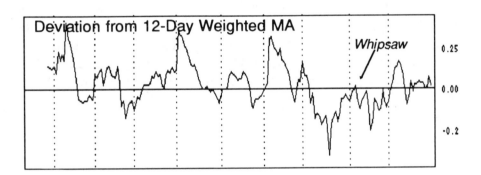

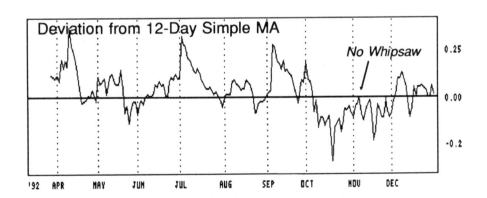

One of the best ways to gain faith in an indicator is to test it to your own satisfaction. Don't take my word for it, prove it to yourself first; after all, it is *you* who will be losing money if you are wrong. If the indicators you use worked reasonably well in the past and are not overly complex, they are likely to help you in the future.

Remember, the most simple trend-deviation method is to compare the closing price to a moving average. The graph representing this calculation is really another way of depicting a price series and moving average surrounded by an envelope. Chart 5.2 shows this concept. The envelope occurs at a vertical distance (i.e., 2% above and below the average). The two envelopes act as support and resistance areas. The lower panel in Chart 5.2 shows how the oscillator is constructed by dividing the closing price by the average price. The overbought and oversold lines have been drawn at the same level as the envelope (i.e., at ±2% of the 30-day EMA). When the closing price falls below the upper envelope on its way back to the moving average, the oscillator also drops below its +2% overbought line on its way back to zero. The placement of the envelopes will vary just as it does for overbought and oversold lines because the same principle applies to both the envelope and trend-deviation calculations.

Chart 5.2   S & P Composite and a Price Oscillator

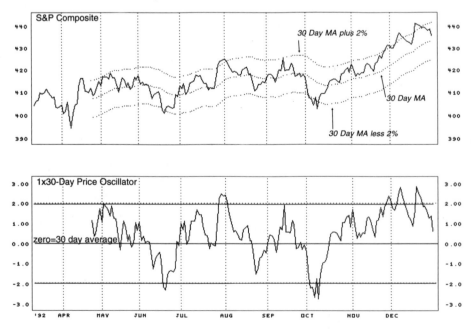

Obviously, if we just consider zero crossovers as buy and sell signals, we are merely substituting an oscillator for a moving-average crossover system, since the moving average and the equilibrium level basically amount to the same thing. In some respects looking at the oscillator can prove to be quite frustrating, since it shows us more vividly the significant number of whipsaw crossovers that can and do happen. Normally, when we look at the same information on a price chart our minds conveniently gloss over this reality.

Apart from keeping us honest, the oscillator also offers an additional advantage over a simple price-versus-moving average presentation. This benefit comes about because the oscillator gives us an inside look at the dynamics of the relationship between the price and the average. Remember, it is a very simple matter to analyze trends in momentum through trendline construction, divergences, price patterns, overbought/oversold analysis, and so on. Using these techniques gives us some advance warning of when a moving average (i.e., the zero level) might be penetrated. Several examples are shown in charts 5.3 and 5.4.

Chart 5.3 Treasury Bonds Three-Month Perpetual
Contract and a Price Oscillator

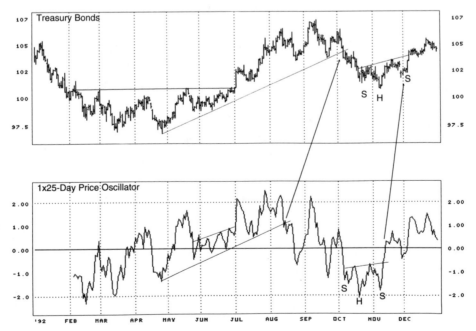

Chart 5.4   39-Week Single Trend Deviation and GTE Corp.

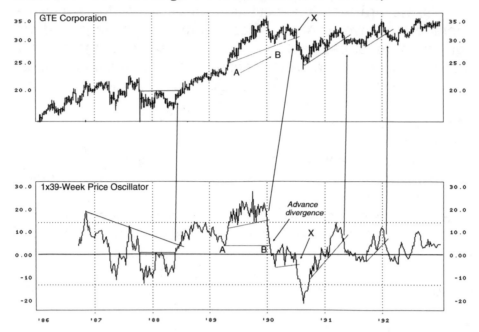

Chart 5.4 shows a 1-week/39-week simple moving-average oscillator of GTEs stock performance. Trend-deviation indicators can be used for any type of data—be it daily, weekly, monthly or even quarterly and annually. In this example, note the completion of the momentum top at Point A, which was confirmed, not by a price pattern in GTE but by a trendline violation instead. Since it occurred at an overbought level, the decline, as might be expected, was quite long and severe. Halfway down, it looked as if the technical position was improving, since the oscillator seemed to diverge positively with the price. However, this constructive action was completely destroyed at Point X as both price and momentum simultaneously broke their small uptrends. This is a good example of the uncontrolled "spring-winding" principle discussed in chapter 4.

There are several techniques that can be used to make the process more efficient. One method is to "lead" the moving average for the purpose of the deviation calculation. Let's say we want to lead the average by five days. This means that instead of dividing today's close by today's average, we divide the closing price by the average five days ago. This technique does have the disadvantage of delaying zero (moving average) crossover signals, but this drawback is often more than outweighed by the elimination of a substantial number of whipsaws. Clearly, the combination of moving-average time spans and periods in which the average is led will affect the efficiency of this approach. This can best be achieved on a trial-and-error basis or though a system-testing module such as those included in the MetaStock or Computrac charting packages.

This concept of leading moving averages was promoted by Gartley in the 1930s. Describing the result, he claimed, "By a slight adaptation in plotting, [moving-average crossovers] can be made into a working tool of considerable significance."[2] He used a 5-day moving average advanced by two days. In other words, the moving average for the seventh day would be plotted on the fifth, that for the eighth on the sixth, and so forth. In Gartley's day, there were no computers in general use so he used a light table and overlaid the moving average on the price. In this way, he was able to see which period offered the most reliable lead. This method allowed him to determine the best candidates visually and to forego the tedium of making a lot of pen-and-paper calculations.

He believed that the best combination of moving average and lead came from a 25-day simple moving average advanced by 3 days. He came to this conclusion from research covering the stock market from the late 1920s to the early 1930s—a period that covered major bull, bear, and transitional markets. Chart 5.5 shows the principle of advancing a simple 25-day moving average by three days for U.S. Treasury Bonds in 1992. Points A, B, and C were all whipsaws under the 25-day moving-average crossover approach, whereas a simple 3-day lead filtered them out. At the same time, we also have to note that the simple lead failed in filtering out the whipsaws at Points D, F, and G. Generally, the leading principle seems to be most effective during a long decline or just after it. At these times quick retracement rallies such as the one that peaked at Point A or base building rallies such as the one at Point B temporarily push the price above the average. However, leading the average seems to provide a quick indication of where the price series is really headed. An additional advantage to this approach is that you know the average value of the moving average for the next three days *ahead* of time. For trading purposes this means you can place stops several days in advance.

[2] Ibid.

Chart 5.5   Treasury Bonds Three-Month Perpetual Contract

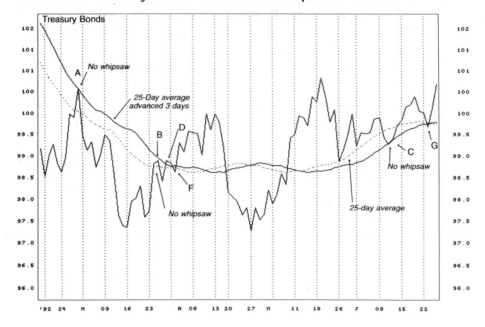

Since this process of advancing a moving average is a useful addition to your moving-average arsenal, it follows that it can be applied equally to trend-deviation analysis. A calculation for a 25-day simple moving average advanced by 3 days is shown in table 5.5. An example of this principle operating in the marketplace is shown in chart 5.6 and described in the caption.

The second method of filtering out whipsaw signals is to substitute a short-term moving average for the closing price in the trend-deviation calculation. The optimum combination of averages can be determined only by trial and error for the type of trend being monitored. Substituting a 2-day moving average for the closing price in a 25-day deviation will not be of much help, since the resulting oscillator will still be quite jagged. You can see this characteristic in the middle panel in chart 5.7. On the other hand, lengthening the averages so that they become too close certainly smoothes out the oscillator but it becomes useless as a timing device. This problem is shown in the lower panel in chart 5.7.

The best approach is to arrange the calculation so that the spread between the averages is somewhere between two and five times. A commonly used combination is a 5-period average divided by a 25-period average. The resulting oscillator generates its best

Chart 5.6   CRB and Two Price Oscillators

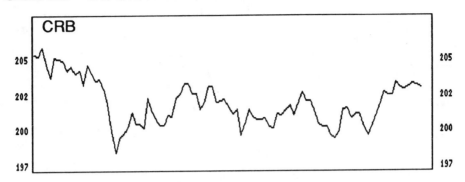

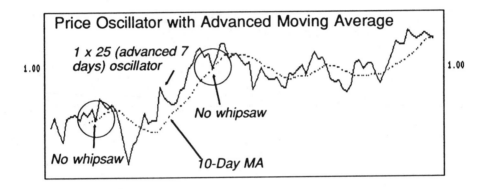

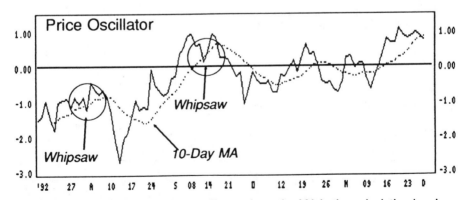

This chart features a 1 x 25 day oscillator where the MA in the calculation has been advanced seven days. The bottom panel shows a simple 1 x 25 day oscillator. Note how this series results in more whipsaw signals when it crosses the 10-day MA than the oscillator with the advanced MA.

Chart 5.7   Sydney All-Ordinary Index and Two Price Oscillators

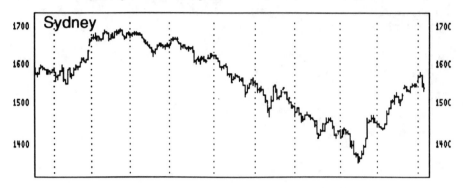

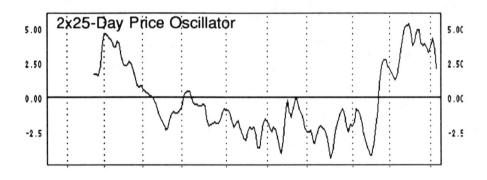

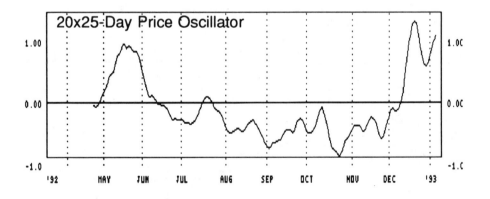

signals from reversals in trend, divergences, and the like. It is also possible to run a moving average through such an oscillator, using crossovers as buy and sell signals.

Because of their characteristic smoothness, these indicators do not normally lend themselves to trendline construction or price-pattern completion. However, on those rare occasions when it is possible to construct a trendline and observe its violation such signals are usually followed by a significant trend reversal. An example is shown in chart 5.8.

So far, we have considered only trend-deviation measurements for short-term movements, but the technique can just as easily be applied to weekly and monthly data. Chart 5.9 shows a 26-week moving average of the closing price divided by a 40-week average. This happens to be a composite index of basic industry stocks such as steels, chemicals, papers, etc. Buy and sell signals are generated when the oscillator crosses above and below its 10-week moving average.

Chart 5.10 shows essentially the same combination, except that the 40-week moving average was advanced by 10 weeks. Note how the late-1985 and 1988 whipsaws are filtered out.

Chart 5.8   DAX and a Price Oscillator

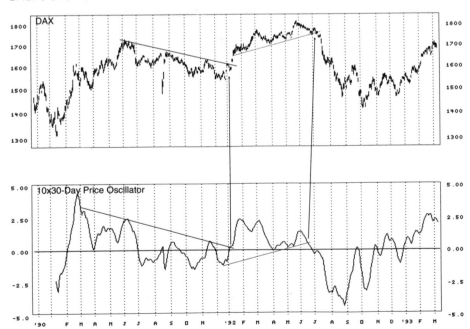

Chart 5.9 Dow Jones Basic Materials Index

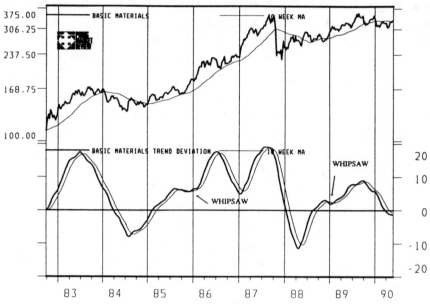

Martin J. Pring, Technical Analysis Explained, 3rd. edition, McGraw-Hill, New York, 1991.

Chart 5.10 Dow Jones Basic Materials Index

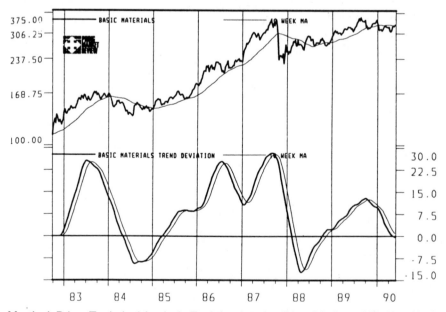

Martin J. Pring, Technical Analysis Explained, 3rd. edition, McGraw-Hill, New York, 1991.

When Colby and Meyers tested for the best combination of moving-average crossovers using weekly data for the S & P Composite, they found that between 1968 and 1986 the combination of a 15/36 week simple moving average worked best. They used the division instead of the subtraction calculation, basing buy and sell signals on a zero crossover. An example of this combination is shown in chart 5.11. Note how the oscillator formed a small base in the 1981–82 period. This was unique to the period covered by the chart and was also followed by an uncommon price move.

It seems that when price patterns and trendline violations are formed by smoothed oscillators, they have much more significance and reliability than those constructed from raw data such as a 1-week average divided by a 40-week moving average. This is because the patterns and lines formed by smoothed indicators more obviously reflect a deliberate trend, whereas formations and lines originating from raw data are more random and therefore less trustworthy.

Chart 5.11   S & P Composite and a Price Oscilator

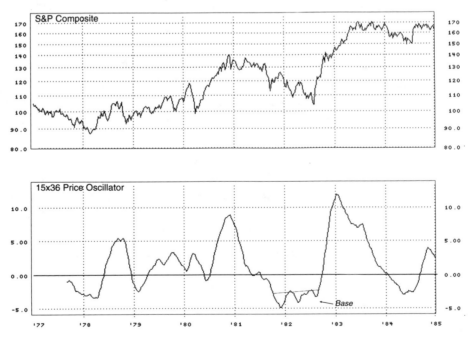

The MACD Indicator

MACD stands for "Moving Average Convergent Divergent" method. This method is simply another way of expressing a trend-deviation oscillator. The system obtains its name from the fact that the two moving averages used in the calculation are continually converging with and diverging from each other. Normally, the two averages are calculated on an exponential basis. Chart 5.12 represents both a figure and marketplace example for the gold price combined with a 9- and 15-day EMA. The top panel in chart 5.12 shows the relationship between the two averages, but this time the closing price has been eliminated. The lower panel shows the oscillator derived from the division of the 9-day by the 15-day average. This oscillator is the MACD.

The zero line represents those periods when the two EMAs are identical. When the MACD is above the equilibrium line, the shorter average is above the longer one and vice versa. The dotted line represents a 15-day EMA of the MACD and is known as the *signal line*. It gets this name because MACD crossovers generate buy and sell signals. In my experience I have not found these crossovers to be particularly reliable, and I regard them as overrated. I prefer to use the MACD from the point of view of trendline violations, or even price-pattern construction. Another possibility is to use the MACD signal-line crossovers as an alert that smoother oscillators based on a longer time span may be poised to give a signal. In this respect I am thinking specifically about the short-term KST constructed from daily data. The KST indicator is discussed in chapter 7.

Obviously, an MACD can be constructed from many different combinations. Gerald Appel of Signalert, arguably its chief proponent, has done a substantial amount of work on the indicator. He recommends a combination of 8- , 17- , and 9-day EMAs, but he believes that sell signals are more reliable using a 12-25-9-day combination. His belief is interesting because the "selling" MACD contains a longer time span. This reiterates the point made in an earlier chapter; namely, that markets spend more time in a rising than in a falling mode. The longer time span effectively delays the sell indications, thereby making them more timely.

Charts 5.13 and 5.14 show some examples of MACD indicators in the marketplace. Here the calculation for the MACD is made by

Chart 5.12   Comex Gold and a 9- to 15-Day MACD

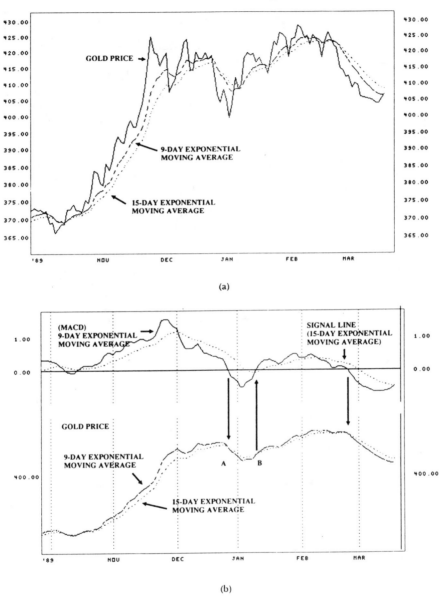

(a)

(b)

Martin J. Pring, Technical Analysis Explained, 3rd. edition, McGraw-Hill, New York, 1991.

Chart 5.13   Three-Month London Lead (in U.S. Dollars) and an MACD

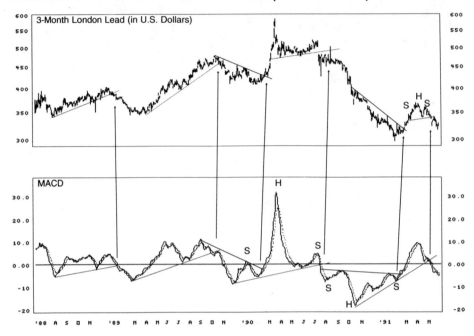

Chart 5.14   S & P 500 and an MACD

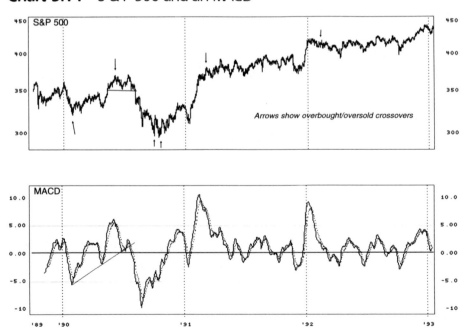

subtracting a 26-day exponential average from a 12-day one. The calculation happens to be the default (standard one) used in the MetaStock charting package. The MACD also can be plotted in a histogram format (See charts 5.15 and 5.16). This arrangement has the advantage of emphasizing the peaks and troughs, but it suffers from the disadvantage that it is more difficult to identify price-pattern formations and trendline violations.

Chart 5.15

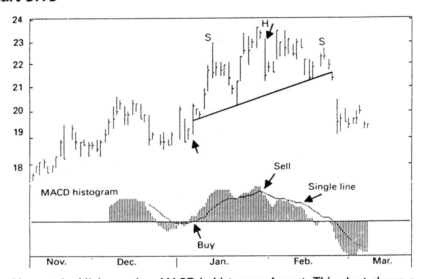

Homestake Mining and an MACD in histogram format. This chart shows a classic up-ward sloping H & S pattern. Note that the MACD histogram gradually became weaker as the pattern progressed. This was only a short-term sell signal, but the price eventually fell below the signal level. Martin J. Pring, *Technical Analysis Explained,* 3rd. edition, McGraw-Hill, New York, 1991, (Original source Telescan).

Chart 5.16

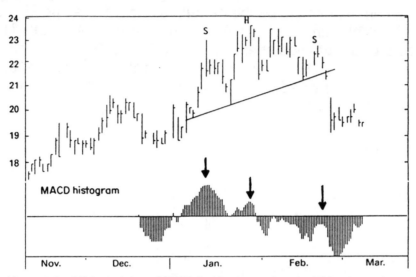

Homestake Mining and an MACD in histogram format. This chart plots a histogram of the difference between the signal line and the histogram in chart 5.15. Zero crossovers occur when the histogram in chart 5.15 crosses above or below the signal line. Note that the momentum indicator in this chart gets progressively weaker to the extent that it is well into negative territory when the right shoulder is being formed. Martin J. Pring, *Technical Analysis Explained*, 3rd. edition, McGraw-Hill, New York, 1991, (Original source Telescan).

Summary

1. Oscillators can be constructed from the relationship of the current price with a trend, usually a moving average.
2. The comparison can be done using either a subtraction or division method. Generally, the division calculation gives superior results.
3. Trend-deviation oscillators are subject to the normal principles of momentum interpretation.
4. Variations can be derived by advancing a moving average or by comparing two moving averages and expressing them in oscillator form.

chapter 6

STOCHASTICS AND WILLIAMS %R

Introduction

The "Stochastic Indicator," invented by George Lane (Investment Educators, P.O. Box 2354, Des Plaines, IL), measures the relative position of the closing price within a given interval. The period is normally a daily one, but a Stochastic Indicator can be constructed for any time period as long as high, low, and closing data are available. The term "stochastic" is actually a misnomer because it is a synonym for "random," which is not a concept that traders feel comfortable with.

This indicator became extremely popular in the 1980s, probably because its simple, deliberate style appears to offer profitable and easy-to-follow signals. The Stochastic method rests on the assumption that prices tend to close near the upper part of the trading range during an uptrend and near the lower part during a downtrend. This range refers to the trading period under consideration. For example, daily data would have a trading range for a day, weekly data for the week, and so forth. As the trend approaches a turning point, the price closes further away from its extreme (i.e., away from the daily high in a rising market and from the daily low in a declining one). The objective of the Stochastic formula is to identify these points in an advancing market when the closes are clustered nearer to the lows than to the highs, since this indicates that a trend reversal is at hand. For down markets the process is reversed.

The indicator is plotted in the form of two lines, known as "Percent D" and "Percent K." An example is shown in chart 6.1. In a June 1984 article in *Technical Analysis of Stocks and Commodities,* Lane explains that he experimented with 28 different oscillators, each using a different letter of the alphabet.[1] It just happened that "D" and "K" turned out to be the best. This thinking also formed the basis for Larry William's %R which, William claims, refines and improves Lane's original. This indicator is described later in this chapter.

The %K is the more sensitive of Lane's two oscillators, but it is the %D line that carries the greater weight and gives the major signals. The formula for the %K is as follows:

$$\%K = 100\left[\frac{C-L_n}{H_n-L_n}\right]$$

[1] Lane, George. "Lane's Stochastics," *Technical Analysis of Stocks and Commodities,* June 1984, pp. 87–90.

Chart 6.1 Matif 3-Month Perpetual Contract and 5%K 3%D Stochastic

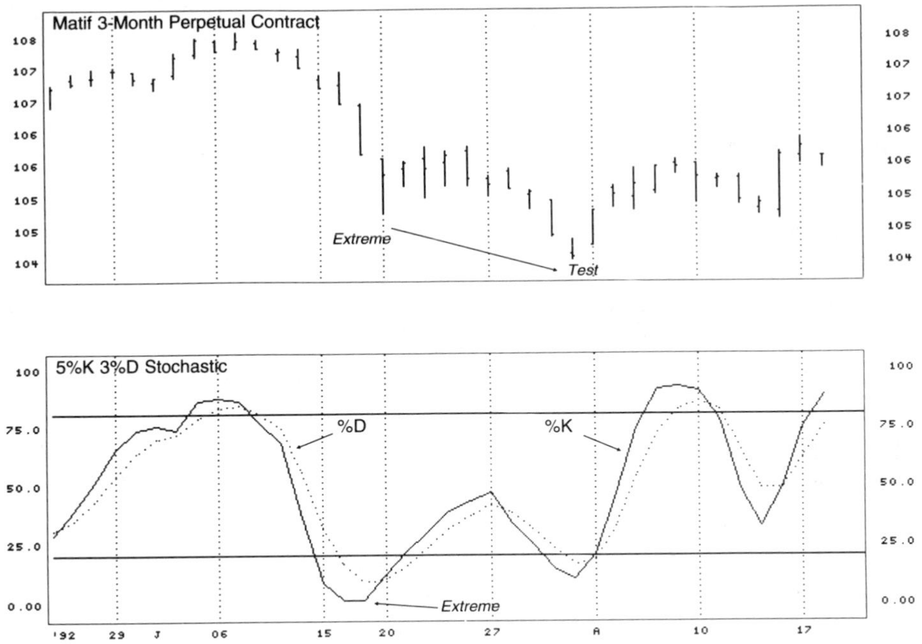

In this equation C is today's close, L_n the lowest low for the last *n* days, and H_n is the highest high over the same *n* day trading period. For short-term trading purposes Lane recommends that *n* should be 3. A 5-period %K line has also become quite popular. Since the time span is longer, the indicator is less volatile than the formula using the 3-period calculation. Of course, other time periods may also be used. In the March 1991 edition of *Technical Analysis of Stocks and Commodities,* editor Thom Hartle uses a 14-day span and makes the point that some traders extend the period as far as twenty-eight days.

It is important to note that the Stochastic differs from other indicators that we have considered so far because it requires the high and low for the trading period in question as well as the closing price. The %D line is a smoothed version of %K. Its calculation uses the following formula:

$$\%D = 100\left(\frac{H_3}{L_3}\right)$$

In this expression, H_3 is the 3-period sum of $(C - L_n)$ in the %K calculation, and L_3 is the 3-period sum of $(H_n - L_n)$. In a sense you could equate the %D line with a 3-period smoothing of %K.

The Slow Stochastic

The Slow Stochastic is a smoothed variation of the regular series. In this calculation the original %K line is eliminated and the old %D substituted. This renamed or "slowed" %K is then averaged by three days to form the %D slow. The resulting indicator is less volatile and subject to whipsaws. The process need not stop there, of course, since there is nothing to prevent the innovative trader from experimenting with other smoothings and time-period comparisons.

The Stochastic Indicator, therefore, takes the form of two oscillators. The %K is usually plotted as a solid line, and its slower %D counterpart is expressed as a dashed or dotted line. I often have trouble remembering which line is which. A useful way to remember is to think of K as K(wick) and D as D(awdling). When plotted, the Stochastic Indicator always falls in the range of 0 to 100, like the RSI. A reading near 80 is generally regarded as overbought and 20 as oversold.

Interpretation

In the article referred to earlier, Lane strongly emphasizes that there is only one valid signal that can be obtained from the %D. This is a *divergence between %D and the price of the security being monitored.* All other signals, he points out, are merely "guideposts or warnings that an important signal is near."[2] My view is that *all* signals from any momentum indicator should be used as an alert or warning of an impending trend reversal. Remember that momentum measures velocity, not price trends. Price measures price trends. Momentum signals are useful primarily because they emphasize the importance of a price trend-reversal signal. As such, they can and should be used in a prudent way for part profit

[2] Ibid.

taking or partial entry of a new position, never as the *sole* basis for a major decision. In most cases a good momentum signal, such as a %D divergence, will be associated with a trend reversal. However, in a large number of "inconvenient" situations the price continues to make one more high or low, bringing on a "stopped-out" position. Alternatively, the trend is of the linear variety, such as the Japanese bull market in stocks in the 1980s. In that event no amount of overboughts or divergences can help.

The one exception to the rule concerning momentum requiring price confirmation occurs with trend-deviation indicators. When they cross through the zero level, this tells us that the trend in price as well as momentum has been reversed. Even so, before entering a position it is important to make sure that prices have not moved significantly away from their ultimate turning point.

Divergence

Divergences between the %D and the price are similar to those discussed in chapter 1. The main difference between a Stochastic and an RSI divergence is that there are usually fewer divergences using the Stochastic Indicator. In fact, it is probably true to say that in the vast majority of cases, the %D experiences only one or, at the most, two divergences, as shown in figure 6.1.

According to Lane, the Stochastic signal requires action when the %K crosses from the right-hand side of the peak in the %D line. Buy signals are triggered when the %K crosses the right-hand side of the low point of the %D line at market bottoms. Figure 6.2 shows crossovers from both the right and left for tops as well as bottoms. In this interpretation the left-hand crossover occurs *before* the turning point in the %D line, and the right-hand crossover occurs after it. Lane emphasizes that the right-hand crossovers are more reliable.

The Hinge

The "hinge" is a slowing down in the velocity of either line. This implies a reversal in the next trading period, which is the next day for daily data, the next week for weekly data, and so forth. (See figure 6.3.) Chart 6.2 shows some hinge examples in action.

Figure 6.1

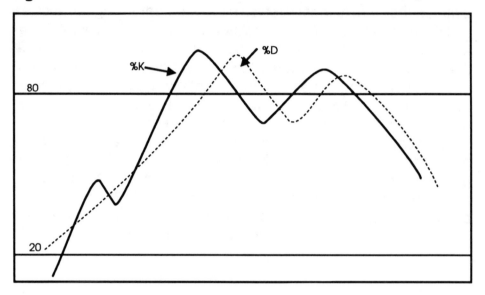

Figure 6.2

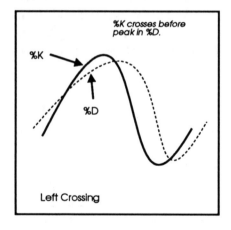

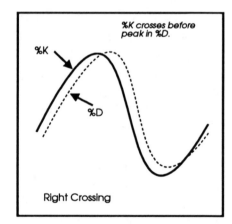

Warning

In the case of a rising market, a warning occurs when the %K line has been rising for a while, and then one day (or week or month, depending on the time frame being used) reverses sharply. (See figure 6.4) In these instances a sharp reversal is defined as one that falls in the range of 2%–12%. This represents a warning that only one or two more days of rising movement are likely prior to a

Figure 6.3

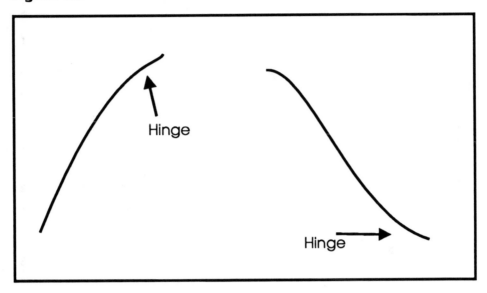

Chart 6.2 S & P Composite and 5%K 3%D Stochastic

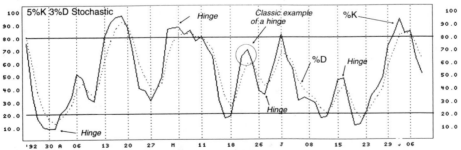

Figure 6.4

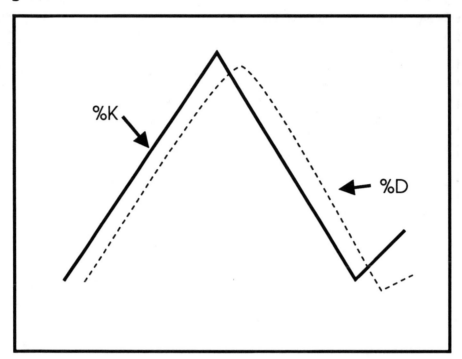

reversal in trend. The opposite, as shown in the right-hand side of figure 6.4, is the case in a declining market.

%K Reaching an Extreme

Normally, when an indicator reaches an overbought or oversold extreme it indicates a possible trend reversal. However, when the %K line moves to the extreme of 0%, Lane emphasizes that this signals "pronounced weakness." Chart 6.1 shows an example. Typically, the %K will bounce up 20% to 25% from the zero level, later falling back toward zero again. He stresses that the odds are extremely good that this testing process will, in fact, take place. Lane estimates that it normally takes 2–4 days (or weeks or months) for the testing process to run its course, after which a small rally should be expected.

The opposite is true of rising markets in relation to the 100% extreme. Lane goes out of his way to underscore the point that the initial 0% and 100% readings in the %K do not signal a top or bottom in the price. In fact, he goes on to point out that they mean the "exact opposite." At most, they indicate that a slight pause or hesitation in the prevailing trend will develop, shortly to be followed by a resumption of that trend.

The Set-Up

In a rising market the "Set-up" occurs as the price makes a low simultaneously with the %D. Both series then go on to make new highs, but on the subsequent reaction the %D breaks below its previous low while the security does not. The implication is that the next rally in price will probably turn out to be an important top. This is known as a "Bear Set-up." Figure 6.5 depicts this concept for both bottoms and tops. Chart 6.3 shows an example of a bullish set-up for 3-month Eurodollar prices at the mid-1992 low.

Figure 6.5

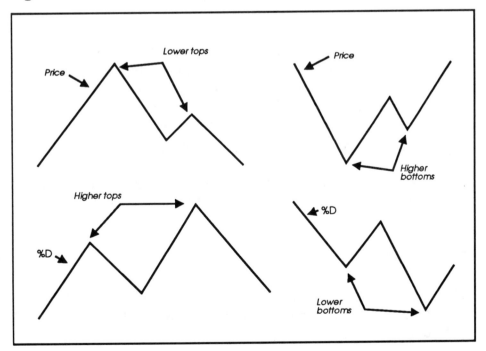

Chart 6.3   Eurodollar 3-Month Perpetual Contract
and a 5%K 3%D Stochastic

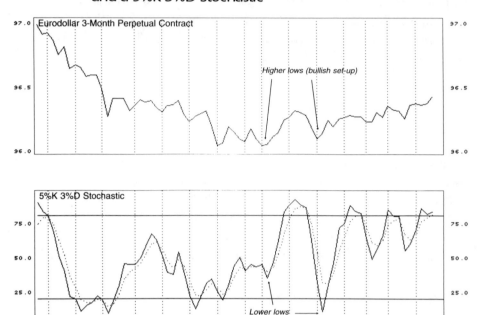

Failure

Rising and falling peaks and troughs reflect the underlying technical strength or weakness in a market. Lane's Stochastic "failure" is
no exception to this principle. At market bottoms failure occurs
when the %K line crosses above the %D and then falls back for a
couple of days while still managing to remain above the %D line.
It represents a kind of test that, if successful, indicates that the new
uptrend is likely to continue. Figure 6.6 also shows this for a market
peak, where the "failure" means that the %K is unable to rally again
above %D. Chart 6.4 shows an actual marketplace example.

Trendlines

Clearly, the Stochastic method works well with divergence and
moving-average crossover analysis. However, it is not normally
suited for trendline construction.

Figure 6.6

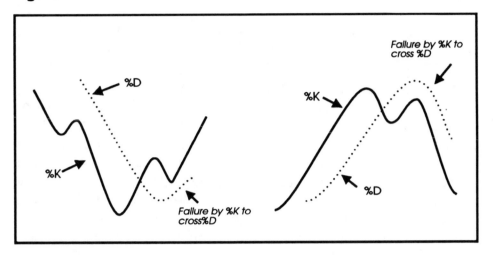

Chart 6.4 S&P Composite vs. a 3%K 3%D Stochastic

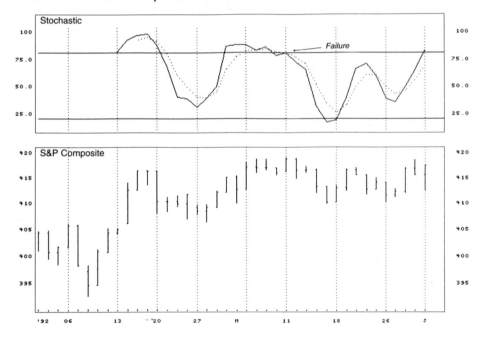

How Does It Test?

In *Encyclopedia of Technical Market Indicators* Colby and Meyers tested the Stochastic Indicator for the effectiveness of a number of rules and parameters, and found that the vast majority of combinations were unprofitable. This research was based not only on 1977–86 weekly data for the NYSE, but also on the experience of Schwager and Strahm (*Technical Analysis of Stocks and Commodities,* July 1986). Colby and Meyers finally discovered a profitable combination, although it did not compare favorably with most of the other indicators that they tested. The rules they established called for a buy signal when the 39-week unsmoothed %K line (n = 39 with no moving average) crosses above 50%, and the %K and closing price are *both* above their previous closing levels. They decided to both sell and sell short when these conditions are reversed (i.e., when %K moves below 50% and the %K and closing prices are below their previous week's levels). They note that fairly consistent profits were achieved for periods (in other words, the *n* value) ranging from 38 to 66 weeks, but they reported that the 39-week span proved to be the most profitable period used. Note that the %D was not used in this particular rule.

How To Use the Stochastic Effectively

The Stochastic is most effective when you keep daily series in conjunction with weekly and monthly. In this way the daily indicator monitors the short-term trend, the weekly indicator the intermediate term, and the monthly the long-term trend. As we will discover in the next chapter on the KST Market Cycle Model System, trading in the direction of the main trend is very important. This approach is not possible with all momentum indicators, but the Stochastic lends itself well to this important discipline. However, it is important to remember that the Stochastic calculation requires period highs and lows in addition to the closing price.

Trading in the direction of the main trend means that buy signals in the daily and weekly stochastics should be ignored if the monthly series is in a topping-out or declining phase. If the decline in the monthly Stochastic is very mature and showing signs of bottoming, and if this condition is confirmed by other long-term characteristics of a primary trend reversal, buy signals in the daily and weekly series will probably result in a profitable trade, as seen in chart 6.5.

Investors can reverse this process by using the two shorter series for more precise timing of a primary low. For example, every bear market ends when the first short-term rally in the new bull market takes place. Consequently, if the monthly series is showing signs of bottoming, wait for the intermediate and short-term Stochastics to reverse direction to the upside. The working assumption is that the strength in the implied short or intermediate rallies will be sufficient to shift the balance for the monthly series as well. Charts 6.6–6.8 show various examples of the Stochastics Indicator in the market place.

Williams %R

This indicator is a variation of the Stochastic method previously described. It is sometimes referred to as the William's Overbought/ Oversold Index. The concept is principally the same for both series. The Williams system also uses a %K based on a 5-period time span. The formula for the %K using 5-periods is:

$$\%K = 100\left(\frac{C - L_5}{H_5 - L_5}\right)$$

where
  C = Today's close
  L_5 = Lowest low in the last 5 periods
  H_5 = Highest high in the last 5 periods.

The %R differs from the %K because the ratios determined in each formula are inverse. In other words, %K compares the close

Chart 6.5   Japanese Yen with Daily and Weekly Stochastics
             Reflecting Short-, Intermediate-, and Long-Term Trends

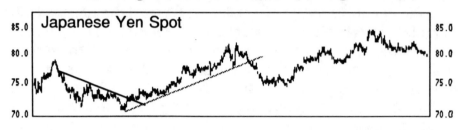

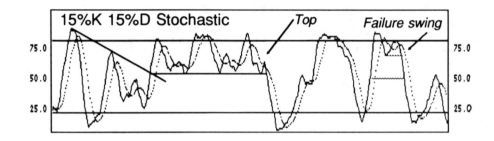

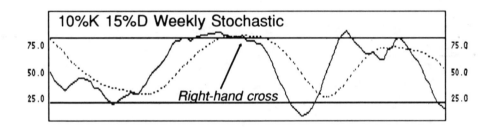

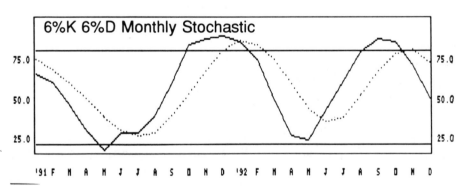

This chart shows a daily, weekly, and monthly stochastic reflecting a short-, intermediate-, and long-term trend. Note the huge top in the daily series in February 1992.

Chart 6.6   S&P Composite, 5%K 3%D Stochastic
              and 15%K 9%D Stochastic

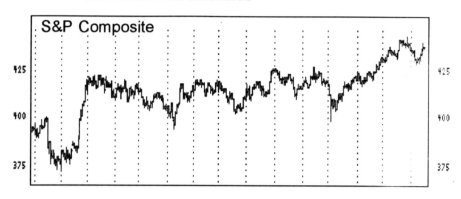

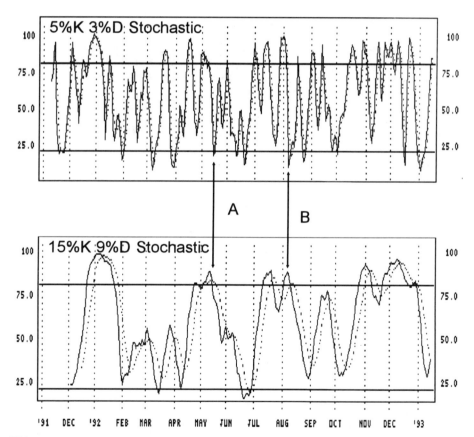

This chart compares two different indicators using different time frames to obtain greater perspective. The first is a 3 x 5 x 3 using a single moving average. The lower panel triples these values for a 9 x 15 x 9 construction.

Chart 6.7   Chevron Corporation and 10%K 15%D Stochastic

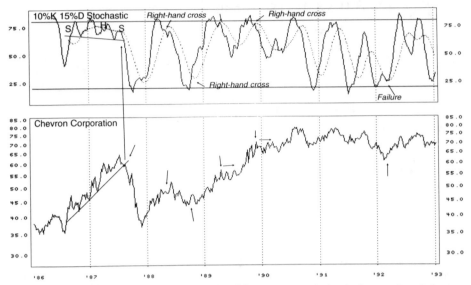

This chart shows an unusual head-and-shoulders top completion in the stochastic just as it violated a 1 1/2 year uptrendline. It also features some right-hand crossovers, two of which were followed by a consolidation rather than a downward correction. Finally, at the beginning of 1992 we see a bullish failure.

Chart 6.8   Amer. Business Products and 10%K 15%D Stochastic

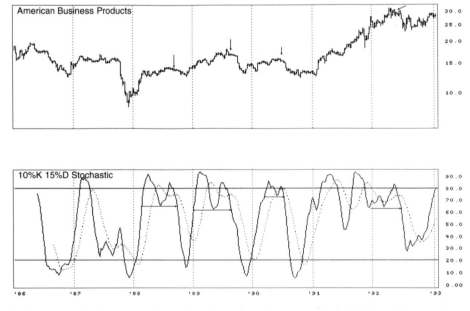

In this example of a 10 x 15 x 15 weekly stochastic, we see four RSI type failure swings each followed by a decline of some magnitude. This is not an "official" way of interpreting stochastics, but often works, which is what really counts.

with the lowest low, whereas %R compares the close with the highest high. The %R formula is as follows:

$$\%R = 100 = \left(\frac{H_r - C}{H_r - L_r} \right)$$

where
  r = The time period selected
  H_r = The highest high of that period
  L_r = The lowest low of that period
  C = Today's close.

When plotted, this means that the Williams formula appears with overbought in the 20 zone and oversold in the 80 zone. In the June 1991 issue of *Technical Analysis of Stocks and Commodities*, Tom Hartle examined the variations between the %R and the %K Stochastics, and found that the only difference between the two is that high readings in the %R are bullish and low readings are bearish.

His point, which is a very valid one, is that too many traders try to use a large number of indicators that essentially accomplish the same task. Obviously, if one indicator is the mirror image of another, overkill has overtaken the analysis. Do we really need two indicators basically telling us the same thing?

Summary

1. The construction of the Stochastic Indicator is based on the assumption that prices close away from their highs as a security is reversing from an uptrend to a downtrend, and vice versa.
2. Stochastics can be calculated for any time frame and are especially useful when daily trends are related to weekly and monthly data.
3. In objective tests the Stochastic underperforms most other indicators.
4. The Williams %R is a mirror image of the Stochastic.

chapter 7

THE KST SYSTEM

- **Introduction**
- **Price Is Determined by the Interaction of Many Cycles**
- **Long-Term Indicators**
- **Short- and Intermediate-Term Indicators**
- **Three Main Trends**
- **Combining the Three Trends (Market Cycle Model)**
- **Some Examples from the Marketplace**
- **Short-Term KST Signals Using Daily Data**
- **The KST and Relative Strength**

    The Concept of Relative Strength

    Relative KST Indicators

Introduction

The KST System combines many of the concepts discussed in earlier chapters into one specific approach. In this chapter you will learn how to create a series that not only combines several different cycles into one indicator, but also acts as a guide offering perspective which is important to both traders and investors. The benefit to investors is obvious. To traders a knowledge of the maturity and direction of the main trend can be of the utmost importance since most mistakes are made moving *against* the direction of the main trend. Even if the direction of the primary trend is obvious, you still need to have some idea of its maturity because if it is in a terminal phase the risks of trading in its direction will be greater with lower odds of success. An additional advantage of the KST is that it also can be used for short-term trading decisions.

Price Is Determined by the Interaction of Many Cycles

We discovered in chapter 3 that when ROC indicators of varying time spans are plotted on one chart different characteristics are highlighted that are not apparent when just one indicator is considered in isolation. This is because any specific time frame used in the ROC calculation reflects only one cycle. If that particular cycle is not operating or is dominated by another cycle or combination of cycles that specific ROC indicator is of little value. An example showing several rate-of-change indicators plotted on one chart is shown in chart 7.1. Note how the 1982 low was associated with an accumulation pattern in the 6-month rate-of-change and that the 24-month series violated its bear market trendline. On the other hand, if we had been looking at only the 12-month series in isolation we would have seen very little evidence that a major reversal was about to get underway.

There is also another major advantage to this arrangement. I have mentioned several times in earlier chapters that the price trend at any one point in time is determined by the interaction of many different time cycles. Sometimes when a trend reverses it is followed by a small price movement; at other times it is followed by

Chart 7.1 S & P Composite Index and 6-, 12-,
and 24-Month Rate-of-Change

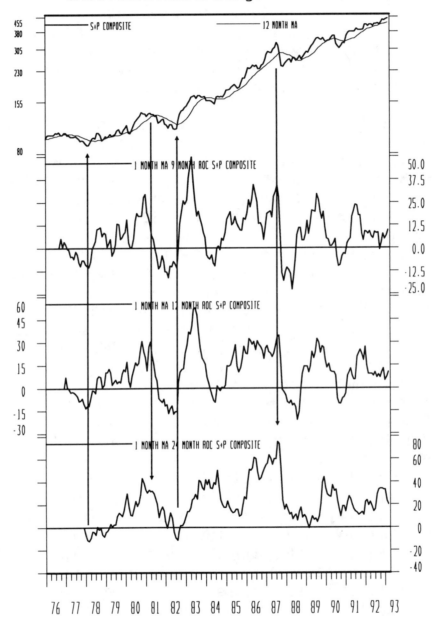

a large one. Why is this so? And is it possible to spot the big turning points? The answer to these questions is found in the number and size of the cycles that are turning at a particular point. If one cycle with a small time span is reversing, it is unlikely to have much influence because it will be offset by all the others. On the other hand, if two or three cycles with a longer-term duration are turning, a significant price movement is likely to follow, other things being equal.

Obviously, it is impossible to track all of these cycles and the varying combinations unless we have a super mainframe computer. Even then the math could be overwhelming. What we can do, though, is arrange several ROC indicators on one chart and observe what happens at major market turning points. This brings us back to chart 7.1. Here we have a 6- , 12- , and 24-month rate-of-change of the S & P Composite Index. Note that there are really five major turning points in the 1976–90 period. The 1978, 1982, and 1987 bottoms and the 1981 and 1987 tops. Also that four of these turning points are associated with sympathetic moves in *all* of the momentum series. I use the word "sympathetic" because sometimes the indicators reverse simultaneously with the price while at other times they have *already* turned. Take the 1981 top, for instance. It was associated with a peak in all three indicators, but it was not immediately followed by a sharp decline because the 12- and 24-month series moved sideways. The 12-month indicator actually traced out a double top. It was only when *all three* were in a declining mode that the S & P began to accelerate on the downside.

A similar situation arose following the 1984 low. In this instance we find that the market advances, but not as aggressively. This is because the very strong 24-month indicator is *declining* while the two shorter series are rallying. However, in the middle of 1985 all three series turn, and the market advances far more sharply. The one major turning point that this arrangement did not explain was the 1987 bottom. This is because of the time frames involved. The 1987 crash was an extremely short-term affair by historical standards. Bear markets usually take a long time to unfold, typically 1–2 years. This means that the longer-term indicators have time to work off their overbought condition and move toward an oversold extreme. In the case of the 1987 bottom, we see three things: the actual low, which occurred in late 1987; a slow but deliberate recovery rally until the end of 1988; and a final accelerated rally into 1989. In this respect the cycles reflected by the three indicators are presenting a relatively true picture of market conditions because all three have bottomed by the beginning of 1989 when the upside acceleration takes place. Obviously, it would have been more convenient if all three had bottomed in October 1987, but the unprecedented brevity of the decline did not permit it. This also illustrates the fact that this approach is far from perfect, but it still points us in the right direction most of the time. The unexpected severity of the 1987 decline was obviously caused by a combination of down cycles that this grouping of three indicators was unable to pick up.

One way to improve this presentation is to smooth the data so that the numbers send more deliberate signals as the momentum series change direction. While whipsaw signals can still occur, they are significantly reduced offering more reliable indications of trend reversals for each of the indicators. Generally, the further the smoothed rate-of-change is from the equilibrium (zero) level, the more reliable the signal.

Chart 7.2 shows the same three momentum indicators calculated for different time spans. The smoothing process gives us a greater perspective on the true trend of each period than we would have had without it. As expected, the 6-month series is usually the first to turn, followed by the 12- and 24-month series. The 6-month ROC is much more sensitive to prices on most occasions than longer-term series and is more timely. At other times it turns way before the data series gives an unduly premature signal. Prices on the 6-month indicator are not always reflected in the 12- or 24-month momentum series because markets experience different cyclical phenomenon simultaneously.

The 6-month series explains virtually every intermediate-trend price movement, but the longer-term 24-month indicator reveals only the major market trends.

On observation these relationships reveal several characteristics:

1. The smoothed 24-month ROC sets the backdrop for the major move.
2. The strongest price trends usually occur when all three curves move simultaneously in the same direction, (e.g., 1973-74, late 1977, early 1975, and late 1982).

Chart 7.2   S&P Composite and 6-, 12-, and 24-Month Rate-of-Change

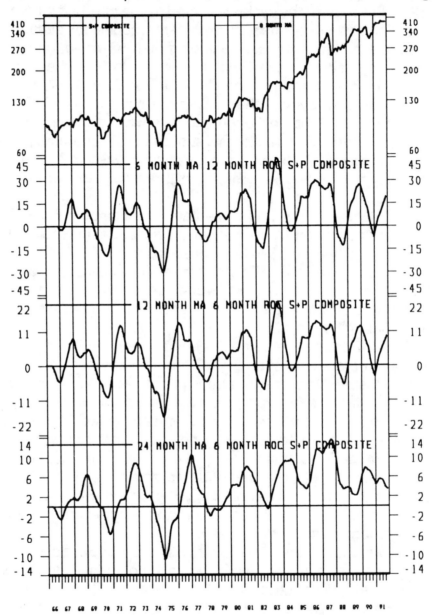

This chart shows three momentum indicators calculated for the 6-month, 12-month and 24-month rate-of-change oscillators. Both the 6-month and the 12-month ROC are smoothed by a 6-month moving average, while the 24-month is smoothed by a 9-month moving average.

3. If the 24-month ROC peaks when either the 6- and/or the 12-month series are rising, the sell-off is normally mild because the cycles are conflicting. A classic example occurred in early 1982 when the 24-month ROC indicator was falling, but the 6-month series had already risen.

4. When the 24-month indicator is in a rising mode but the 6- and 9-month indicators peak, the implied decline is usually mild. An example occurred in 1971 when a decline was signalled by the peaking action of its 6- and 12-month indicators. But the 24-month indicator was only beginning to cross above its zero reference indicating that the bull market was in a relatively early stage. The ensuing reaction proved to be an intermediate decline within a bull market. A similar instance occurred in 1976 when the 24-month momentum made a strong upturn, but the 6- and 12-month ROCs were falling sharply. The result was a distributional top.

The same principle can be applied to daily and weekly data. Chart 7.3 shows the daily close for the S & P Composite between January and July 1990. Note how the late April low was associated with a bottom in all three indicators. However, the market did not respond negatively to the May peak in the 10-day indicator because the 15- and 30-day oscillators were still rising. The result was a stand off between them and the S & P responded with a modest rally. Just after the 15-day ratio peaked, the market experienced its final run-up.

Later, in mid-June all three indicators were finally in downtrends and the S & P experienced a sharp sell-off. The July peak was once again associated with a top in all three momentum indicators when the market underwent a very sharp decline. These examples show quite clearly that the strength and sustainability of a market trend is determined by the simultaneous, combined reaction of a number of different cycles.

Long-Term Indicators

It is a very complicated process to plot and follow indicators reflecting many different time spans, but it is possible to come up with a satisfactory compromise. This alternative involves the

Chart 7.3   S&P Composite vs. 10-, 15-, and 30-Day Rate-of-Change

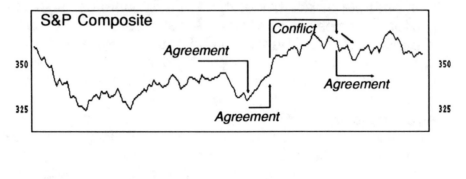

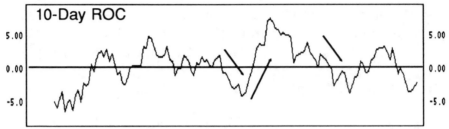

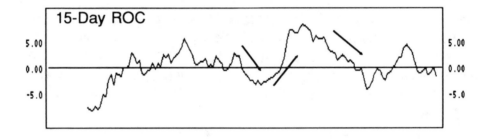

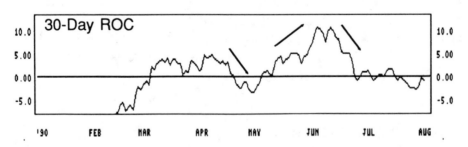

This chart shows the daily close for the S & P Composite between January and July 1990. Note how the April low appears to be associated with a bottom in all three indicators.

construction of *one single indicator* that combines four different ROC series and weights them according to the length of their time span.

If we closely study chart 7.4A we can see that movements of the 9-month moving average of the 24-month rate-of-change in the bottom panel closely monitor the primary bull and bear swings of the market. However, since the market is slow to reverse direction, signals of trend reversals are often given well after the fact. Consider the late 1989 reversal, for example. It occurred just in time to catch the tail end of the rally, hardly great for timing purposes. One way around this problem is to combine four smoothed rates-of-change in one indicator, weighting each one in rough proportion to its time span. This approach enables the longer-term smoothed momentum to turn faster as it keeps whipsaw signals to a minimum. In effect, it still retains its ability to reflect the major trends, but it signals such reversals on a more timely basis. Because such an indicator also includes several rates-of-change covering different time spans, it also reflects the interaction of several time cycles.

Chart 7.4B shows a summed ROC for the S & P Composite using this concept. The momentum series has been constructed from smoothed 9-, 12-, 18-, and 24-month rates-of-change. In this calculation, the first 3 periods are smoothed with a 6-month moving average and the 24-month time span with a 9-month moving average. These series are then weighted in proportion to their respective time spans. This means that the 24-month ROC has a far larger weighting of (4) than its 9-month counterpart which is (1).

Direction reversals of the indicator alert traders to most of the major movements in the stock market on a relatively timely basis without suffering too much from whipsaw activity. Note how the combined indicator reverses direction almost a year earlier than the smoothed 24-month rate-of-change following the 1987 low.

Periods of accumulation and distribution occur between the time that the summed ROC and its moving average change direction. There are three levels of signals. The first level is triggered when the indicator changes direction, the second when it crosses its moving average, and the third when the average also reverses direction. *In most cases the moving-average crossover offers the best combination of timely signals with a minimum of whipsaws.*

Chart 7.4A   S&P Composite and 3 Rate-of-Change Indicators

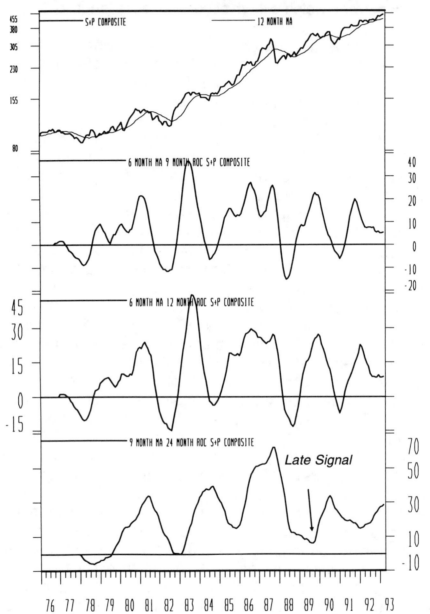

Three smoothed rate-of-change indicators are presented below the S & P 500 Composite Index. The 9-month moving average of the 24-month rate-of-change closely follows the primary bull and bear market swings but can lag important market turns as it did in late 1989.

Chart 7.4B   S & P Composite and Long-Term KST

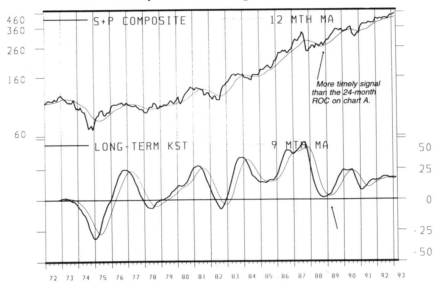

The KST indicator is a weighted summed rate-of-change oscillator that is designed to identify meaningful turns. Various smoothed rate-of-change indicators can be combined to form different measurements of cycles. The long-term KST crossed above its 9-month ROC is shown above.

The indicator generally offers timely signals and an accurate perspective, but as with any technical approach, it is not perfect. For instance, during a prolonged uptrend (as occurred for Japanese equities in 1980s), this method is bound to give false or very premature signals. We can see this occurring in chart 7.5, where false signals were triggered in 1985 and 1987.

Another drawback is the fact that the indicator turns very slowly and is unable to respond to random events. Two examples that come to mind are the effect of the 1989 Tiananmen Square massacre on the Hong Kong stock market and the abrupt change in Federal Reserve policy that occurred in 1981 when interest rates reversed their primary downtrend on a dime. The Hong Kong experience is shown in chart 7.6.

Fortunately, the vast majority of market movements operate within the normal business cycle, so the summed Rate-Of-Change concept gives us a reasonably accurate picture of what is happening in a market. For this reason I have called this indicator the KST. The letters stand for "Know Sure Thing." Most of the time it is reliable, but it's also important to know that this approach is not a sure thing.

Chart 7.5   Nikkei and Long-Term KST

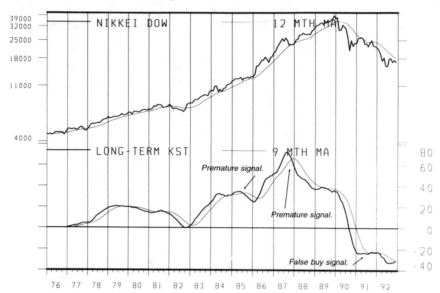

As with any technical indicator, the KST is not infallible. If there is a prolonged trend, the indicator may give false signals of a trend reversal.

Chart 7.6   Hang Seng and Long-Term KST

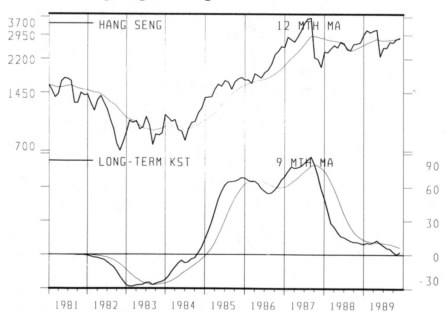

Short- and Intermediate-Term Indicators

Chart 7.7 shows that the same concept can be applied to daily charts for short-term swings, and chart 7.8 demonstrates that it can be used for intermediate-term price movements as well. The short-term KST constructed from daily data is particularly useful for *filtering* out entry and exit points when trading in the futures markets. I emphasize the term "filtering" because I strongly believe that trades should be based on the condition of more than one indicator. When the KST reverses its prevailing trend, especially from an extreme overbought or oversold zone, this is a signal to take a look and see what the other indicators are saying.

It is also *mandatory* to ensure that KST signals are confirmed by some kind of trend reversal in the price series. This could take the form of a moving average crossover, trendline violation, or similar confirming signal.

Chart 7.7   S & P Composite and Short-Term KST

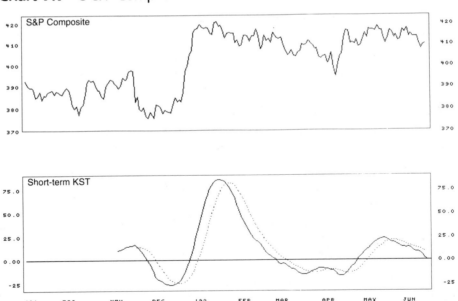

The KST can be tailored for any time frame. Here the daily KST is presented with the S & P Composite. The daily KST indicator should be used as a complement to additional technical indicators.

Chart 7.8   Deutsche Mark and Intermediate-Term KST

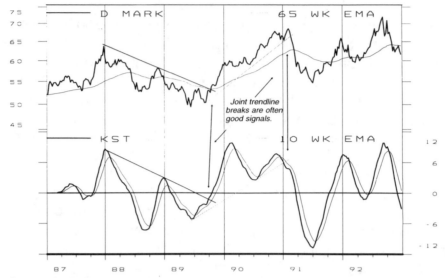

One method of using the KST is to apply trendline analysis to the indicator. Here, the intermediate KST has trendlines drawn upon it along with trendlines drawn on the Deutsche mark. Joint trendline breaks are often reliable signals.

The KST should be interpreted using the same principles that you would apply to other oscillators. Divergences, overbought and oversold conditions, trendline violations, and price-pattern analysis are as relevant to the KST as they are to the rate-of-change, RSI, MACD, and so forth. Trendline violations in the KST do not occur very often; but when they do, they have the effect of strong reinforcment for the KST moving average crossover signals previously discussed. Chart 7.9 demonstrates this effect quite clearly. Since the long-term KSTs based on monthly data are far more smooth and deliberate in their movements, trendline construction and price-pattern configurations are rarely, if ever, apparent. On the other hand, we can see that the short-term KST indicators are far more susceptible to such possibilities because of their more volatile nature.

The formulae set out in table 7.1 are not the last words on the KST. I am sure that someone who wants to optimize the time frames, moving averages, and weightings could come up with statistically superior results. Even though they are offered here as a starting point for additional experimentation, remember there is no Holy Grail. Substituting the impossible objective of statistical

Chart 7.9 Toronto Stock Exchange and Daily KST

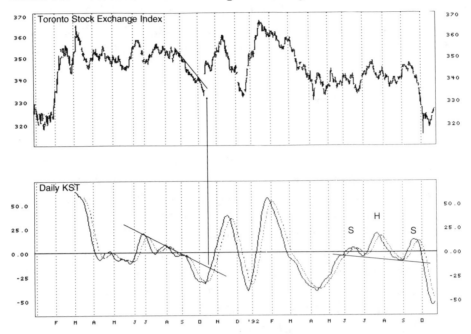

Table 7.1 Suggested KST Formulas*

	ROC	MA	Weight	ROC	MA	Weight	ROC	MA	Weight	Roc	MA	Weight
Short-term†	10	10	1	15	10	2	20	10	3	30	15	4
Short-term‡	3	3¶	1	4	4¶	2	6	6¶	3	10	8¶	4
Intermediate-term‡	10	10	1	13	13	2	15	15	3	20	20	4
Intermediate-term‡	10	10¶	1	13	13¶	2	15	15¶	3	20	20¶	4
Long-term§	9	6	1	12	6	2	18	6	3	24	9	4
Long-term‡	39	26¶	1	52	26¶	2	78	26¶	3	104	39¶	4

* It is possible to program all KST formulas into MetaStock and the Computrac Snap
  Module (see Resources, at the end of the book).
† Based on daily data.
‡ Based on weekly data.
§ Based on monthly data.
¶ EMA.

perfection for sound and reasoned analysis is certain to lead to
trouble.

Now we can proceed to what I think is the most valuable part of
the KST System and that is to combine three KST indicators into
one overall arrangement in order to gain a better understanding of
the complete market cycle. Think of the combination in this way: If

you were in a strange city and did not have a map for guidance, you would have a problem getting from the train station to the hotel on your own. Most of us operate in the marketplace without such a map. Let's see how the KST System can help in this respect.

Three Main Trends

We have already discussed the fact that there are several trends operating in the market at any particular time. They range from intra-day and hourly trends to very long-term or secular ones evolving over a 20- or 30-year period. For investment purposes the most widely recognized are short-, intermediate-, and long-term trends. Short-term trends (3 to 6 weeks) are usually monitored with daily prices, intermediate (6 weeks to 6 months) with weekly prices, and long-term (1-3 years) with monthly prices. Figure 7.1 shows a hypothetical bell curve incorporating all three trends.

From both an investment and trading point of view, it is important to understand the direction and maturity of the main, or

Figure 7.1

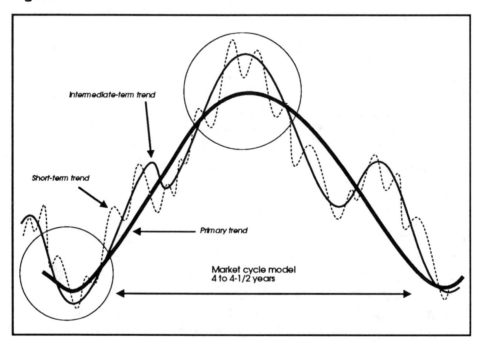

primary, trend. It is said that a rising tide lifts all boats. In a similar vein, short-term rallies are much more profitable in a bull market than they are when the market tide is retreating (i.e., in a bear market). If you want proof, try comparing the results of short-term buy signals for mechanical trading systems in a bull market and then in a bear market. An indicator that can give you reliable evidence of not only the direction but also the maturity of the primary trend can be of invaluable help.

Combining the Three Trends (Market Cycle Model)

Ideally, it would be very helpful to track the KST for monthly, weekly, and daily data on the same chart, but plotting constraints make this difficult. It is possible, though, to simulate these three trends by using different time spans based on weekly data. Chart 7.10 shows how this is done for the S & P Composite Index. These indicators differ from those presented earlier because they are smoothed by *exponential* rather than simple moving averages. This arrangement, which is possible using the popular Metastock Professional charting software, facilitates identifying both the direction and the maturity of the primary trend (shown at the bottom of the chart), as well as the interrelationship between the short and intermediate ones. Reversals in trend are signaled some time between the point where the KST and its moving average change direction. The best signals are given when the KST crosses above or below its exponential moving average (EMA). This alternative construction gives a very good indication for the prevailing stage of the specific trend that it is measuring. Like any indicator, however, it is far from perfect, especially in highly volatile markets or markets that fail to undergo a specific cyclic correction.

The long-term KST monitors the primary trend of the market; that is, price movements lasting one, two, or three years. Its current position gives us some perspective on the maturity of the trend. The intermediate- and short-term indicators are used more for timing purposes. For example, if a short-term "buy" is triggered when the long-term indicator is rising from just above the zero level, this indicates a bull market rally. On the other hand, a short-term "buy" that occurs when the long-term indicator is declining tells us that a bear market rally is underway. The difference is important, since

Chart 7.10   S & P Composite and Three KSTs

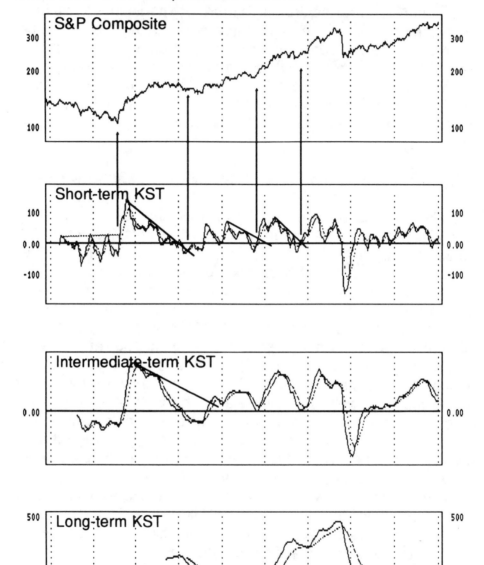

The best opportunities occur when the primary trend is in a rising mode but is not overextended and the intermediate- and short-term KSTs are turning up. You can draw trendlines on the short-term KST to identify important turns. The short-term KST uses an 8-week exponential moving average for the crossover, the intermediate-term uses a 10-week moving average and the long-term a 26-week moving average for the crossover.

the former is usually profitable and the latter deceptive, unreliable, and unprofitable. This arrangement of three KST oscillators into what I call the "market-cycle model" not only helps the trader or investor to position himself in the *direction* of the main trend, but also gives some indication of the trend's maturity. An example is when a long-term KST is overextended on the upside and an intermediate sell signal is generated, the odds are fairly high that the implied intermediate correction will turn out to be the start of a major reversal formation or the first downleg of a new bear market.

The best trades and investments are made when the primary trend is in a rising mode but is not overextended and when the intermediate- and short-term market movements are bottoming out. During a primary bear market, shorting is best accomplished when intermediate- and short-term trends are at their final peak. In a sense, any investments made during the early and middle stages of a bull market are bailed out by the fact that the primary trend is rising, whereas investors have to be much more agile during a bear market in order to capitalize on the rising intermediate-term swings.

Bullish intermediate signals that met the two criteria of correct positioning on the long-term indicator and moving average cross-over on the intermediate-term indicator occurred in late 1985 and December 1986, shown in chart 7.10. Both signals were followed by powerful rallies. The last one in 1990 did not do the same primarily because the long-term indicator reached its peak in early 1990.

Intermediate-term sell signals are less powerful when they occur against a backdrop of a rising primary trend KST. These signals occurred in 1985, early 1986, and early 1987.

This arrangement is helpful for trying to assess the maturity of a primary bull or bear market. In the classic conceptual sense, a primary bull market consists of three intermediate uptrends and, in certain cases, a fourth. During the 1984–87 period there were, in fact, three rallies in the intermediate-term indicator.

During a bear market the same conditions should work in reverse, by having three intermediate-term declines. However, during the 1983-1984, and late 1987 periods, the primary declines were accompanied by only one downtrend. The position of the long-term indicator can also provide a valuable clue to the maturity of a primary trend. Other things being equal, the further it is from the equilibrium level, the more mature the trend.

The intermediate- and short-term momentum series can also flag positive and negative divergences and occasionally can help in constructing important trendlines. This is especially true of the more volatile short-term KST. For instance, it was possible to construct four trendlines in the 1982-89 period, each of which was followed by an important rally.

Obviously, it is not easy to determine when the long-term KST will reverse direction, but if it is in an overbought condition at a time when both the short-term and intermediate-term series are also reversing, the odds of a long-term reversal are that much better. If you can spot some trendline violations in these intermediate- and short-term KSTs, so much the better.

I have found this KST arrangement to work well for virtually all markets, whether it be individual stocks, currencies, commodities, and so forth. As with any indicator, some entities work better than others, so the KST market cycle should not be blindly adopted for everything. See if it has worked historically; if there is a good fit, the chances are good that it will work well in the future.

Some Examples from the Marketplace

Chart 7.11 shows weekly data for First Michigan Bank. The first thing to note is the fact that it is possible to construct some pretty good overbought/oversold zones with this data at ±100. This is not always an option; but in this case, we can see that virtually every time this series reverses from one of these boundary lines a new short-term trend gets underway. The magnitude of the price movement depends on the position of the other two indicators; that is, are they in an uptrend or a downtrend, or in an overbought or oversold condition? Another factor is the nature of the change in the trend for the short-term KST indicator. For example, the horizontal lines marked A, B, and C above the price indicate those times when the short-term KST has violated a small rising trendline. In these instances the price did not reach a new high until about a year later. Trendline breaks, therefore, have the effect of emphasizing a breakdown in momentum and imply a larger correction than would normally be signaled by a short-term sell signal alone.

The same concept, but in reverse, occurred in late 1990 and early 1992. In the first example the short-term KST violated a

Chart 7.11   First Michigan Bank and Three KSTs

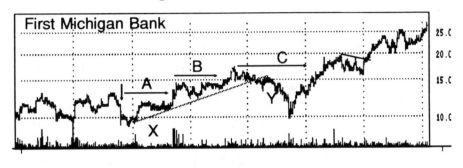

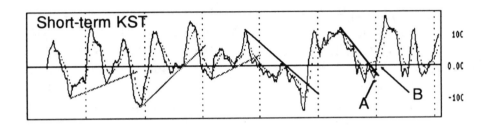

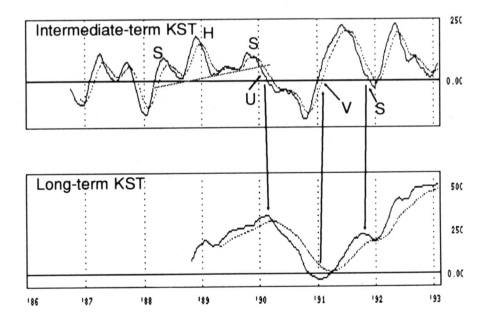

downtrendline, and in the second it completed a small base. Both were followed by a larger than average rally.

The intermediate series can also help to gauge the potential for a new trend. At the beginning of 1990 this series completed a head-and-shoulders top. The nature of the sell signal—at a time when the long-term KST was in a relatively overbought condition—indicated that a fairly important decline or consolidation was likely. This breakdown was associated with a violation of trendline (XY) in the price and was followed by the worst decline in the whole period. This major sell signal was also preceded by a small trend break in the short-term indicator.

Because it requires nearly three years of data to calculate, the long-term KST does not appear on the chart until late 1988. As you can see, it pretty well reflects the primary-trend ups and downs after this point. One of the key questions that needs to be addressed is: When will the long-term indicator reverse trend? Unfortunately, there is no clear-cut answer. Obviously, the more overextended (i.e., overbought or oversold), the greater the odds of a reversal. In many cases, I have learned to expect a reversal in the long-term trend when the intermediate series, having been above or below zero for a considerable time, crosses through the equilibrium point. Examples occurred at Points U and V. Point S was an exception, because the long-term indicator did not violate its EMA, even though it did reverse direction.

This underscores the fact that the zero-intermediate crossover is not a hard-and-fast rule. It seems to work most of the time, but there are a lot of exceptions. Examine the security you are monitoring to see how accurate this method has been in the past. If it has failed quite often, do not use it. On the other hand, if it has been reasonably accurate there is a good chance that it will continue to work.

Quite often, the long-term KST will move toward its EMA, looking as if it is about to cross. If the short- and intermediate-term series have begun to reverse, the chances of a crossover will be greatly reduced. The experience of the early 1992 period exemplifies this point. During that period the long-term indicator fell toward its EMA, but the short-term series broke out from a base and the intermediate gave a buy signal. In this instance the long-term series was not very overbought so it was able to recover. If this positive short/intermediate combination had occurred when the long-term was overextended, the outcome would probably not have been as positive.

Chart 7.12 shows a market cycle model for First Virginia Bank. Note again how the zero crossovers of the intermediate series correspond with reversals in the long-term KST. We can also see some important trendline applications at work for the short-term KST. For example, there was a joint break in both the short and intermediate series at the beginning of 1989. Both series hardly fell below their zero lines just before the take-off in prices. The reverse set of circumstances developed at the end of 1989. Not surprisingly, this action was followed by the most severe decline in the chart.

Finally, the short-term KST traced out a head-and-shoulders top at the beginning of 1991. This should have resulted in a fairly important short-term decline, however, there are two points to bear in mind. First, the trendline that was later violated was quite steep. Normally, steep trendline violations are followed by consolidations, not reversals. In this case the horizontal line at Point A, just above the price, indicates a consolidation. Second, there were two signs that a bull market was in its early stages. The first indication was that the long-term KST had clearly reversed to an upward direction. The reversal was also associated with a positive zero- intermediate KST crossover. The second sign was that the short-term and intermediate series managed to reach unusually high readings, typical of the early stages of a bull market.

Chart 7.13 shows the short- and intermediate-term KSTs for the Lehman Bond Index, a benchmark for the U.S Government bond market. This period brings out several interpretive principles. First, in early 1989 the short-term KST completed and broke down from a head-and-shoulders top. By rights this should have been followed by a sharp down move, but it was not. I have included this example to show that not all momentum breakdowns are followed by serious declines. This one just happened to be an exception. The time to have concluded that it was a whipsaw was when both the AB trendlines were violated on the upside.

Second, there was a marginal short-term buy signal at the end of 1989. Taken on its own merit, this signal should have produced a worthwhile rally. It did not because the intermediate series not only was very overextended, but also was in a clear-cut downtrend at the time.

Chart 7.12   First Virginia Bank and Three KSTs

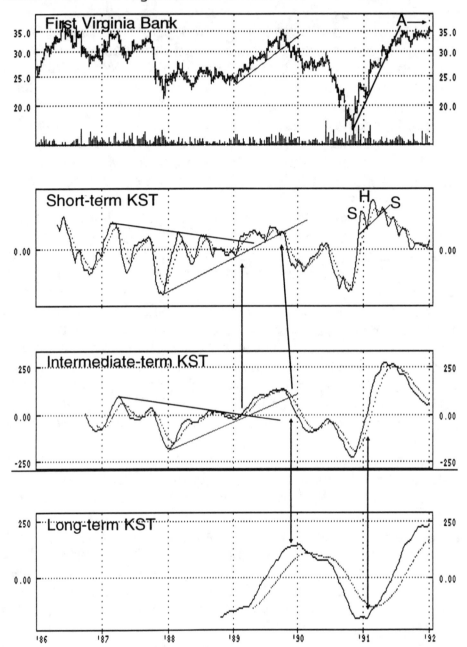

Chart 7.13   Lehman Bond Index with a Short-Term and
                 Intermediate-Term KST

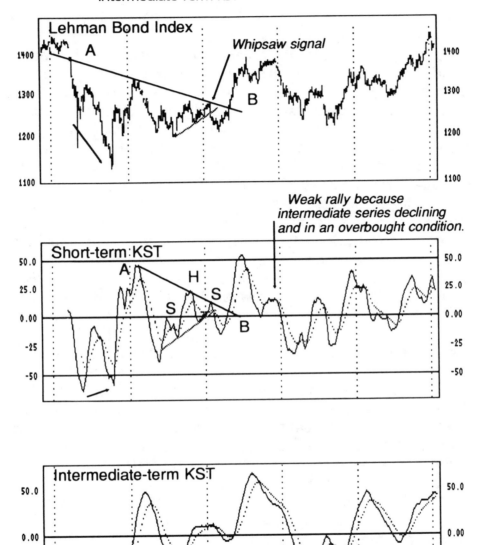

Short-Term KST Signals Using Daily Data

The formula for a short-term KST based on daily data is included in table 7.1. It is shown here to indicate that, apart from helping traders to gain perspective, the KST system can also be used as a short-term trading tool in its own right. I often use it in conjunction with an MACD indicator as shown in chart 7.14. The MACD is used because it is a more sensitive series than the KST, and it usually reverses direction ahead of it. This can be of invaluable help when the KST is very overextended, as it was in August 1992. It makes sense to look at the MACD to see when it reverses direction, because it is quite likely that the KST will soon follow.

The MACD is also helpful because it often lends itself to trendline construction, more so than the KST. In this way, we are better able to discover when important reversals in momentum are likely to get underway. When this occurs in conjunction with a KST buy or sell signal, the strength of the signal is emphasized.

Finally, I have noticed that when the short-term KST crosses zero it is often signaling that a relatively sustainable short-term trend is underway. The quality of the signal will depend largely on how close to the bottom or top in the actual price it is triggered. In chart 7.15 featuring the gold price, we can see that the zero crossovers set the scene for bullish and bearish environments. The June buy signal developed very close to the final low and could have been used with great benefit. On the other hand, although the August zero crossover was associated with a major decline, it unfortunately came after most of the sell-off had taken place. The same was true, but in reverse, for the next buy signal. The rule then is to use zero crossovers as an indication that an important short-term trend reversal is underway, but to take no action if the price has already moved a great deal.

The KST and Relative Strength

The Concept of Relative Strength

So far we have considered the KST indicator from the standpoint of the absolute price, but the analysis can also be extended to relative pricing as well. As we have learned in chapter 4, relative

Chart 7.14   Treasury Bonds Three-Month Perpetual Contract
with a Short-Term KST and an MACD

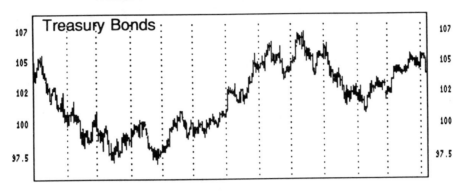

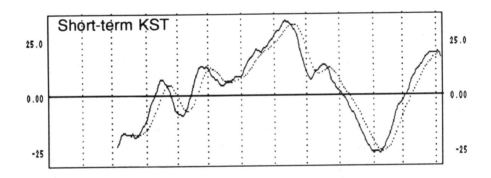

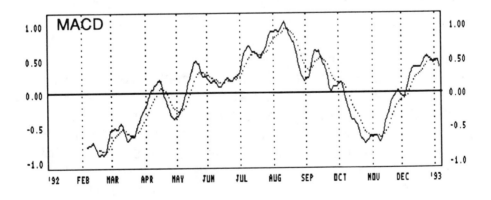

Chart 7.15 Comex Gold Three-Month Perpetual Contract
and Short-Term KST

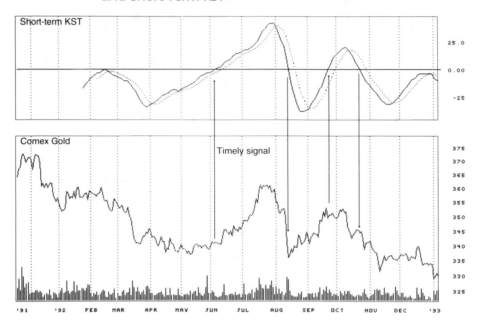

strength (RS) measures the relationship between two price series and should in no way be confused with the relative strength indicator (RSI), which compares the current price of a security with its past price. An RS line typically compares a specific item such as a stock with a base; normally some measure of the market. The line is calculated by dividing the stock by the market; the result is plotted as a continuous line as shown in figure 7.2. When the line is rising the stock is outperforming the market, and when the line is falling the market is outperforming the stock. A rising RS line does not tell us that the *absolute* or *actual price* of the stock is appreciating, only that it is outperforming the market. For example, the market may decline 20% but the stock loses only 10% of its value. Both are losers, but the stock's losses are less than those of the market.

Relative strength can also be used to compare two different price series. The gold/silver ratio is a relative strength relationship; so too is the "Ted Spread," where T-bill prices are compared with those of Eurodollars. Even currencies are an expression of relative strength: the dollar vs. the yen, the yen vs. the pound, and so forth.

Since relative strength moves in trends just like absolute prices, it follows that the KST market cycle model approach can be

Figure 7.2

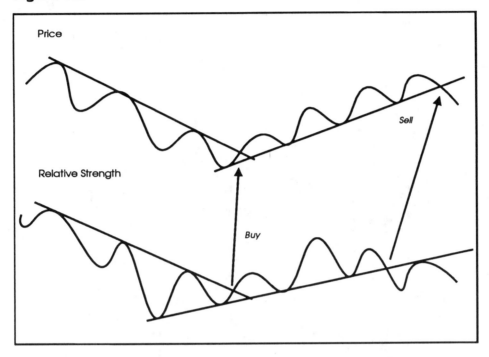

extended to this area as well. In my analysis I take a "top-down" approach. This involves an examination of the long-term position of the market as a whole, followed by industry groups and finally the individual stocks included in the group. Let's consider the second stage; that is, isolating potentially attractive stock groups.

Relative KST Indicators

In many ways the KST approach is more suitable for analyzing trends in *relative* than *absolute* prices. This is because the group rotation process that occurs as the business cycle unfolds is normally far more subject to cyclic rhythms than the actual prices of the various indexes and stock prices themselves. Chart 7.16A shows the market-cycle model for the Dow Jones Financial Sector relative strength. The series in the top panel is the RS; the other three are the KST indicators. When the line is rising, it indicates that finacial stocks are outperforming the market and vice versa. The best buying opportunities occur when the long-term KST of the RS

Chart 7.16A   Dow Jones Financial Relative Strength and Three KSTs

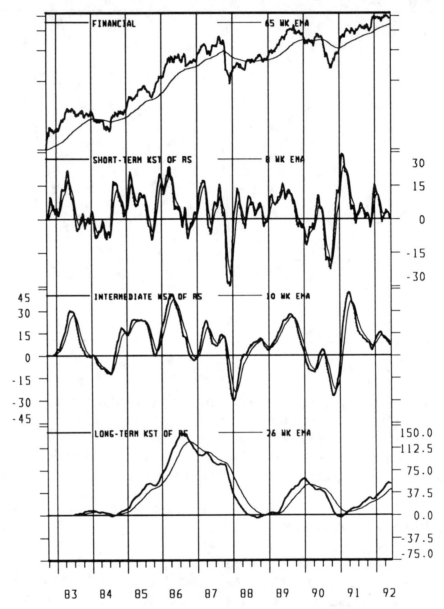

Rates-of-change analysis can also be applied to a relative strength chart. The most reliable buying opportunities are when the long-term KST indicator is below zero and is turning up. Negative indications occur when the long-term KST is above zero and turning down.

is below zero and has started to cross above its moving average while the short- and intermediate-term series are simultaneously consistent with a trend that has yet to reach overextension. It is also important to make sure that the RS has generated some kind of buy signal such as an EMA crossover or trendline break. In a similar vein, the probabilities of success do not favor situations in which the long-term KST is in an overextended reading way above zero. At such junctures the indicators are telling us that the trend of superior RS is well advanced. It could well continue for some time, but the law of averages does not favor such a development. At this juncture it would be far better to search for a group in which the long-term KST is depressed and turning up.

The best approach is to isolate those groups for which the market cycle model is in a positive mode not only for the relative price (Chart 7.16A), but also for the absolute price (Chart 7.16B) as in late 1988 and early 1991. Each instance was followed by superior results. In mid-1986 and early 1990 both conditions reversed since both long-term KST indicators peaked out.

In any given situation there is a constant rotation among the various industry groups in terms of RS action. This can be appreciated by comparing two groups that traditionally perform at different stages in the cycle. At the beginning of a bull market, interest-sensitive issues such as financials typically outperform the market. As the cycle matures this leadership gives way to inflation-sensitive issues such as those in the energy sector as shown in chart 7.17. Chart 7.18 compares the long-term KST of RS for both series. Note that there is a tendency for them to move in opposite directions. For example, the KST for the financial series peaked in late 1989 while energy was bottoming. The reverse held true in early 1991. For the next few years after 1991, financial issues outperformed and energy lagged.

The relative KST analysis can be used not only for timing the purchase and sale of securities that make up industry groups, but also for determining the prevailing stage of the market cycle. When the long-term KST for the RS of financial securities is bottoming, this indicates that a new cycle is beginning; and when the energy sector is reversing to the upside, this is a warning that the cycle is rapidly maturing.

Chart 7.16B   Dow Jones Financial Sector and Three KSTs

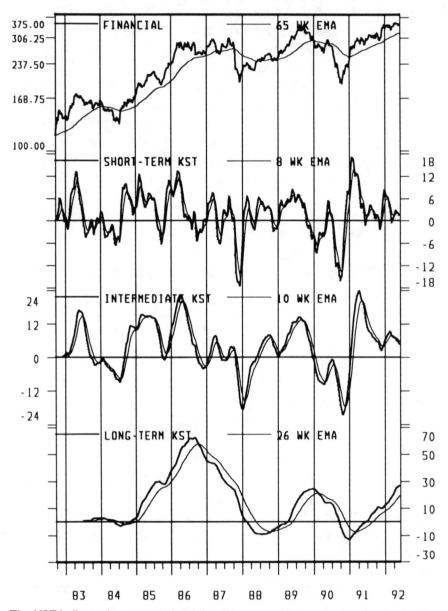

The KST indicator is a summed weighted measure of rate-of-change. Varying the weights and the rates-of-change can produce indicators that measure rate-of-change for short-term, intermediate-term and long-term time horizons.

Chart 7.17   Dow Jones Energy Sector Relative
Strength and Three KSTs

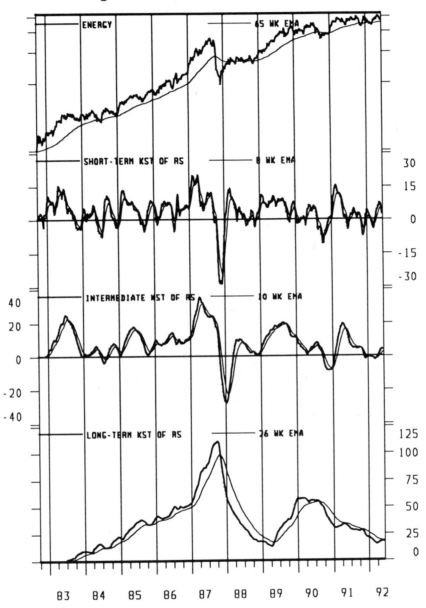

When a bull market in stocks begins to mature, energy stocks tend to take over
the leadership role. The long-term KST should begin to turn up, indicating better
relative performance by the energy group.

Chart 7.18   Dow Jones Financial vs. Energy Relative Strength

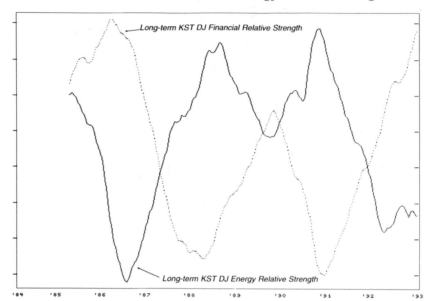

Plotting the long-term KSTs for both the financial relative strength line and the energy relative strength line displays the rotation of these two stock groups. Strength in one group coincides with weakness in the other.

In this chapter I have barely been able to scratch the surface of KST analysis. The concept is far from perfect, but it does provide suitable *long-term* perspective of a specific market, enabling us to make well-informed, *short-term* decisions.

chapter 8

VOLATILITY AND THE DIRECTIONAL MOVEMENT SYSTEM

- **Volatility**
- **What Is Directional Movement?**
- **True Range**
- **Average Directional Movement Index Rating**
- **Plus and Minus Directional Movement Crossovers**
- **Interpretation**
- **Alternative Interpretation**

Volatility

In a very brief but informative article in the January 1991 issue of *Technical Analysis of Stocks and Commodities,* Arthur Merrill considered the question of whether the degree of volatility in the stock market is a useful indication of the market's future course. Based on a 10-year study, he wrote that day-to-day volatility does have good "crystal ball" characteristics, and there is no reason that Merrill's conclusions could not apply to other types of markets or even individual stocks.

Testing for a 1-day ROC, Merrill multiplied the result by 1,000 to create a meaningful scale. The data were also smoothed by a 33% exponential moving average, which roughly corresponds to a 5-week time span. He then tested for unusually high and low data points using the standard deviation method above and below the mean. The indicator proved correct 70% of the time in predicting 13- and 26-week periods. The accuracy rate for the 52-week period was 78%.

One of the key problems faced by all traders is whether the security they have chosen to be involved with will experience trending or trading range characteristics. The distinction is very important. A trading-range market would be attacked by selling into an overbought reading and buying into an oversold one. Short positions would be initiated with an overbought condition and covered with an oversold one. On the other hand, if it is known ahead of time that a market is likely to trend, greater emphasis could be placed on trend-following devices such as moving averages and trendlines with less significance on oscillators.

After all, if you believe that a market will continue to rally, why make trading decisions based on a momentum indicator that is likely to undergo several negative divergences with the price before the final peak?

Of course, there is no precise way to foresee with any consistency whether a market is likely to fall into either the trending or trading range. However, in *New Concepts in Technical Trading* Welles Wilder outlines an approach that tries to determine at least when a market is likely to break out of a trading range. He calls it the "Directional Movement System." The objective of the system is to categorize a number of different markets or stocks by their trending characteristics. The directional movement system measures each security on a scale of 0 to 100. Those with likely trading-range characteristics are ranked at the lower end of the range and those with trending-range characteristics at the higher end. Knowing where a specific security may fall enables you to decide intelligently whether to trade the stock from a trending or trading range perspective. Any security that falls into either extreme offers good opportunities for low-risk profits because trading tactics can be adapted to suit the indicated characteristics. Those securities that fall in the middle would be ignored. Since all securities alternate between trading and trending range characteristics, the system is dynamic because it monitors these characteristics on a continual basis.

Most of the approaches described in this book explain how various technical systems work, but the directional movement approach tries to match the right system to the likely market action. In other words, if we apply a particular system to a market it's rather like trying to ski regardless of whether it's summer or winter, which is really putting the cart before the horse. The Directional Movement System, on the other hand, tries to tell us what the prevailing season is likely to be, so we can decide whether to get out the skis (momentum indicators) or the sail boat (e.g., moving averages).

What Is Directional Movement?

To measure directional movement, two periods of data are needed in order to make a comparison. In most futures trading the period would be in days, but there is no reason why it could not be in weeks or even months. Taken to the other extreme, the comparison could be made between hourly bars in an intraday chart and so forth.

In this explanation I will use days, but please remember that these directional principles can be applied to any time series. In essence the directional movement is defined as the difference between the extreme part of the current period (today) that falls outside the range of the previous period (yesterday). Let's consider some examples.

In figure 8.1 the range of day one is line AB and of day two, line ED. Part of the price range in day two, namely the distance between

Figure 8.1

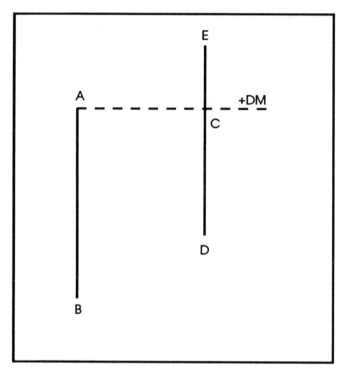

C and D, retraces some of the ground covered in day one. It is the distance between C and E in day two that really earmarks the directional movement (DM). The difference between Point E, or the high, in day two and Point A in day one is called "plus DM" (+DM) because the price is moving up. Minus DM (–DM) would occur when the price declined between the two periods as in figure 8.2. In effect, the distance between the low today and the low yesterday would represent the minus DM.

There are some other possibilities to consider, and these are shown in figures 8.3 and 8.4. In these examples the trading range in day two is so great that it encompasses all of day one and then some. These are known as "outside" days and often warn of short-term reversals in price. How should these be treated? In essence, this situation offers both a +DM and a –DM, so for the purposes of the calculation we take the *greater* of the two. In figure 8.3 this is a +DM (CE) and in figure 8.4 it is a –DM (CD).

The opposite of an outside day is an "inside" day where the trading range of day two is completely encompassed by that of day

Figure 8.2

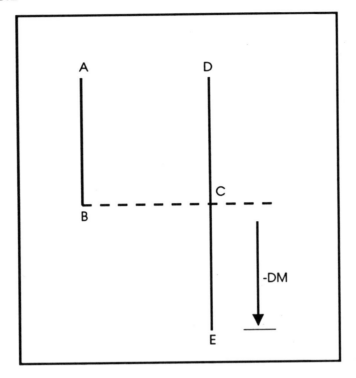

Figure 8.3

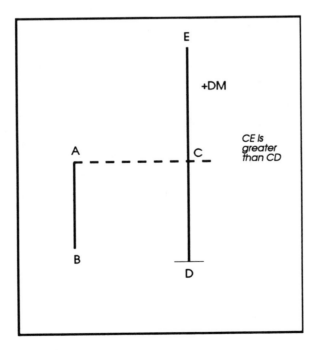

Figure 8.4

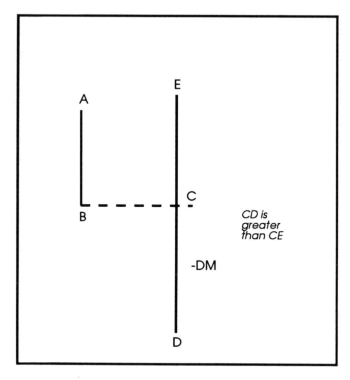

one. Alternatively, we might get an example of two identical trading ranges. These two possibilities are shown in figures 8.5 and 8.6, respectively. In each of these instances there is no directional movement, so the DM value is zero.

In futures trading many contracts are subject to "limit" moves that also must be addressed. Figures 8.7 and 8.8 show limit up and down days, respectively. In an up day, the +DM is *not* the extent of the limit; in other words, it is not the distance between day one's close and CD in day two. Rather, it is the difference between day one's high (Point A) and the limit itself. In this example, it is assumed that the price trades "limit up" all day. Figure 8.8 shows an example of a –DM in which both day one and day two represent limit moves.

Figure 8.5

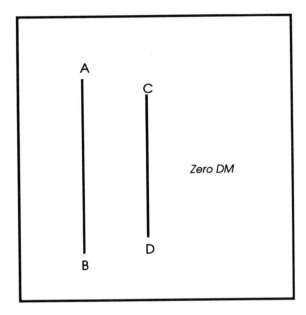

Figure 8.6

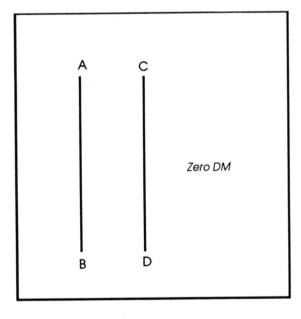

Figure 8.7

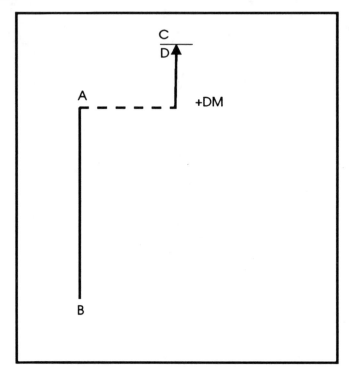

Figure 8.8

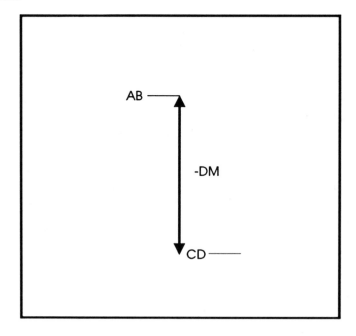

True Range

Price movement is best measured in proportions rather than arithmetic numbers. This enables us to make a more realistic comparison between two periods or two securities of differing price magnitude. For example, a +DM measurement of $1 for IBM stock trading at $100 would have a very different implication than a $1 move for an issue worth $2, since the former would represent a 1% move and the latter a 50% one.

Wilder deals with this problem by comparing the +DM and −DM with what he calls the "true range." He defines this as the maximum range that the price has moved either during one day's trading or from the close of the previous day's trading to the extreme point reached the following day. This means, in effect, that the "true range" in price is the greatest of the following:

1. The distance between today's high and today's low.
2. The distance between yesterday's close and today's high.
3. The distance between yesterday's close and today's low.

The directional indicator (DI) is calculated by dividing the directional movement by the true range. The formula for one day is:

$$+DI_1 = \frac{+DM_1}{TR_1}$$

and

$$-DI_1 = \frac{-DM_1}{TR_1}$$

TR_1 reflects the true range for today and the DM_1 the directional movement for day one. The $+DI_1$ formula would be used for the up days and the $-DI_1$ for the down days, since directional movement can occur only in one direction during one day. It is also important to note that directional movement can only be *positive*. This means that the −DM refers only to a down day, not a negative number.

One day does not make a trend, so it is normal practice to calculate the formula over a number of days. Wilder recommended 14 days, since that represents half the 28-day lunar cycle. This formula reads as follows:

$$+DI_{14} = \frac{+DM_{14}}{TR_{14}}$$

and

$$-DI_{14} = \frac{-DM_{14}}{TR_{14}}.$$

Here the DM_{14} is the sum total of 14 days of directional movement and TR_{14} the sum total of 14 days of true ranges.

The accumulation method gives us the formula for day 15. That method works like this: Take yesterday's $+DM_{14}$, divide it by 14 and subtract this quotient from yesterday's $+DM_{14}$ then add back today's DM_1. This sum is the DM_{14} for today. Calculating the TR_{14} is done in the same manner. Of course, there is no reason why other time spans such as 30-day or 10-day periods cannot be used, or even other forms of data such as weeks, months, etc. The advantage to using this method of calculation is that it does not require us to process and maintain 14 days' worth of back data once we have made the first DI_{14} calculation. A second benefit is that it gives the final indicator a smoothing effect. The actual formulas are as follows:

$$+DM_{14}(today) = Previous \ +DM_{14} - \left[\frac{Previous \ +DM_{14}}{14}\right] + DM_1$$

and

$$-DM_{14}(today) = Previous \ -DM_{14} - \left[\frac{Previous \ -DM_{14}}{14}\right] + -DM_1$$

These two formulas are then each divided by the TR_{14} and multiply the result by 100 to get the plus and minus directional indicators. If the answer to the +DM formula, for example, is 15% and the $-DI_{14}$ is 25%, this means that 15% of the true range prices over the last 14 days were up and 25% were down. Thus, 40% of the 14 days was directional and the balance of 60% was nondirectional.

The figure we are looking for, though, is the difference between $+DI_{14}$ and $-DI_{14}$ because that figure reflects the true direction of the price movement. For instance, if $+DI_{14}$ and $-DI_{14}$ are identical it would mean that up days more or less offset down days. In other words, there was no directional movement at all. By the same token, if the direction is up for 10 to 12 days the +DI would have a high value and the –DM would be very low, resulting in a very high directional movement.

All of these calculations result in an indicator called the directional movement index (DX) that measures the difference between the two DIs. The DX is calculated by dividing the difference between $+DI_{14}$ and $-DI_{14}$ by the sum of the DI_{14} and $-DI_{14}$. The sum reflects the total of the percentage of days that experienced directional movement; the difference is the net result of the type of movement, either plus or minus. By the very nature of the calculation, the DX will always fall between 0 and 100. The higher the number, the greater the directional movement. The *direction* of the price movement has no bearing on the DX itself, since the DX indicates only the trending characteristics. In chart 8.1 note that each of the two highs at Points A and B in the index are associated with a top and bottom.

Let's examine the DX further to see how it works. If the price moves down sharply and then stabilizes, the DX will move from a high number as it did between Points B and C in chart 8.1. Then, as the price continues to rally or starts to decline again, as it did in this example, the DX rallies once again. The low DX numbers between Points C and D indicate low directional movement. Only

Chart 8.1   Swiss Franc and 14-Unit Directional Movement Index

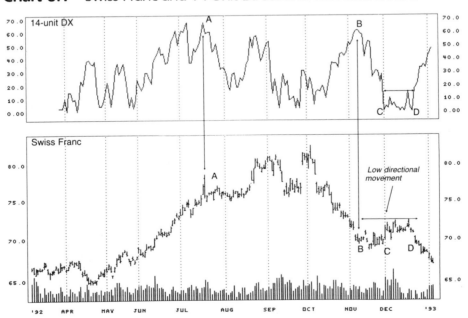

after prices resume their decline does the DX rally once more. This low reading between C and D is because the difference between $+DI_{14}$ and $-DI_{14}$ is decreasing, occasionally touching zero.

The time span used in the construction of the DX has important implications for directional movement in the same way that changes in the time span of a moving average, ROC, or stochastics do. If the standard time span of 14 days is used, the assumption is that the 28-day lunar cycle is the predominant one for short-term trends. However, all cycles can and do fail to operate because price trends are determined by the interaction of many different cycles, each of which has a varying influence on the trend. Thus, if other cycles in a combination have a larger than normal influence because of the way in which they are combined, it will mean that the 28-day cycle will fail to have its normal strong influence. Consequently, indicators constructed to reflect this cycle will not have their usual reliable characteristics.

Wilder recommends smoothing out the action of the DX in order to make it indicative of price movements to both the high and low extremes. To do this he suggests calculating DX using a period twice as long as the one used for calculating DI_{14}.

A short-cut is to take a 14-day average of DX. This average is known as the average directional movement index (ADX).

Average Directional Movement Index Rating

Another feature of the directional movement system is the calculation of the average directional movement index rating (ADXR). The ADXR is the indicator used to rate the directional characteristics of all of the securities we might want to trade. The formula for the ADXR is as follows:

$$ADXR = \frac{ADX_{Today} + ADX_{14\ Days\ Ago}}{2}$$

I have used 14 days as the Wilder-recommended default. It is possible, of course, to substitute any time period you prefer. According to Wilder, the first step is to identify securities that have a high directional movement, and then to determine when that directional movement is likely to develop. The ratio is calculated by dividing the sum of the ADX today and the ADX 14 days ago by 2.

When the ADX and ADXR are plotted together, the ADXR has the appearance of a moving average running through an indicator (the ADX) that is fluctuating around it, or a sort of sine curve as in chart 8.2. The chart shows that peaks and troughs in the ADX indicate changes in direction. Remember, though, that *the ADX measures directional changes only and not the direction of the change*. Thus, in a bull market a peak indicates a reversal to the downside, but in a bear market it reflects a change from down to up. The larger the difference between the highs and lows in the ADX, the greater the reactions resulting in greater trending characteristics. In general, it is usually wiser to trade only in the direction of the main trend, but if the amplitude of the movements in the ADX are substantial it means that profitable trend-following trades could be made in either direction.

The ADXR according to Wilder, is exclusively a rating device and should only be used as a measurement of directional move-

Chart 8.2   Swiss Franc and 14-Unit Average Directional
Movement Index Rating

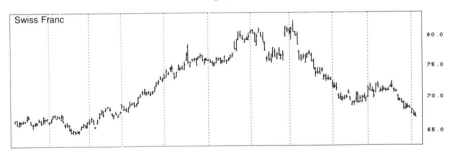

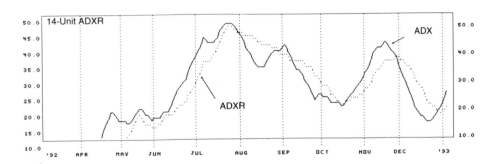

ment. The greater the distance between the ADXR and zero the greater the directional movement of the security being monitored.

Plus and Minus DI Crossovers

The "equilibrium point" is when $+DI_{14}$ and $-DI_{14}$ are the same level. Buy and sell signals are generated when $+DI_{14}$ and $-DI_{14}$ cross. This means that good tradeable directional movement is not only just a question of straight up and down price movement, but also movement in excess of the equilibrium point.

In figure 8.9 Points A, B, and C represent the equilibrium points (i.e., the places where the DIs cross). This example shows that there is a fair degree of volatility, but unfortunately the profit potential from buying at A, selling at B, and selling short at B while covering at C is not very great. According to Wilder, this type of market would have a *low* ADX rating.

Figure 8.10, on the other hand, shows a situation where the profit potential between the equilibrium points is pretty good. In this instance the ADX is assumed to have a *high* rating. In other words,

Figure 8.9

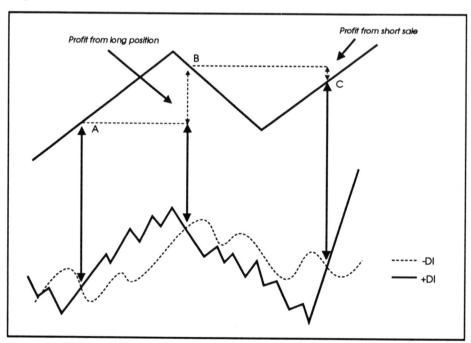

Figure 8.10

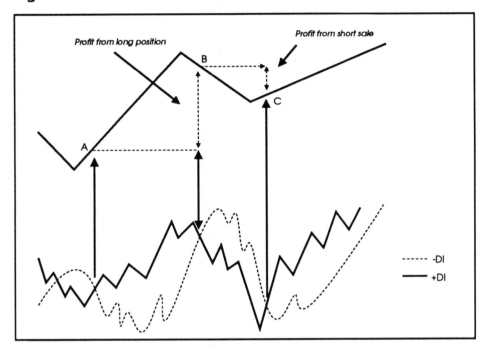

the high ADX reading indicates not only that a market is volatile, but also that this volatility enhances the market's tradeability.

Figure 8.11 shows the best situation of all. This occurs in a strong-trending market where the two DIs are continually moving toward each other but rarely cross. At Points W, X, Y, and Z they almost cross, but at the last moment they diverge once again so that the position is maintained. According to Wilder, this type of market condition indicates a very high ADX rating.

Finally, in figure 8.12 we see an example of a volatile but unprofitable market. The AB long trade breaks even but the BC short sale loses money. In *New Concepts* Wilder points out that this type of market action reflects a situation in which the ADX is less than 20. He argues that when the ADX rallies above the 25 level the equilibrium points widen.

Interpretation

Wilder believes that the first step in interpreting the directional movement system is to select a security with a high ADX and ADXR

Figure 8.11

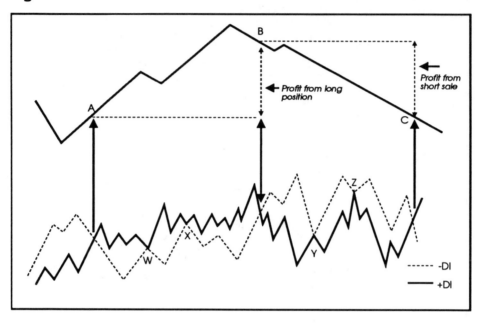

Figure 8.12

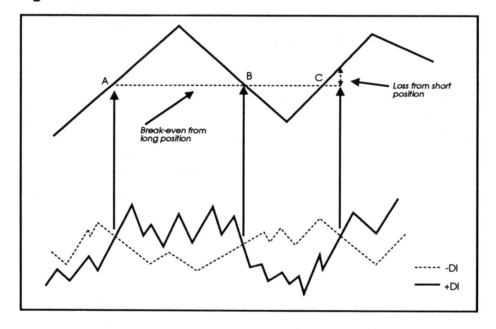

reading. This provides sufficient directional movement to make tradeable profits from trend-following signals. Buy signals in an up market are generated when the $+DI_{14}$ crosses above the $-DI_{14}$ and sell signals when the $+DI_{14}$ moves below the $-DI_{14}$. In a declining market, negative crossovers would be used to take short positions that subsequently would be covered when the $+DI_{14}$ crosses back above the $-DI_{14}$. In short, ADX is used to identify securities that are likely to trend, and the DIs are used for actual timing purposes, just as we might use a moving average crossover, trendline violation, or price pattern completion.

There is one more feature of the directional movement system called the "extreme point rule." This rule states that on the day that the DI's cross, use the extreme price that the security reached that day as the reversal point. Long positions would use the low of the day; short positions the high. These are shown in figure 8.13. These positions are the stop points that should be used for the next several days, *even if the DIs signal that the position should be liquidated.*

Figure 8.13

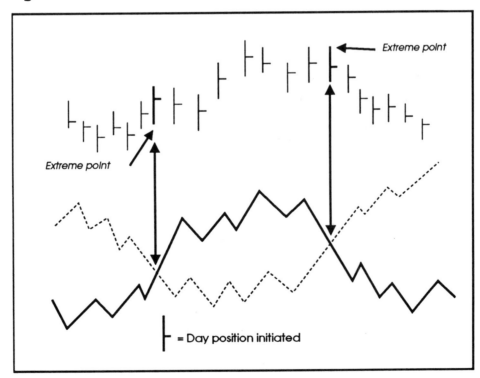

Wilder rationalizes taking this action on the basis that the initial equilibrium or crossover day tends to be an important one, regardless of whether or not a market is going to reverse. As a result, the extreme price point reached on that day is not normally breached.

Important turns are often indicated when the ADX reverses direction *after* it has moved above both DI's. In figure 8.14, the ADX reverses direction at Point A, and after one more rally the price also peaks. The actual signal would have occurred when the $+DI_{14}$ crossed below the $-DI_{14}$, but it would not have been a bad idea to take some profits at A since the timing was better. In a really strong market, like the one shown in figure 8.14, the ADX will reverse direction from a high level, decline, and then move back up, yet the DIs do not cross until much later as at Point B. Conversely, when the ADX line moves below both DIs, Wilder recommends staying away from trend-following systems.

In summary, it is possible to set out a series of rules as explicitly proposed by Wilder:

1. Trade only trend-following systems in securities with a high ADX rating. The ADX level reflects the degree of directional movement, not the direction itself.

Figure 8.14

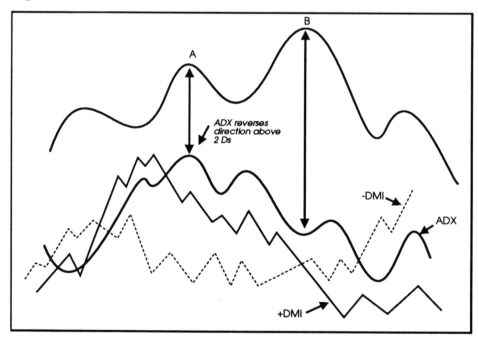

2. Use crossovers of the $+DI_{14}$ and $-DI_{14}$ as timing points for entering and exiting the markets.

3. The exception to rule 2 occurs when the extreme-point trading rule takes effect. This states that on the day of the DI cross-over, use the extreme price point in the *opposite* direction to your position as a stop point. Long positions should use the low of the day and short ones the high. This becomes the stop point even if the DIs subsequently re-cross.

4. An early indication that a trend reversal is about to take place and some profit-taking is in order is when the ADX moves above both DIs and reverses direction. Final liquidation would occur in the event of a DI crossover or an extreme point violation. If the $+DI_{14}$ is above the $-DI_{14}$ at the time of the ADX reversal, this would mean a change in trend from up to down. The same principle works in reverse.

5. If the ADX is above both DIs and is at an extreme reading, this means that the trend has been in force for some time. This is not a good point for entering new trades, because the DIs could re-cross in the direction of the prevailing trend. In other words, the high reading in the ADX is a form of overbought or oversold reading where new trades in the direction of the prevailing trend are usually not profitable.

6. When the ADX is below both DIs avoid trend-following systems because little directional movement is indicated.

7. When the ADX is below the 20-25 area avoid trend-following systems, since little or no directional movement is indicated, regardless of the ADX position relative to the DIs.

Alternative Interpretation

Technical analysis is an art rather than a science, so it would not be surprising if other methods of interpretation of the directional movement system were to evolve. In my own research I found different ways to use the DM system. These comments are in no way intended to denigrate Mr. Wilder's contribution; they are meant more to elaborate and expand on his ideas. You, of course, are free to choose whatever principles you find most useful.

Chart 8.3 takes us back to the DI arrangement. This chart shows that buy signals are generated when the solid +DI crosses above the dashed −DI, and vice versa. The arrows show that this approach would have worked quite well for the Canadian dollar

Chart 8.3   Canadian Dollar Spot and 14-Unit
Directional Movement Index

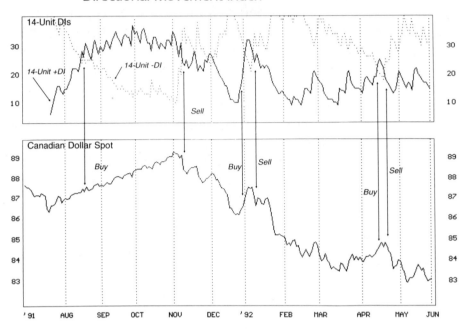

between 1991 and 1992. There were some whipsaw signals, but by and large the "system" would have kept you in for the major trending moves. After all, this was a very trendy period for the dollar so virtually any technical system would have done quite well.

Chart 8.4, shows a trading range market for the S&P Composite Index in 1992. Here we see that the system was not very successful because a substantial number of whipsaw signals were generated (indicated by the circles). One way around this drawback is to smooth the DIs. This has been done in chart 8.5, where we can see that most of the whipsaws have been filtered out. The system barely makes money, but we have to remember that this was an extremely difficult period. However, when the market does begin to trend in the last quarter of 1992 the system participates in a large part of the move.

These simple crossovers form only part of the system, of course, and should be related to the ADX. From my own observations I have not found the concept of a high ADX rating as a selection tool for securities with a strong directional movement to be particularly helpful. Any momentum indicator in an overbought or oversold extreme can tell you that a market has been trending.

Chart 8.4   S & P Composite and 14-Unit Directional Movement Index

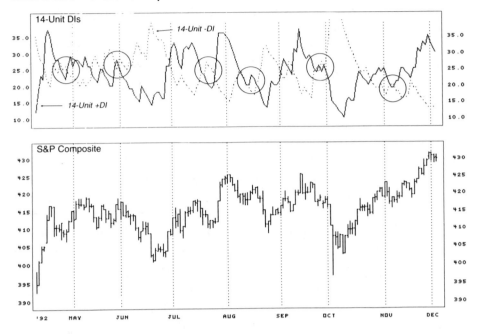

Chart 8.5   S & P Composite and 8-Day EMA of a Positive Directional
Movement Index vs. 8-Day EMA of a Negative Directional
Movement Index

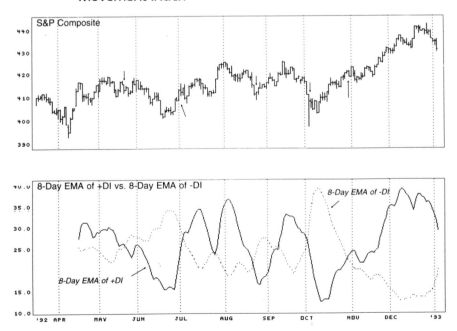

It is a fact that once a market has had a good run that the chances are also good that it will subsequently consolidate its gains or losses. In most cases I find that a reversal in the ADX from an extreme high level is followed by a consolidation. Reversals can be of invaluable help if you are selling options because the price of an option declines over time if there is no price movement.

Take a look at charts 8.6 and 8.7. Almost every time the ADX peaks from an extreme the security in question experiences some kind of consolidation. This was especially true for the U.S. stock market in the 1990-92 period. Every time the ADX topped out this was followed by some kind of sideways movement in the price.

Conversely, I have found that some of the best trend following moves begin when the ADX is at a low number and *starts to reverse* to the upside. In chart 8.8 we can see that four important trending moves are all signaled by a DI crossover that occurs *when the ADX is at or below a 25 reading.* I find that *low* readings are very useful since they tell us in a fairly graphic way those times when a market has *not* been trending. For other oscillators, such as an RSI, directionless markets are reflected in dull activity around the zero

Chart 8.6   CRB Index and 14-Unit Average Directional
                        Movement Index

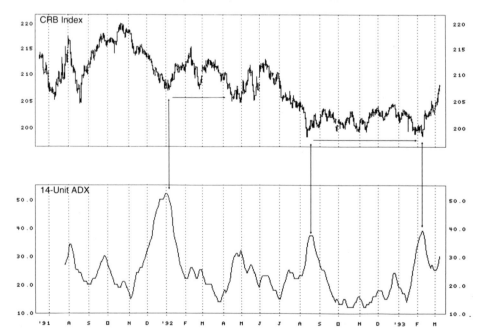

Chart 8.7   S & P Composite and 14-Unit Average
               Directional Movement Index

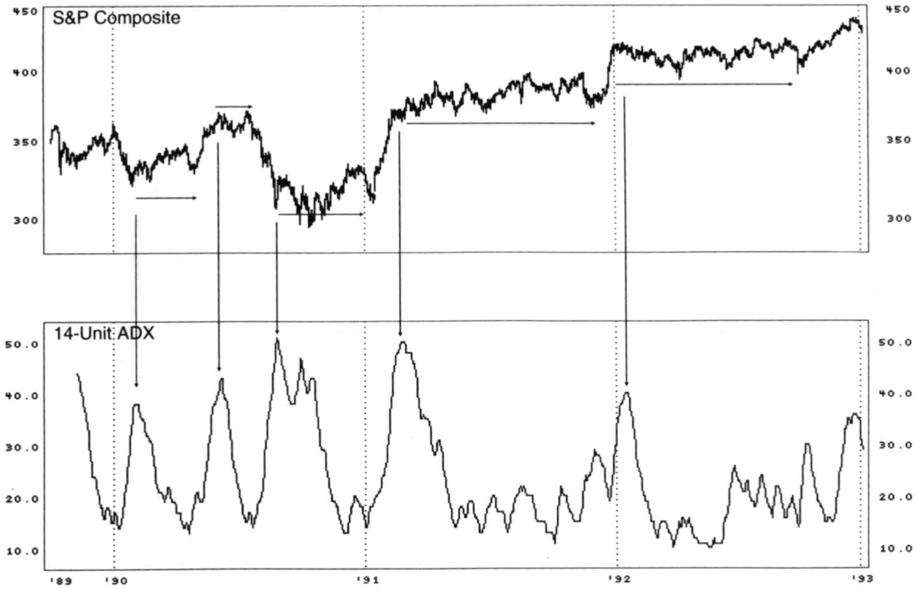

This chart shows that the ADX peaks from a high level the price will often consolidate before continuing in the direction of the previous trend.

level, which is relatively difficult to spot. In the case of the ADX it is easier to detect because the indicator falls close to zero. The near-zero readings tell us to be on the alert for a trending move to begin any time. When the ADX starts to rally it warns us that a directional move is on the way. The nature of the direction can be obtained from a review of other momentum series.

In figure 8.15 we can see that good trending DI signals come from points when the ADX is low and begins to turn. Quite often the DI crossovers occur before the ADX reverses to the upside. In such situations it is usually best to wait for a reversal, even if this means giving up a little potential profit. This is because the declining ADX indicates that the directional movement is still in a declining phase. Only when it turns up is it telling us that a directional move is underway.

If we refer back to chart 8.8 we can see that most of the best DI crossover signals occurred when the ADX was at a very low reading and then began to turn. These signals are marked by the letters A, B, C, and D. Not all signals generated in this way resulted

Chart 8.8   Sydney All Ordinary and Average Directional Movement
Index and Negative Directional Movement Index

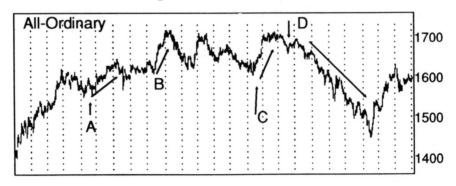

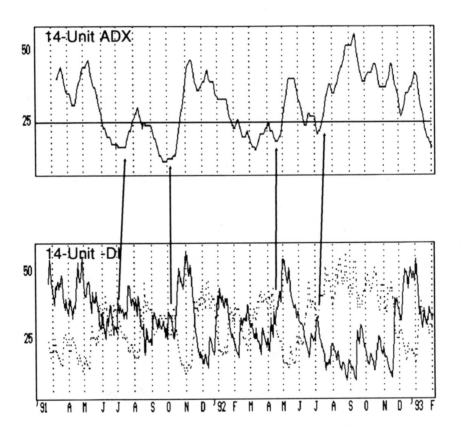

Figure 8.15

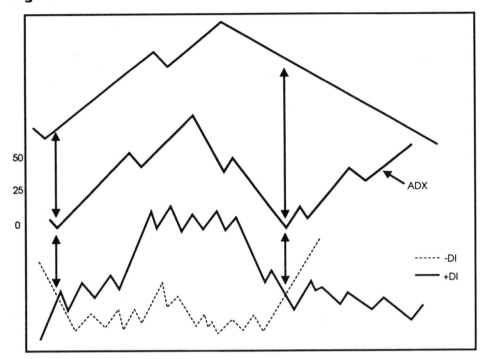

in such strong moves. Chart 8.9 represents part of the period covered in chart 8.8 in a little more detail. Note that the two indicated signals were generated not at the time of the crossover but *after* the ADX had begun to rise. Here the DI crossover was an alert which was later confirmed by the turn in the ADX. In most instances these types of signals will be triggered with a lag, as the ADX plays catch up.

The DI system should always be used in conjunction with other momentum indicators. In this way, it is possible to gain some valuable clues as to the nature of the forthcoming trend. For example, we would expect to see a far stronger trend develop after a momentum indicator has reached an oversold condition and perhaps diverged positively with the price several times. A low and reversing ADX in combination with a positive DI crossover would probably be followed by a healthy advance.

Chart 8.9   Sydney All Ordinary and 14-Unit Average Directional
Movement Index and 14-Unit Negative Directional
Movement Index

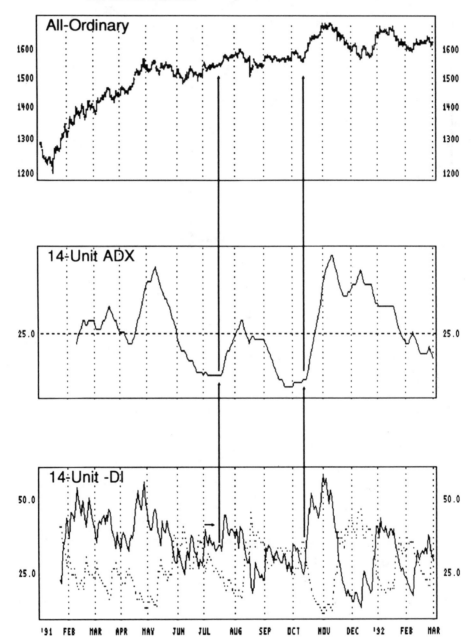

In his excellent book *Trading for a Living* (John Wiley & Sons, 1993), Alex Elder gives an excellent account of the directional movement system. He regards the best signals as those that occur when the ADX falls beneath the two DIs. As he says, "The longer it stays there, the stronger the base for the next move."[1] Once the ADX begins to rise by about 4 points to, say, 8–12 points from its low, it signals the beginning of a major new trend. Under his rules traders should buy if $+DI_{13}$ is above $-DI_{13}$ (note that he uses a different time frame) and place a stop beneath the previous minor low. Short sales would be instigated if the $-DI_{13}$ is above the $+DI_{13}$. The stop point would be the previous minor high.

A buy-signal of this nature was given by the mark in May 1992. This signal is shown in chart 8.10 at Point A. The ensuing price move was extremely worthwhile. Later, a sell signal was triggered

Chart 8.10   Deutsche Mark and 13-Unit Directional Movement Index

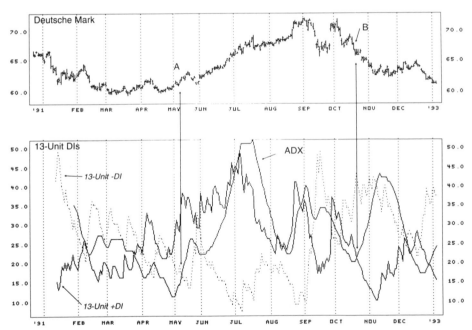

[1] Elder, Alex, *Trading for a Living.* New York: John Wiley & Sons, 1993, pgs. 135-141.

at Point B. Note how the ADX had begun to rise from below both series. Since the $-DI_{13}$ was on top, this move by the ADX constituted a sell signal.

It should be noted that these should be used *only* as general signals that an important change in trend is likely. Consequently a trader would not buy at point A with a view to selling at B. Instead he would buy at A and look for a point to sell based on other criteria. This is because a sell signal of the B variety may not come for many months after. In short, the two signals (A and B) are *not* related. They just tell you when the environment is changing.

There is no doubt that the directional movement system can offer some fairly accurate trading signals. However, as with all technical indicators, this approach is best used in conjunction with other momentum indicators.

The Commodity Selection Index

The Commodity Selection Index is another Welles Wilder innovation. The original name "commodity" can apply to any security for any time frame. Wilder points out in *New Concepts in Technical Trading* that volatility is a measurement of movement, since it is always accompanied by movement; but movement is not always associated with volatility. A security can advance or decline very slowly in a firm direction but still lack volatility.

The objective of the Commodity Selection Index is to identify which securities will get the greatest bang for the buck. The characteristics measured by the indicator are basically directional, but it also takes into consideration volatility, margin requirements, and commission costs. The result, in theory at least, is an indicator that allows for comparison and selection.

Calculation

The formula for the Selection Index uses a number of the concepts used in the directional movement system:

$$CSI = ADXR \times ATR_{14}\left[\frac{V}{\sqrt{M}} \times \frac{1}{150+C}\right]$$

Where $ADXR$ = Average Directional Movement Index Rating
ATR_{14} = the average true range for 14 periods
M = margin requirement (in dollars)
V = conversion factor (value of a 1 cent move in dollars),

and

C = commissions (in dollars).

Interpretation

According to the system's rules, trading activity should be concentrated in those securities that have the highest selection rating, since they will offer greater directional movement and substantial volatility than those with low selection ratings. In other words, the objective of the Selection Index is to direct the trader to the place where the greatest action is likely to be.

In *New Concepts* Wilder uses the example of coffee vs. soybeans to illustrate how the system operates. Coffee, it is assumed, has an ADXR of 70% and soybeans an ADXR of 50%. However, in Wilder's example he assumes that a trader would have been exposed to both contracts for 10 days. The coffee contract has an average true range of 3.75 cents. At that time a 1-cent move was worth $375. This would mean that the average dollar move per day would be $375 x 3.75, or $1,406.25. For beans the assumed dollar range was $750 per day. At first glance it would be reasonable to conclude that coffee is the commodity of choice because the average dollar movement for each day is almost twice as much. This is where the margin-requirement component benefits because coffee had a margin requirement of $9,000, whereas the requirement for beans was only $3,000. In effect, it was possible to trade three contracts of beans for the same margin requirement needed to trade one contract of coffee. This meant that the average leveraged dollar movement for a margin requirement remained at $1,406.25 for coffee, while for beans it increased to $2,250, or $750 x 3.

This indicator was not originally designed to be used as a timing device, but as a method for determining where the most leverage can be obtained in relation to the implied volatility and trending characteristics of various contracts. My view is that this is a poor method for selecting potential trades because it places emphasis on the greed factor; that is, "How quickly and easily can I make money?" Anyone who has studied the psychology of trading or who has learned from their own errors in the markets knows without a doubt that objectivity is one of most important psychological attributes for a trader to possess. (For further reading see chapter 2 of my book *Investment Psychology Explained* [John Wiley & Sons, 1992].) Any hint of the greed factor substantially increases the odds of failure. Patience and discipline, not greed and speed, are the orders of the day for a successful trader. Having said that though, I have noticed that in some cases the Commodity Selection Index, when used in conjunction with other momentum series, can aid in timing decisions.

Chart 9.1 shows the Nikkei from 1989 to 1993. Extreme peaks in the Selection Index often occur at very important turning points. Here we see that the two highest readings in 1990 were associated with two intermediate-term lows illustrating the fact that changes in the direction of this series at virtually any point is associated with

Chart 9.1   Nikkei Stock Index and a 14-Day
                 Commodity Selection Index

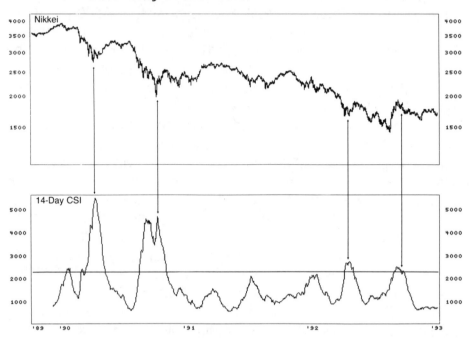

a market turning point. What it does not tell us is *which* direction, since the mid-1992 peak in the indicator corresponded to a short-term top in the index. Remember, direction can only be ascertained in regard to the prevailing trend. For example, if the market has been rallying and the Selection Index has begun to turn in either direction, we should expect the market to reverse direction as well.

I feel that an efficient way of using the Selection Index is to combine it with other momentum series, so in chart 9.2, a short-term KST has been included. The first thing to notice is that both the April and October 1990 lows were associated with extreme peaks in the Selection Index and KST buy signals. The same was true at the April 1992 low and the September high, except that the latter was accompanied by a sell signal. Now, if we consider the two significant declines in the Nikkei that began in mid 1990, we see two very similar technical characteristics. These are a bottoming in the Selection Index and an extremely weak rally in the KST at Point A

Chart 9.2   Nikkei Stock Index, Short-Term KST, and
14-Day Commodity Selection Index

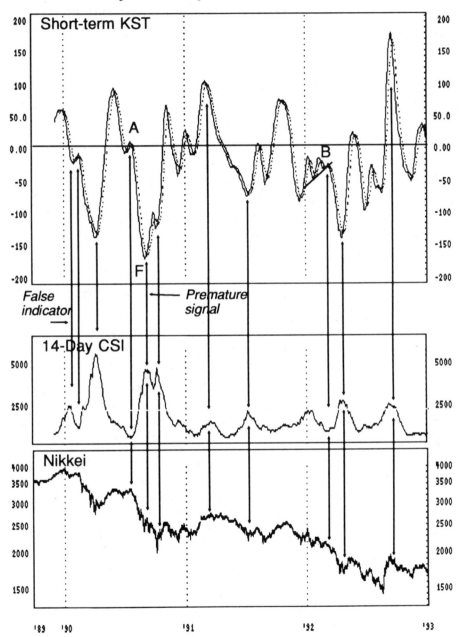

that barely moved it from the zero level. The decline in the Selection Index reveals the fact that the market is losing its sense of direction, while the subsequent rally indicates that it has regained it. However, the weak KST buy signal followed by a sell signal indicates that this new direction is down. A similar situation developed in March 1992 (Point B) where the KST, after a series of weak rallies, violates a small trendline at the same time the Selection Index reverses to the upside. In this example the market had experienced a small consolidation with a downward bias. However, when the Selection Index reverses and the KST violates the line, the decline in the Nikkei accelerates.

Not all turning points are flagged in this way. The final bottom in late August was associated with a KST buy signal, but the Selection Index continued to rally. Also the signals do not always work as well as we may want them to do. For example, the KST and Selection Index both "did their bit" in July 1991 by confirming each other. However, the subsequent rally did not amount to very much. This is because the main trend was down. If a momentum indicator is going to fail, it probably will when moving in a contra-trend fashion, as it did here. A second failure occurred at Point F in September 1990 when both the Selection and KST Indicators gave clear, but, as it turned out, false indications. Unfortunately, such incidents are a fact of life that cannot be explained or avoided. The one warning is that the direction of the primary trend was down. Once again, we need to stress the fact that if a failure is going to take place, it is likely to be in a contra-trend direction.

Chart 9.3 shows a similar combination, only this time for the S & P Composite Index. Note that the most precipitous decline of the entire period, in August 1990, occurs in a technical environment similar to that of the Nikkei in the previous example. This was a failed KST rally from around zero, combined with a Selection Index reversal from a low level. A similar reversal failure occured when the Selection Index appears to reverse direction in late August just as the KST gives a buy signal at point F. In this instance the primary trend is down and the signal is a contra-trend one. The actual bottom does not materialize until Point J, when the Selection Index reverses from an even higher high and the KST is still in a moderately oversold, but bullish position.

Chart 9.3   S & P Composite, Short-Term KST, and
14-Day Commodity Selection Index

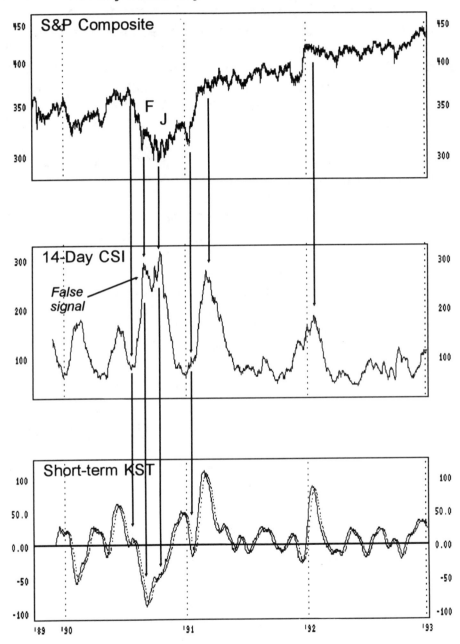

A final point brought out by this chart is the fact that an extreme reading in the Selection Index is not necessarily followed by a reversal in trend. A consolidation can, and sometimes does, follow. All that the reversal from an extreme high reading really tells us is that the strong directional move is over. In the case of bottoms this is usually followed by an upmove. However, because tops are often more lengthy affairs, a reversal to the downside by the Selection Index may be followed by a period of consolidation. For those who write options either scenario is a recipe for profits as can be seen in early 1991 and 1992.

Chart 9.4 shows this principle in action for the Hong Kong market. Here the time frame has been changed from 14 days to 28. Notice how all the extreme peaks except that of (the circled) March 1992 were followed by a sideways correction. You can also see that the low points in the Selection Index, which occurred around the 1000 level, were all associated with a meaningful rally.

Finally, chart 9.5 shows how it is possible to use the Selection Index with a moving average to generate buy and sell points. The center panel shows a 14-day Index with a 15-day simple moving average, and the lower one depicts a 28-day series with a 25-day

Chart 9.4   Hang Seng and 28-Day Commodity Selection Index

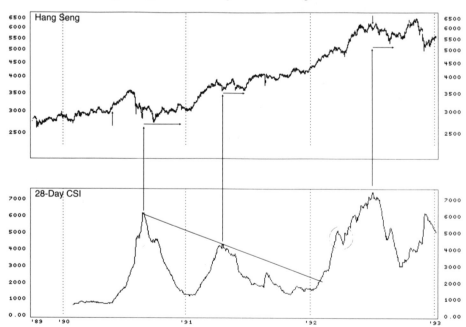

Chart 9.5   Hang Seng and Two Commodity Selection Indexes

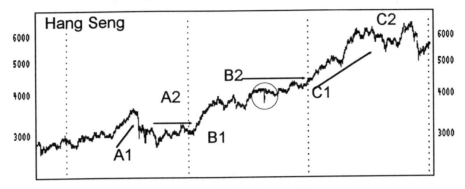

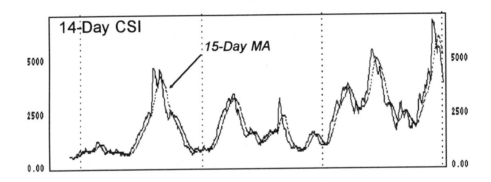

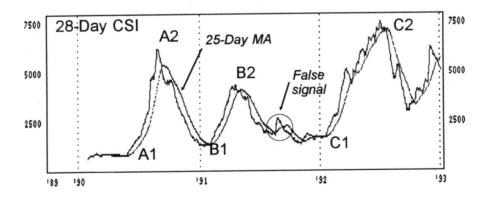

average. The 28-day series gives a number of very good moving average signals, at A1, A2, B1, B2, C1 and C2. Just to be fair, you should look at the false moving-average crossover signal in the middle of 1991. This signal relates to the direction of the CSI *not* the Hang Seng.

Summary

1. The original concept of the Commodity Selection Index was to identify the commodity markets where a combination of volatility relative to margin requirements would offer the best returns.
2. An alternative is to use changes in direction of the Selection Index in combination with other momentum indicators. This practice often leads to better-timed trading decisions.

The Parabolic System

Introduction

In the previous chapter we examined the concept of directional movement and discovered that there are two steps involved when putting on a trade. The first is to select a security with a high directional weighting; the second is to wait for that particular security to signal that a new trend is underway. This is a wonderful concept in theory which often works in practice. Welles Wilder estimates that the market is only trending about 30% of the time and from my own observations, I cannot quibble with this estimate. "Directional" signals filter out a lot of trading-range activity, but like all technical tools they can and do fail to operate reliably. Consequently, some kind of escape mechanism is required to help protect the trader from such failures.

This is where the parabolic system comes in. Since it is not a momentum indicator, the system does not really fall within the scope of this book. However, I am mentioning it briefly because it has become a very popular trading mechanism and can be used successfully with momentum indicators.

One of the most valid criticisms of any trend-following system is that the implied lags obliterate a significant amount of the potential profitability of the trade. The Parabolic System is designed to address this problem by increasing the speed of the stop after the first few trading days. The stop is a function of both price and time and it never goes backwards. So whenever prices reach new highs or lows the stop moves a certain incremental amount each day depending on the direction of the trade. The concept draws on the idea that time is an enemy, and unless a trade can continue to generate more profits over time it should be liquidated.

I said earlier that the Parabolic Method can be used in conjunction with the Directional Movement System. However, since it is a stop-loss system it can theoretically be used with any momentum series once that indicator has been used to filter out a good entry point for a trade.

Parabolic Stop Reversal

The Parabolic Stop Reversal System (SAR) is a trailing stop technique. The formula is designed so that the stop is constantly being tightened as the market moves in your favor. When the position is first initiated, it is given a relatively long leash, so to speak. Then, as time passes, the stop is gradually tightened. The expression "parabolic" derives from the shape of the curve the stops create as they appear on the chart. In a rising market the stop is continually raised, never lowered. In a declining market the opposite holds true.

The Parabolic System is termed a "stop-and-reverse" system because it assumes that you are always in the market. Every short sell stop, for instance, is expected to produce a long position when activated, and each long stop induces a short trade. Wilder termed these stop points SARs for "stop and reverse."

Calculation

The calculation works as follows: The first step involves establishing a reference point. Wilder instructs us to take the extreme high or low from the previous trade. For example, if you had been short earlier and now are long, the reference point would be the extreme low for the previous (down) move. Every trade has to start somewhere, so if there was no previous trade the logical point ought to be the previous minor low. In figure 9.1 this would come at Point X on day 4.

Figure 9.1

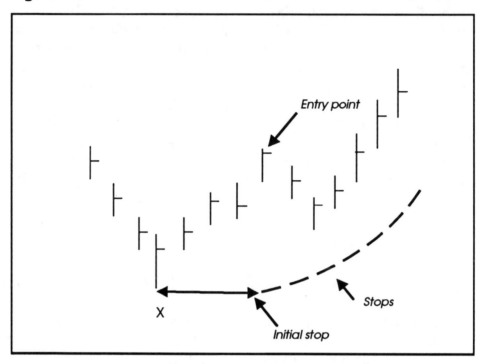

For the sake of argument, our trade is initiated on day 8. On this particular day the SAR would be placed at the previous minor low established on day 4. The SAR for the next day, day 9, will be the high experienced on day 8 minus the SAR multiplied by an *acceleration factor.* Wilder stated that the acceleration factor should begin at 0.2 on the first day of the trade. This factor is gradually increased by 0.2 each day *that a new high for the trade is recorded,* until the position is either stopped out or the maximum of 2.0 is reached. After that, the acceleration factor remains constant at 2.0. This means that in our example if the price continues to make new highs the acceleration factor rises to 0.8 on day 12. If a new high for the trade is not recorded between, say, days 8 and 12 the acceleration factor remains constant at 0.2. Then, if on day 13 a new high is achieved, the acceleration factor would increase by 0.2 above its previous level.

The formula can be summarized as follows:

$$SAR_{(tomorrow)} = SAR_{(today)} + \text{Acceleration Factor } [(\text{the extreme point for the trade} - \text{the } SAR_{(today)}].$$

In the case of a long trade, the extreme point is the high for the trade, and for a short position the extreme point is the lowest low that occurred since the trade was made. This means that in a long trade, even if the price does not reach a new high, the stop point will continue to rise because the acceleration factor is still part of the calculation. In effect, this makes the formula return an exponential average of the SARs. Only after the price makes a new "post-trade" high is the acceleration factor again raised until the maximum of 2.0 is reached.

There are really three ways to set an SAR. The first two have already been covered. The initial stop is set at the extreme point for the previous trade. Then the stop is moved in the direction of the trade, with reference to the extreme price for the new trade and the acceleration factor. The final rule for long positions states that you should never move the SAR for tomorrow above the yesterday's or today's low. In the event that the calculation calls for the SAR to be plotted above the previous day's or today's low, then use the lower of today or the previous day. The next day's calculation should then be based on this SAR. The reverse is true for short positions.

Acceleration Factors   Wilder recommends using an acceleration factor of 0.02 with a maximum of no more than 0.2. In the December, 1989 edition of *Stocks and Commodities*, Peter Aan tested several markets for various acceleration factors from 0.01 to 0.03 and maximum values from 0.10 to 0.30 for the 5-year period covering January 1984 to December 1988. He used $100 for commissions and slippage and found the combinations presented in table 9.1 to be the most profitable.

These are the most profitable optimizations, and we must recognize the fact that they will probably change over time. Nevertheless, as Mr. Aan points out the tests he performed "indicate that the Parabolic remains one of the most unique and interesting concepts in trend-following trading systems...and is very worthy of careful consideration by serious traders."[1]

Interpretation

The interpretation of the Parabolic System is purely mechanical. Chart 9.6 shows the S & P Composite Index during the 1990 mini-

[1] Aan, Peter, "Parabolic Stop/Reversal," In *Stocks and Commodities*, November 1989, pp. 411–413.

Table 9.1   Parabolic Time/Price Performance Results

Commodity	AF	Maximum AF	Total Profit	# Trades	% Wins	Average Win	Largest Win	Largest Loss	Maximum Drawdown	Closed Drawdown
Soybeans	0.010	0.20	3,690	84	41	1,490	8,102	−3,016	−14,074	−12,023
Live cattle	0.030	0.20	−7,148	139	44	573	2,120	−1,348	−15,500	−14,432
Coffee	0.022	0.10	104,870	91	47	4,211	31,370	−8,755	−23,290	−14,183
Sugar	0.016	0.10	8,139	83	36	1,084	3,999	−973	−6,340	−5,362
Cotton	0.026	0.10	10,045	102	60	1,360	7,785	−2,260	−7,645	−6,700
Silver	0.030	0.20	3,070	105	44	1,620	10,935	−7,930	−21,760	−14,815
Gold	0.010	0.20	−20	67	31	1,945	5,340	−2,790	−17,140	−15,050
Crude Oil	0.014	0.10	24,510	68	44	1,939	12,090	−1,920	−8,710	−7,740
Swiss Franc	0.010	0.30	42,512	75	45	2,703	9,437	−2,812	−11,399	−10,324
J. Yen	0.012	0.10	47,516	66	47	2,854	10,412	−2,700	−7,887	−5,562
T-bonds	0.024	0.10	37,740	105	44	2,456	13,970	−4,750	−13,100	−9,940
S & P 500	0.026	0.30	13,310	133	33	4,132	37,750	−6,945	−53,955	−32,065

Test results based on January 1984-December 1988 perpetual contracts, $100 per trade for slippage and commissions.
Cotton produced the highest percentage of winning trades under the parabolic stop method, although coffee showed the greatest profit between 1984 and 1988.
Peter Aan, "Parabolic Stop/Reversal," *Technical Analysis of Stocks & Commodities*, Nov. 1989, pg 412.

Chart 9.6   S & P Composite and Parabolic Stop Points

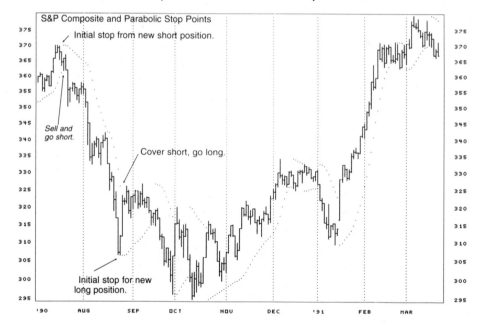

bear market and the beginning of the subsequent bull market. During the sharp August decline and the advance in early 1991, the system did remarkably well but during the intervening trading range it did not. This is not surprising since the system is supposed to be a trend-following and not a trading-range scheme.

One problem I have with the system is that the initial stop point can often occur a long way from the entry point. In chart 9.7, for example, a trader would have gone long at the mark near the 70-cent level in late September, but the stop would have been close to 65 cents. That's a very wide margin of error for a system that has the objective of tight stops. Because of the acceleration factor the position would have been stopped at 67 cents, still a sizeable loss. The short sale from which the long position was reversed would have involved even more risk, since the stop point was the 72-cent high. As it turned out, this trade was profitable because of the very sharp decline that followed and was eventually covered at around 64 cents. However, when you consider that the initial risk was close to 5 cents and the eventual profit about 3 cents, you can readily appreciate that the risk reward was not particularly attractive.

I believe that the SAR should be used as a stop only (SO) method. In other words, it should be used in conjunction with other indicators. For example, if the violation of a price and an RSI downtrendline generates a buy signal then the Parabolic System could be set in motion, using the previous low as the stop point. The system would be used only if the stop were fairly close. If it is necessary to enter a trade using a wide stop, this automatically

Chart 9.7 Deutsche Mark and Parabolic Stop Points

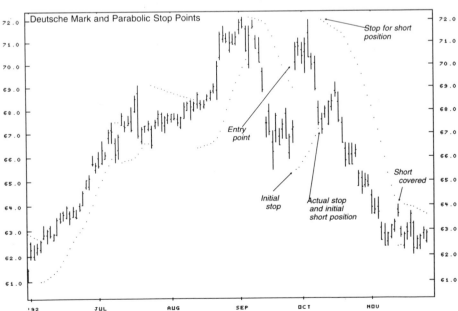

means that the potential risk-reward equation has shifted in favor of the risk side. Under such circumstances the best advice is to stand aside.

It is also possible to calculate the parabolic stop for the previous trade and use that as the stop point. In either case the only way to trade successfully in any systematic way is to use *low-risk* ideas, meaning low risk relative to a potentially high reward. Consequently, even if the trade does look promising in terms of positive momentum characteristics and price-trend reversals, other indicators won't touch it if the logical stop point is a long way off. Remember, technical analysis is not a science, and your interpretation or the market may be wrong. This means the stop that *couldn't possibly* be triggered almost always will be.

Chart 9.8 shows the Nikkei Index with a Commodity Selection Index and a Parabolic. Points A1 and A2 represent the entry and SAR points, respectively. The vertical distance between the two mean that the trade involves a high degree of risk. In this particular instance the trade never stays on long enough for the SAR to begin its acceleration process and as a consequence a large loss is taken.

Chart 9.8   Nikkei Stock Index and a 14-Day
Commodity Selection Index

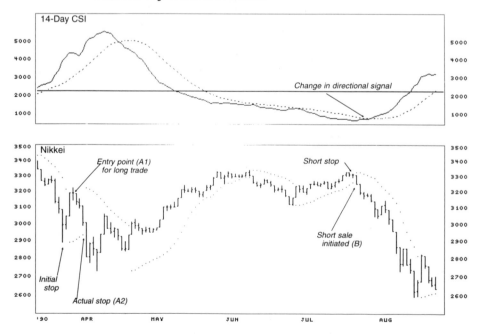

On the other hand, in July we see how a Selection Index can be used profitably in combination with the Parabolic. The Selection Index bottoms out and the Parabolic gives a sell signal. We learned earlier that reversals in the direction of the Selection Index can offer indications that a new trend is about to begin. In this case the sell signal from the SAR (at B) indicates that the trend would be down not up. The critical point is that the stop indicated by the SAR is an extremely close one. Since this is also accompanied by a sell signal and weak rally by the MACD indicator, as well as a timely negative DI crossover, the whole situation amounts to a low-risk trade with a high-reward potential. The latter two indicators are shown on Chart 9.9. Note how neither the MACD nor the DI combination confirm the Parabolic by giving a decisive buy signal in March.

Combining Parabolic with Directional Movement

The Directional Parabolic System (Welles Wilder Chart Trading Workshop 1980 Trend Research, Greensboro, NC, 1980) is the name given to the combination of the Directional Movement and Parabolic Systems. It involves the integration of the following indicators:

$+DI_{14}$—The upward directional indicator based on a 14-day time span.

$-DI_{14}$—The downward directional indicator based on a 14-day time span.

ADX — The Average Directional Movement

DPS — The Directional Parabolic Stop

The first three concepts are discussed at length in chapter 8. The DPS is effectively half of an SAR which is a stop that calls for the reversal of the position when it is triggered. The DPS, on the other hand, is a one-directional stop.

The Directional Parabolic System comprises the following rules:

1. If the ADX is up (i.e., if $+DI_{14}$ is greater than the $-DI_{14}$), trade from only the long side when a parabolic stop is triggered.
2. If the ADX is down (i.e., if $+DI_{14}$ is less than the $-DI_{14}$), then trade short only when indicated by the Parabolic System.

Chart 9.9   Nikkei Stock Index, MACD, and 14-Day
                Directional Movement Index

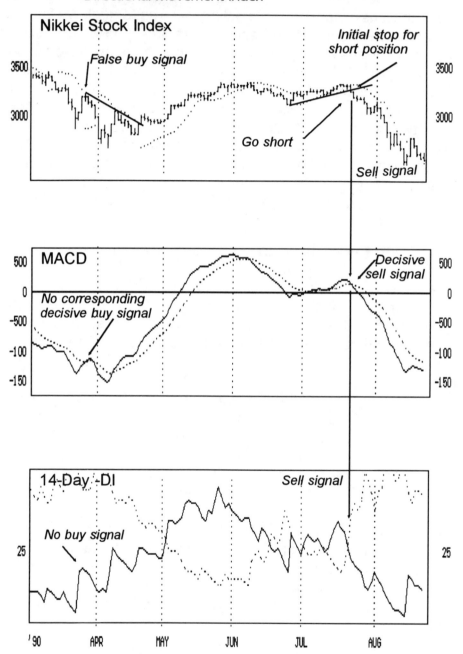

This chart shows how parabolic signals can be used effectively when combined with the other momentum indicators.

3. If the systems conflict stand aside until they agree. This follows the tried-and-true maxim: "When in doubt stay out!"
4. Liquidation of positions is executed through the DPS (i.e., parabolic stop).
5. If no position is held use the Directional Movement equilibrium point (i.e., the high or low on the day), the $+DI_{14}$ crosses above or below its $-DI_{14}$ counterpart.

Wilder later added a rule that involved the ADX. Briefly stated, if the ADX is above the two DI_{14}s liquidation should begin when the ADX reverses direction. This rule is based on the theory that the ADX is really an oscillator in its own right, so reversals in its direction represent a leading indicator of a trend reversal. If the ADX subsequently reverses prior to the DI_{14} crossover, this indicates a very strong trend, and final liquidation should wait for such a crossover. However, a reversal of the actual trade from long to short or short to long should not be undertaken until the DI crossover is confirmed by a parabolic signal.

This formal combination of oscillator and trend-following system often permits traders to close out at a more favorable price than they would have gotten using normal trend-following signals. The main criticism is that if the trade is stopped out prematurely a convenient low risk re-entry point may not present itself. This drawback again reminds us of the age-old conflict between sensitivity and timeliness.

chapter 10

MISCELLANEOUS MOMENTUM INDICATORS

- **Introduction**
- **Herrick Payoff Index**
  - **Rules for Interpreting Open Interest**
  - **Calculation**
  - **Interpretation**
- **Accumulation Swing Index**
  - **Calculation**
  - **Interpretation**
- **TRIX Index**
- **Commodity Channel Index**
  - **Calculation**
  - **Interpretation**
- **The Ultimate Oscillator**
  - **Calculation**
  - **Interpretation**

Introduction

In a book of this kind, there is always the temptation to try to cover the waterfront by describing as many indicators as possible. However, I have always believed that technical analysis—if it is to be practiced in a successful and profitable way—should adhere to simple principles and common-sense interpretation. For this reason the assortment of indicators described here in general focus on those that show the most promise.

In the last few years traders and technicians have developed a host of new momentum indicators, many of which are based on complicated mathematical formulas. Ironically, there seems to be an inverse relationship between the complexity of these formulas and their reliability. In this chapter we will consider some of the lesser known indicators that add new dimensions to the technical approach. I have deliberately avoided mentioning the more complicated varieties, since for the most part I have never found them to be any more reliable than their more basic counterparts.

In describing indicators, many of their enthusiastic instigators use sophisticated sounding terms such as "measuring money flow," "moving from strong hands to weak hands," and so on. In almost all cases such terminology has more of a foundation in sales and promotion than in trading and research. Sometimes these indicators do deliver what they promise, but on most occasions they do not. My advice is to adopt a skeptical attitude and never accept these claims at face value. Let the indicators described in this book prove their worth to *your* satisfaction. Only then will you be in a position to fully appreciate their true strengths and weaknesses.

Herrick Payoff Index

Calculating the Herrick Payoff Index (HPI) requires the use of "open interest." This indicator is designed only for futures markets where open interest data is available. Open interest is defined as "the total number of contracts outstanding for all months of a futures market."

Rules for Interpreting Open Interest

1. If prices are rising and open interest is increasing at a rate faster than its five-year seasonal average, this is a bullish sign. More participants are entering the market, involving additional buying and any purchases are generally aggressive in nature.
2. If the open interest numbers flatten following a rising trend in both price and open interest, take this as a warning sign of an impending top.
3. High open interest at market tops is a bearish signal if the price drop is sudden, since this will force many "weak" longs to liquidate. Occasionally, such conditions set off a self-feeding, downward spiral.
4. An unusually high or record open interest in a bull market is a danger signal. When the rising trend of open interest begins to reverse, expect a bear trend to get underway.
5. A breakout from a trading range will be much stronger if open interest rises during the consolidation. This is because many traders will be caught on the wrong side of the market when the breakout finally takes place. When the price moves out of the trading range these traders are forced to abandon their positions. It is possible to take this rule one step further and say that the greater the rise in open interest during the consolidation, the greater the potential for the subsequent move.
6. Rising prices and a decline in open interest at a rate greater than the seasonal norm is bearish. This market condition develops because short-covering and not fundamental demand is fueling the rising price trend. In these circumstances money is flowing out of the market. Consequently, when the short-covering has run its course prices will decline.
7. If prices are declining and the open interest rises more than the seasonal average, this indicates that new short positions are being opened. As long as this process continues it is a bearish factor, but once the shorts begin to cover it turns bullish.
8. A decline in both price and open interest indicates liquidation by discouraged traders with long positions. As long as this trend continues, it is a bearish sign. Once open interest stabilizes at a low level, the liquidation is over and prices are then in a position to rally again.

Calculation

The Payoff Index uses open interest to achieve its objective of measuring the money flowing in or out of a futures market. It does this by computing the difference in dollar volume in each period (usually one day). The formula is:

$$HPI = \frac{K_y + (K_1 - K_y)S}{100,000},$$

where

K_y = Yesterday's HPI

S = User - entered smoothing factor (0.1 is the default)

y = Yesterday's value

and

$$K^1 = CV(M - M_y)\left[1 \pm \frac{2I}{G}\right]$$

In this case M represents the mean and is calculated as half the value of the high plus the low. C = the value of a 1 cent move, V = volume, and I = the absolute value of today's open interest or yesterday's open interest, whichever is greater. G = the greater of today's or yesterday's open interest.

The plus in the right-hand part of the formula occurs if M, or the mean price, is greater than M_y (yesterday's mean). It would be minus if yesterday's mean was less than today's mean (M_y < M). Fortunately for those of us who are not mathematically inclined—and I count myself as a leading contender—the Herrick Payoff Index is featured on most popular charting software such as MetaStock and Computrac. In the MetaStock package, the user is required to enter just two variables; the amount of a 1 cent move and the multiplying or smoothing factor. The latter more or less corresponds to a moving-average time span. A 10-day multiplying factor corresponds to a 10-day moving average, an 11-day factor to an 11-day moving average, and so on.

The Payoff's calculation assumes that the amount of money active in a contract is represented by the volume of trading. It monitors the flow of money in and out of a market by calculating the difference in the dollar value for each period. Again, periods are measured usually in days. This is represented in the formula as "mean price times volume." The figures for money flow are subsequently adjusted by changes in open interest and then smoothed exponentially by the smoothing factor previously discussed. The second user-determined variable is the value of a 1 cent move for the futures contract being monitored, (e.g., $400 for cattle or $50 for soybeans).

One problem in calculating this indicator stems from the fact that most data services provide statistics only for total volume and open interest on *all* contracts. This causes a predicament for many agricultural commodities, where for seasonal reasons, price movements in the nearby contracts can differ considerably from more distant ones. This dilemma is not as acute for financial futures because their price movements are more interrelated between the various contract months, generally fluctuating because of changes in interest rate differentials. Where commodities are subject to such seasonal differences, a single-contract system is recommended. In other words, use the volume and open interest pertaining to that specific contract.

This can be quite an onerous task unless the data can be conveniently downloaded electronically from a data vendor. If that is not possible, it is probably better to limit Payoff analysis to financial futures and other markets not seriously affected by seasonal variations. Except when it nears expiration, the nearby contract typically attracts the bulk of the trading volume. For most futures contracts where there is little or no seasonal variation, a three-month perpetual contract provides a satisfactory compromise. The perpetual contract is a continuous contract with a theoretical life of three months. Carrying costs and other differentials are calculated with reference to more distant contract months. This arrangement is a good compromise because it offers a continuous series for contracts that would otherwise expire every three months. CSI Data of Boca Raton, Florida, is one firm that provides data for these contracts.

Finally, one should always be on the lookout for contracts that often undergo a sharp reduction in open interest purely because of quarterly contract expiration. This occurs fairly regularly, for example, on the S & P Stock Index Futures Contract. (See chart 10.1).

Interpretation

The first step in interpreting the Herrick Payoff Index is to determine whether the indicator is above or below zero, since this gives a

Chart 10.1 S & P Composite and Open Interest

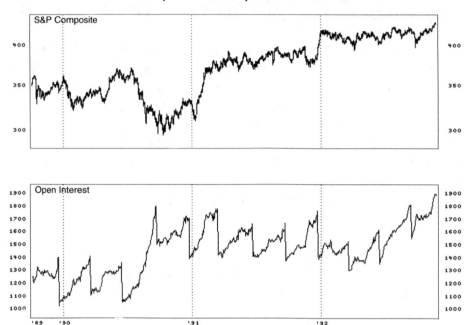

good long-term indication of whether money is flowing in or out of the market. Readings above zero indicate that interest in the market in question is growing and are regarded as a positive sign. Readings below zero are a bearish sign indicating a contraction of activity.

The Index often shows whether a rally signaled by other short-term indicators will turn out to be worthwhile or not. The reverse is true for short positions during declines. *Decisive* zero-crossovers, therefore, can be of invaluable help when combined with momentum indicators constructed from a larger time span.

For example, if a weekly ROC indicator gave an intermediate-term buy signal a confirmation by the Payoff Index would add substantial weight to the view that the market was likely to rally for the next six weeks or so. Clearly, the time span used in the construction of the Index will play an important part. A Payoff Index using an 8-day smoothing as shown in chart 10.2 would not carry the significance of one constructed from a 26-day span (chart 10.3). Notice that the number of whipsaw zero-crossovers increases in inverse proportion to the time span. The arrows on chart

Chart 10.2 British Pound (Spot) and 8-Day Herrick Payoff Index

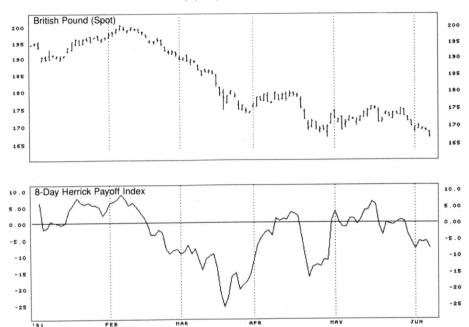

Chart 10.3 British Pound (Spot) and 26-Day Herrick Payoff Index

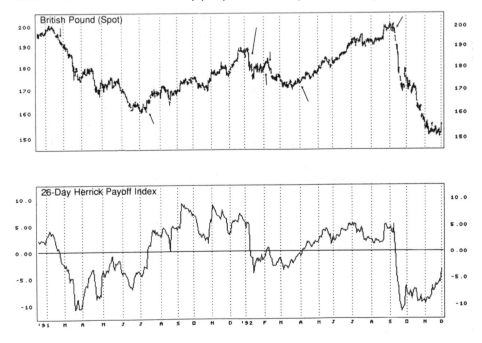

10.3 show how reliable zero-crossovers would have been for the pound sterling between 1991 and 1992 based on a 26-day time span. This is an extreme example of reliability, and you should not expect to see this degree of accuracy repeated too often.

Generally, decisive zero-crossovers tend to give long-term signals relative to the time frame under consideration. In any event, each security needs to be analyzed on its own merits from the point of view of the reliability and timeliness of zero-crossovers. If a particular time span or market proves undependable, then disregard or significantly downplay the zero-crossover concept. While I regard zero-crossovers as a useful concept for analyzing many markets, it should be noted that John Herrick, the innovator of the Payoff system, has discounted their importance.

Here, then, is where supplementary analysis plays a role in assuring both reliability and timeliness. This analysis can utilize positive and negative divergences as well as trendline violations and price configurations. It is also possible to look for moving average crossovers. The degree of usefulness will depend on the smoothing factor used in the formula. This is because Payoff Indexes calculated over a long time span are much smoother and more deliberate than those based on a short one. You can see this by comparing the difference in characteristics between charts 10.4 and 10.5, which are constructed from spans of 2 and 10 weeks, respectively. Chart 10.4 uses a 13-week moving average crossover; Chart 10.5, a 26-week crossover. There is little doubt that the longer term one is more reliable.

Noted technician Tom Aspray, in a March 1988 article in *Stocks and Commodities* magazine, recommends a 21-day period. He places great importance on the zero-crossover mechanism as a good starting point for payoff analysis. His market letter *Boardwatch* (P.O. Box 2141, Spokane, WA 99210-2141) is one of the few that I have seen that regularly features this indicator.

One other important characteristic of the Payoff Index that appears to be very useful from a short-term trading aspect is the fact that from time to time the Index moves to an extreme, then often reverses quite sharply. This can be seen in chart 10.6, which shows a 10-day Index for Italian government bonds traded on the LIFFE exchange in London. Five examples of extreme reversals are presented on the chart. On each occasion they indicate that the price reached a short-term buying or selling climax. Chart 10.7 shows the same market but in the November 1991 to June 1992

Chart 10.4 British Pound (Spot), 2-Week Herrick Payoff Index,
and 13-Week Moving Average

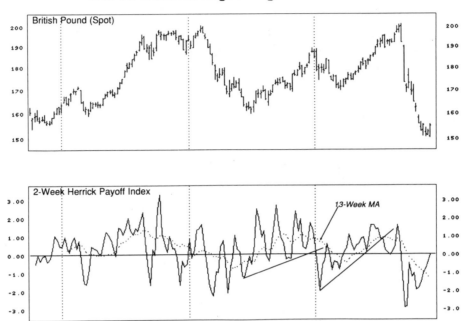

Chart 10.5 British Pound (Spot), 10-Week Herrick Payoff Index,
and 26-Week Moving Average

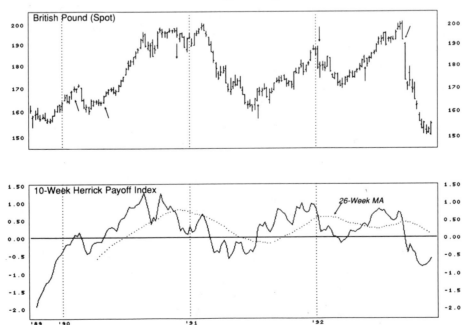

Chart 10.6 Italian Government Bonds Three-Month Perpetual
Contract and 10-Day Herrick Payoff Index
(Oct 1991 to Dec 1992)

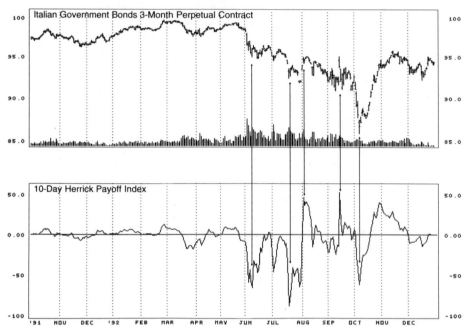

period. The chart demonstrates that trendline violations in the
Payoff Index, when accompanied by a similar break in the price,
can offer very good short-term buy and sell indications.

While zero-crossovers are not particularly useful, here we can
see three instances at Points A, B, and C where they emphasize
the importance of trend breaks in both the indicator and more
importantly the price. In the cases of A and B the zero crossovers
occur almost to the day that the price broke above the declining
trendlines.

The arrows on chart 10.8 indicate decisive zero-crossovers.
Some work quite well because they occur close to a turning point.
The mid-June buy signal (A1) is a good example. On the other
hand, the mid-August sell signal (B) occurs well after the fact and
is totally useless. The important point to grasp about these examples is that the best signals occur in conjunction with the
completion of a pattern in the price. Using them in combination with
price-trend reversal signals is I believe, the best way to treat zero-

Chart 10.7 Italian Government Bonds Three-Month Perpetual
Contract and 10-Day Herrick Payoff Index
(Oct 1991 to Jun 1992)

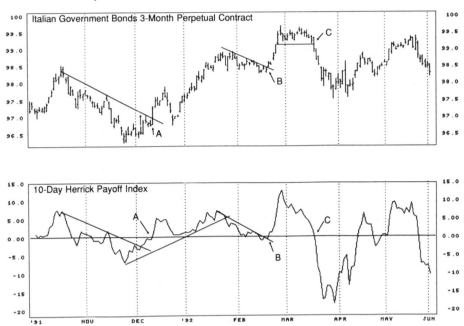

Chart 10.8 Comex Gold and 21-Day Herrick Payoff Index

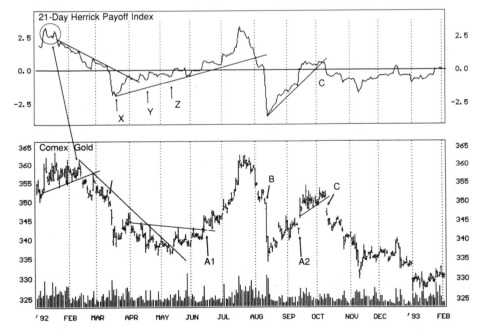

crossovers. The chart also shows some positive divergences at work in the form of Points X, Y, and Z, which clearly emphasize the bullishness of the zero-crossover and the price breakout at Point A1 when it finally occurs.

This period also brings out one of the characteristics discussed earlier. This is the tendency of the HPI to reach an extreme reading from time to time and then reverse on a dime. We see this happen at the July peak and the August bottom. In these instances the movements are too sharp to offer any indications of a trend reversal such as a trendline break or a moving average crossover. In most instances of a parabolic rise or precipitous drop, it would seem that a one- or two-day move in the opposite direction is usually sufficient to signal a reversal. In any event, the fact that the indicator has moved to such an extreme should be important enough to short-term traders to at least take some profits.

Chart 10.9 shows a 21-day Payoff Index for U.S. Treasury Bond prices. In this example the two decisive zero-crossovers are

Chart 10.9   Treasury Bonds Three-Month Perpetual Contract and 21-Day Herrick Payoff Index

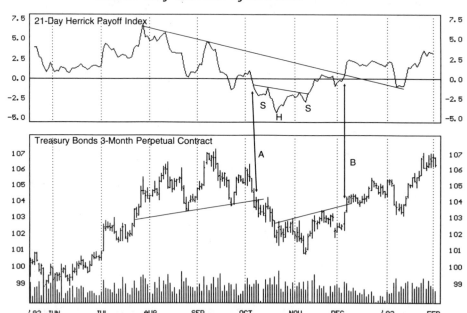

accompanied by important short-term moves *and* price breakouts at Points A and B. Normally, it would be reasonable to anticipate a more substantial decline than the one that occurs in the chart during October 1992. After all the Payoff Index shows a significant number of negative divergences and the price traces out an impressive head-and-shoulders top. However, the November low actually touches the bull market trendline that began two years earlier, and the primary trend is still positive. In effect, bond prices reached important support within a bull trend, thus reducing the negative influence of short-term factors. This example shows how very important it is to integrate short-term trends into the longer term technical environment.

Accumulation Swing Index

This indicator is a variation of Welles Wilder's Swing Index (SI), so I will begin this section with a few words on the Swing Index itself. The objective of this indicator is to determine the true market direction and changes in direction by comparing the most significant changes between today's price action and yesterday's price moves. The formula uses open, high, low, and closing data, so the indicator can be used only with securities where opening price data is readily available. For this reason the Swing Index is principally associated with the futures markets.

The manual provided with the MetaStock charting package describes the indicator's three basic characteristics:

1. It provides numerical value-quantifying price swings.
2. It defines short-term swing points.
3. It simplifies the relationships between high, low, open, and closing prices, indicating the real strength and direction of the security in question.

Calculation

In *New Concepts* (pages 87–95), Wilder describes in detail the theory itself and how to calculate the indicator. More mathematically inclined readers may wish to look it up. The actual formula is:

$$\text{Swing Index} = \left[\frac{C_2 - C_1 + 0.5(C_2 - O_2) + 0.25(C_1 - O_1)}{R} \right] \frac{K}{L}$$

where

C₁ and C₂ = The closing prices yesterday (C_1) and today (C_2)

O₁ and O₂ = Opening prices for yesterday (O_1) and today (O_2)

K = The greater of H_2 (high for day 2) minus C_1 or L_2 (low for day 2) minus C_1

L = The value of a limit move in one direction

R = The largest of $H_2 - C_1$, $L_2 - C_1$, or $H_2 - L_2$.[1]

The plotted result is a very volatile and at times spiky line that fluctuates between −100 and +100 as shown in chart 10.10. Extreme spikes indicate short-term exhaustion points. They are normally reversal points and are followed by a reaction in the direction opposite to the previous trend. In some cases a swing spike is followed by a near-term consolidation. At first glance it looks as though this indicator is of limited use because it gives the impression of simply triggering signals of a very short-term nature. If that were the case, its use would be restricted to highly leveraged traders with a time horizon of no more than a few days. It is, however, of greater use when used in conjunction with the Accumulation Swing Index (ASI).

The ASI is calculated from a cumulative running total of the Swing Index. On days when the Swing Index is rising, this will have a positive effect on the Accumulation Index and vice versa.

Interpretation

According to Wilder's interpretation, the ASI sends out a buy signal when it exceeds its value on the day a previous significant high in the Swing Index was achieved as shown in chart 10.10 at Point B.

This concept does not always work out as one can see from the XY combination. The price does rally a bit after the Y buy signal. This was the day the ASI exceeded its value and the Swing Index made its previous important peak, shown here at Point X. A downside breakout develops when the value of the ASI drops below the level that it achieved when a significant low was seen in

[1] Ibid.

Chart 10.10 Comex Gold Three-Month Perpetual Contract, Swing Index, and Accumulation Swing Index

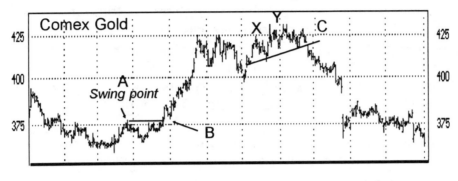

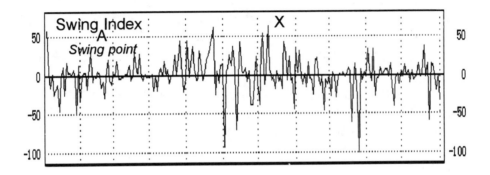

the raw Swing Index. In effect *an emotional extreme point in the Swing Index is regarded as an important pivotal point,* similar to a support or resistance area. When the ASI moves through the price achieved on this extreme swing day, the system assumes that this psychological barrier has been breached and will no longer represent an obstacle to the prevailing trend in prices.

Wilder also set up specific rules for the Swing Index System where price and the ASI were related. These rules are:

1. Go long when the ASI moves above the level it attained on the day of the previous significant high in the Swing Index (Point C in figure 10.1).
2. Use the value of the ASI on the day of the previous important low in the Swing Index to set an initial stop level and the point at which the position would be reversed (Point B in figure 10.1). Wilder calls this the SAR (i.e., the index stop-and-reverse point).
3. Set a trailing stop 60 (ASI) points below the extreme high in the ASI. These appear as rising and horizontal dots in figure 10.1, depending on whether new highs are being recorded or the

Figure 10.1

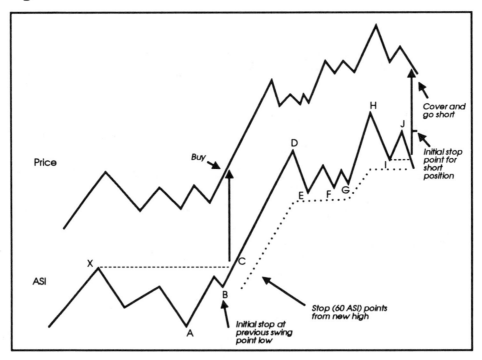

ASI is in a congestion mode. Note that the trailing stops are based on the action of the ASI rather than the price.

4. The first low swing point after a high swing point (Point E in figure 10.1) should be used to raise the level of the Index SAR. This remains the stop point until the ASI goes on to make a new high. When in doubt, take the closer of the higher of the 60 point rule or the low swing point (i.e., the tighter of the two stops). In this instance both forms of stops will result in a reversal in the position from long to short.

5. Once a short position has been triggered by the stop point, the previous swing high becomes the initial SAR.

6. Rules 1–5 are reversed during declining markets.

Normally, the reversal in the ASI and the price occur on the same day so there is no problem translating ASI interpretation into market-oriented action. However, on occasion the price may make a new intraday low *after* the ASI. This occurs when the price closes higher on the day and causes the ASI to rally. In figure 10.2, the ASI

Figure 10.2

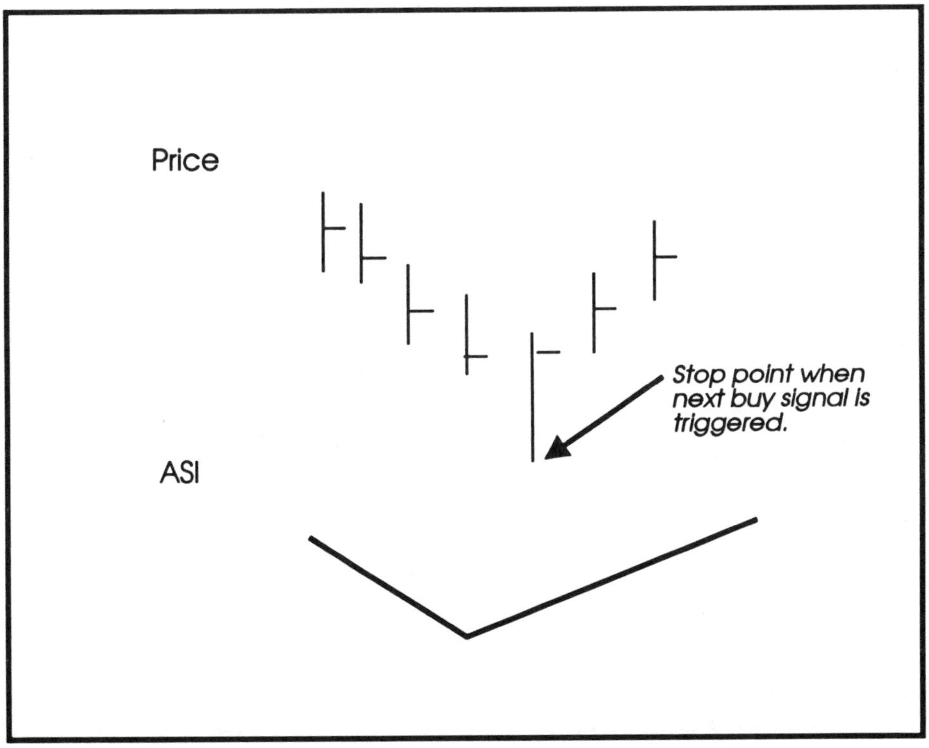

bottoms out on the fourth day, but the intraday low occurs on the fifth. In this example the stop would be based on the low for the fifth day and not the low on the day the ASI bottomed. Figure 10.3 shows how this would look in a down market.

One final way to use the ASI is to compare trendlines on the ASI with price trendlines. When each line is violated, it is often a good sign of a trend reversal. The nature of the reversal will, of course, be a function of the length of the lines, the number of times they have been touched or approached, and the angle of ascent or descent.

TRIX Index

The TRIX index was introduced to the world in *Stocks and Commodities* Magazine by then editor Jack Hutson. It is a 1-day rate-of-change calculation of a triple exponentially smoothed moving average of a closing price. Triple-smoothing involves repeating the exponential smoothing process discussed in chapter 5 an addi-

Figure 10.3

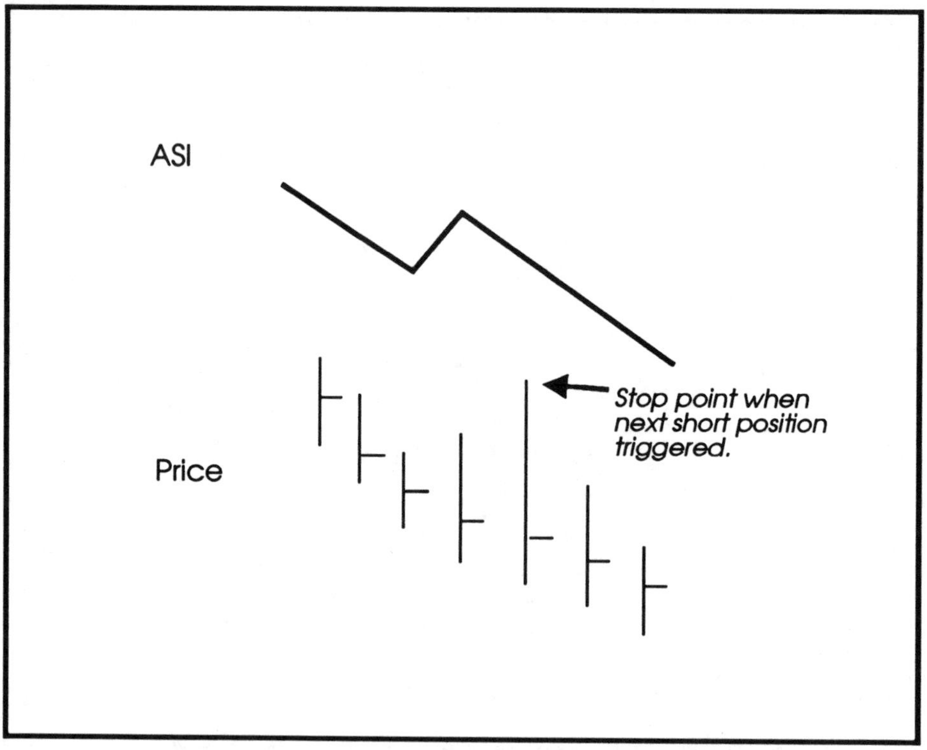

tional two times. The result is an oscillator that essentially reflects the slope of the smoothed price search. Some traders use the subtraction method for the ROC calculation, then multiply the result by 1,000 in order to obtain a meaningful scale. I prefer using division (i.e., day two divided by day one, day three divided by day two, and so on).

Whichever method is selected, the result is a very smooth curve that filters out all cycles that are less than the time span chosen for the EMA. As I have said before, indicators always represent a trade-off between sensitivity, or reliability, and timeliness. One would think that the triple-EMA smoothing would give the indicator good reliability characteristics but leave it lacking in the timeliness department. Obviously, the longer the time span, the less timely an indicator will be. Nevertheless, it is surprising how well the Trix can balance these conflicting characteristics.

Chart 10.11, shows that a daily TRIX based on a 12-period EMA catches most of the moves in the gold price for 1992. A 9-day EMA has been superimposed on the TRIX to offer a kind of signal line similar to the MACD discussed in chapter 5. As always the choice

Chart 10.11   Comex Gold Three-Month Perpetual Contract, 12-Day TRIX, and 9-Day EMA

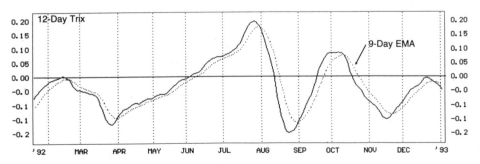

of time span is critical to the interpretation. Chart 10.11 uses the default value of 12 in the MetaStock charting package.

Chart 10.12 shows a 30-day TRIX. This series reflects the broad price swings in the yen between late 1989 and 1992. This time span is good for showing intermediate-term price swings, but it is occasionally late. In this respect, it is sometimes a good idea to relate movements in the 30-day span to those of a shorter-term one, in this case twelve days. Since the 12-day span is much more sensitive, it often gives an advance warning of when the 30-day series is about to reverse direction. This sometimes occurs when the shorter average is just about to cross zero, as at Point A. This also coincides with a trendline violation in the 12-day TRIX and a very important trendline violation in the price. At the end of 1990, a trendbreak in the price and 12-day Trix also takes place at a time when the 30-day Trix is reversing from an extreme level. This combination serves to underscore the point made earlier that the greater the number of indicators that are in agreement the more reliable the buy and sell signal.

This concept of a trendline violation in price can also be taken a step further. If a series such as the slow-moving 30-day TRIX is overbought but still rallying, then a trendline violation in the price will almost certainly lead or correspond with a peak in the TRIX. This is because a trendline violation signals a break in upside momentum. The penetration will be followed by either a decline or a temporary sideways move. In both cases this implies that the additional upside momentum required for an advancing TRIX is no longer available. This principle is not limited to TRIX but can apply to any momentum indicator, whether it be a raw ROC closely hugging a trendline, a smoothed Stochastic or a KST.

Finally, chart 10.13 shows the TRIX Indicator using weekly data. The second panel is a 26-week series and an 8-week indicator. At first glance, it looks as though the indicator calls turns in the price of Gannet stock very well, but on closer scrutiny we can see that the 1987 and 1989 reversals are somewhat late. In both cases the price traces out and breaks down from a head-and-shoulders top. These distribution patterns in themselves are not that significant, but when they are compared with the extremely high readings in the TRIX they tell us two things. First, they indicate

Chart 10.12   Japanese Yen, 30-Day TRIX and 12-Day TRIX

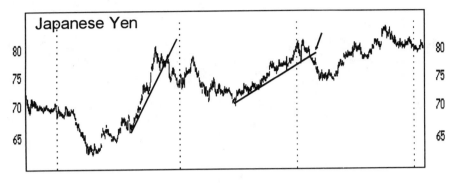

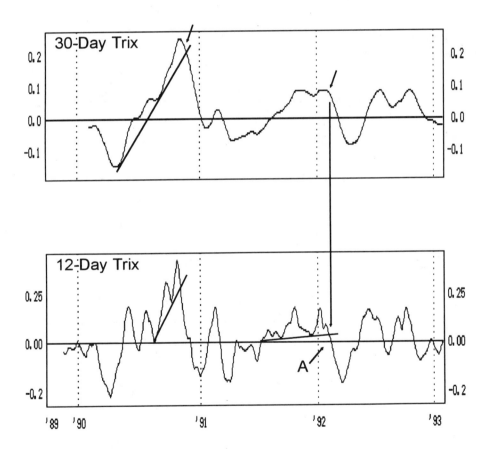

Chart 10.13   Gannett, Inc., 26-Week TRIX and 8-Week TRIX

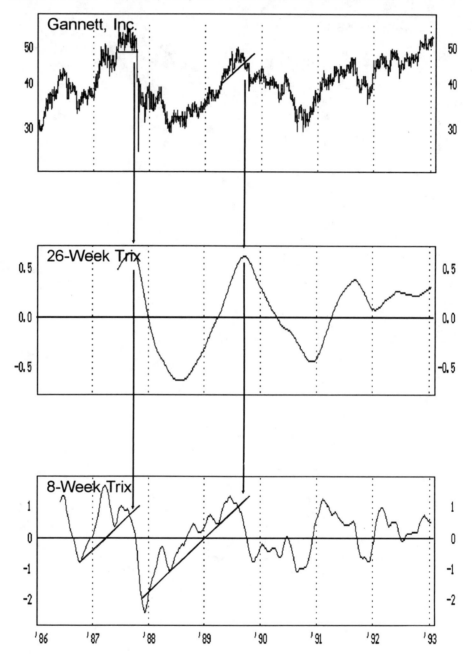

that even a small downward move following the completion of the formation would be of sufficient force to reverse the upward direction of the TRIX. Second, the very fact that the TRIX, an important intermediate-term indicator, is peaking from an extreme level itself serves as a warning that the downside potential from the head-and-shoulders top is far greater than its size suggests. The violation of the two uptrendlines in the 8-week Trix further underscores the fact that the technical situation is precarious.

Commodity Channel Index

The Commodity Channel Index (CCI) was developed by Donald Lambert and made public in an article in the October 1980 edition of *Futures* magazine. The CCI is a momentum system that was originally designed for futures contracts that demonstrated cyclical or seasonal characteristics. Its noble objective is to detect when these cycles start and finish using a statistical technique that incorporates a moving average divisor reflecting both the possible and actual trading ranges. In recent years it has been adopted to monitor securities other than those traded in the futures markets.

The Index is calculated by establishing the difference between the mean price of a security and the average of the mean price over a previous time period. Lambert used a moving average as opposed to an EMA for the averaging process because, as he says in his article, "To be useful in cyclical markets, an index must examine current prices in the light of past prices but must not allow data from the distant past to confuse present patterns."[2]

Calculation

The first two steps involve finding each day's "typical price" by taking an average of the high, low, and close and then calculating a moving average of the result. Step 3 is more complex and

[2] Lambert, Donald, "The Commodity Channel Index," *Futures*, October 1980.

involves computing the mean deviation for the number of days desired from each day's new updated moving average.

A 0.015 constant in the CCI formula means that the vast majority of fluctuations fall in the range of plus and minus 100.

Lambert believes that the 5-day CCI has the "highest theoretical efficiency level," but he concludes that such a short time span makes the indicator unduly subject to whipsaws. He recommends any span between 5 and 20 days but chooses 20 as his default.

For those interested in the math the formula is:

Four steps to calculate CCI

1. Compute today's "typical" price, using high, low and close:

$$X_1 = \frac{1}{3}(H + L + C)$$

2. Compute a moving average of the N most recent typical prices:

$$\overline{X} = \frac{1}{N}\sum_{i=1}^{N} X_i$$

3. Compute the mean deviation of the N most recent typical prices:

$$MD = \frac{1}{N}\sum_{i=1}^{N} \left| X_i - \overline{X} \right|$$

4. Compute the Commodity Channel Index:

$$CCI = \frac{\left(X_1 - \overline{X}\right)}{.015 \times MD}$$

where
N = number of days in data base
X_1 = today's typical price
X_2 = yesterday's typical price
X_3 = day before yesterday's price...
X_N = oldest typical price in the data base

$\sum_{i=1}^{N}$ Stands for the sum of items following the symbol, starting with 1 and ending with N, e.g.

$$\sum_{i=1}^{N} X_i = X_1 + X_2 + X_3 \ldots + X_N$$

$\left| \ \right|$ signifies "absolute value"; difference should be added as if all were positive numbers.

Source: Computrac Manual.

Interpretation

The above description sounds fine, but the bottom line is, does it work? The answer, as far as I can see, is that the CCI is no more incisive than a simple ROC indicator or an RSI. The generally accepted methods of interpretation are divergence and over-bought/oversold analysis. In this respect the basic idea is that the CCI gives a buy signal when it moves through its oversold level on its way back to zero. Sell signals are generated when it re-crosses the overbought line on its return to zero. Chart 10.14 shows that its forecasting ability appears to work reasonably well over very short terms, since most of the signals are followed by a reversal in trend lasting at least several days. Some last much longer in their effect. Generally, I can find little difference between the performance of the CCI and, say, the RSI. The two do differ in price movement quite a bit for any given time span, which in chart 10.14 is 20 days. In this way it makes sense to compare the two in order to obtain a more complete understanding of the underlying technical structure. The bottom panel features a 9-day RSI. A comparison with the 20-day CCI shows that the broad swings are almost identical, and the only differences except the positive divergence in the CCI of the April 1991 low appear to be those of magnitude.

The Ultimate Oscillator

This seems to be a great way to end a chapter on miscellaneous indicators. The title "Ultimate Oscillator" (UI) would appear to allow us to end on a note of glory. Let's see whether the UI lives up to its description.

The concept is certainly very sound. Larry Williams, its inventor, contends that an oscillator based on one time span is subject to a number of false signals. By combining three such oscillators, each based on different time frames, the "ultimate oscillator" should offer more reliable signals.

Williams describes this indicator in the August 1985 edition of *Stocks and Commodities.* He begins by explaining that Owen Taylor, one of the pioneers of momentum analysis in the 1920s, used a 7-day oscillator based on breadth data. The problem with Taylor's approach was that the maximum price move that could be caught by such a brief time span was about nine days. This meant that the indicator peaked well ahead of the price, usually setting up

Chart 10.14   Toronto Stock Exchange Index,
                  20-Day CCI and 9-Day RSI

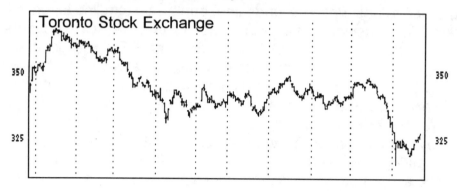

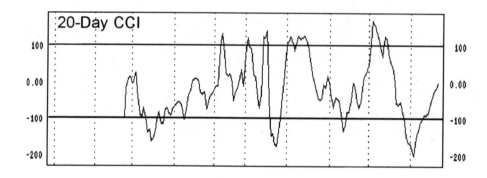

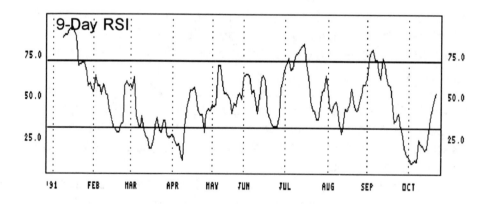

several divergences prior to the ultimate peak. On the other hand, Williams notes, indicators based on longer time spans do catch the big swings but often reverse direction well after market turning points. To quote Williams: "As an example, if the market shows a tremendous amount of strength your oscillator would expand the *time base,* thereby not allowing the short-term fluctuation to influence the fact that the market has turned the corner on a long-term basis."[3] The reasoning is similar to my own for the KST market cycle model discussed in chapter 7. Charts 10.15 and 10.16 show the oscillator in action for the Australian an U.S. stock markets for 1992.

Calculation

Williams chooses three different time spans that he believes reflect the dominant cycles for most commodities. They are 7, 14, and 28 days. He then weighted the 7-day series by 4 and the 14-day indicator by 2. The 28-day indicator was not weighted. This meant that all cycles were "equalized." The individual oscillators are calculated as follows:

1. Establish today's *buying pressure* (B_t), by subtracting the "true low" from the close. The "true low" is today's low or yesterday's close, whichever is lower.
2. Calculate the "true range" (R_t), which is either the greatest of one of the following: today's range (the high minus the low), today's high and yesterday's close, or yesterday's close and today's low.
3. Total the buying pressure (B_t) separately over the three cyclic intervals (i.e., 7, 14, and 28 days [SB_7, SB_{14}, and SB_{28}]).
4. Repeat the totaling process for the true range over the same periods (i.e., SR_7, SR_{14}, and SR_{28}).
5. Finally, divide the buying pressure by the true range for each cycle (i.e., SB_7/SR_7 and so on). They are then weighted by the aforementioned factors 4, 2, and 1.

In their book *Encyclopedia of Market Indicators*, Colby and Meyers point out that the nearest seven values for the buying pressure and the true range are each used on seven different

[3] Williams, Larry, "The Ultimate Oscillator," *Stocks and Commodities,* August 1985.

Chart 10.15   Sydney All-Ordinary and the Ultimate Oscillator

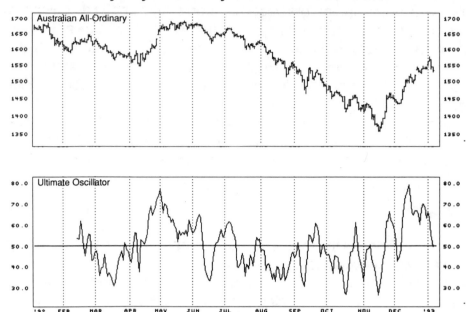

Chart 10.16   S & P Composite and the Ultimate Oscillator

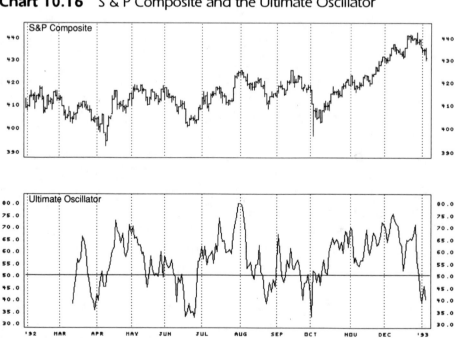

occasions. In other words, they are the sum of their weights. They go on to point out that the indicator is a step-weighted momentum, where the values 7, 3, and 1 are assigned to the first 7 days, second 7 days, and last 14 days, respectively. This means that the last 14 days account for only 10% of the total. They regard this as an important flaw in its construction.

Interpretation

Buy and sell signals have basically two requirements. The first is the presence of a divergence between the price and the oscillator. The second is a trend break in the oscillator itself. Williams does not define the trend break in the UO specifically, but we may infer that for long positions it is the breaking of a previous high in the indicator and the violation of a low in sales or the initiation of short positions.

1. A buy signal is triggered when the oscillator moves below the 30% oversold line, subsequently rallies and then fails to take out its previous bottom on the next decline. A buy order is executed when it is apparent that the indicator has diverged positively.
2. Sell signals develop when the indicator crosses above the 50% area, declines below 50%, and the following rally reaches a lower high than the first one. When it is apparent that a negative divergence has occurred, execute a sell order.
3. Long positions are closed out either when a sell signal is generated as the indicator moves up to the 70% level or when it falls below 30% (having previously been above 50%), whichever comes first. The last rule is a stop-loss mechanism.
4. Short positions are closed out when a buy signal is triggered, when the 30% level is reached, or when the indicator rallies above 65% after moving below 50%, whichever comes first. The 65% rule is also a stop-loss mechanism.

Colby and Meyers criticize the Ultimate Indicator for two other reasons. The first is the subjectivity of the interpretation. I do not find this a problem, since many of the indicators and approaches described in this book are very subjective. If we treat technical analysis as the *art* of building a picture from many *scientifically* derived indicators, this aspect should cause no problem. Since their book is concerned with mechanically testing a number of indicators, the subjectivity problem is an insurmountable one for them.

Their second criticism carries more weight. They point out that the stop-loss rules apply only after the oscillator has crossed 50%. If the oscillator immediately goes against the position, there is no risk control.

chapter 11

VOLUME MOMENTUM

- **Introduction**
- **Principles of Volume Interpretation**
- **Rate-of-Change of Volume**
- **Volume Oscillator**
- **Upside/Downside Volume**
- **Demand Index**

Introduction

Most of the indicators that we have looked at so far are constructed from a statistical manipulation of price alone. This means that each of them is a variation on a theme. Volume, on the other hand, not only monitors the enthusiasm of buyers and sellers, but it also acts as a variable that is totally independent from price. Therefore, it makes a great deal of sense to examine the velocity or momentum of volume in order to gain additional insight into the underlying technical picture.

I mentioned earlier that it is *mandatory* to use the weight of the evidence when attempting to identify market turning points. Inserting volume into the analysis is one way to get some new evidence from a dimension that is not bound to price-manipulated statistics. This provides two benefits. First, when we look at indicators that measure both price and volume momentum, we can see whether the two are in agreement. If they are, this increases the odds that any trend-reversal signals will be reliable. Second, when they disagree it warns us of an underlying weakness in the prevailing trend. In this way an *advance notice* of a potential trend reversal is given.

Volume is usually represented as a series of histograms appearing just under the price series. This arrangement is generally acceptable because it highlights significant expansions and contractions in trading activity. These, in turn, confirm or question the sustainability of the price trend. Volume may also be expressed in a momentum format, which has the effect of accentuating fluctuations in activity levels more graphically.

Before we examine some of these volume-momentum indicators, I would first like to describe some of the principles governing the relationship between price and volume.

Principles of Volume Interpretation

The most important principle is that *volume normally accompanies the trend.* In a rising market, volume should be expanding and in a declining market it should be contracting. Rising volume refers to the average daily, weekly, or monthly transaction level relative to itself. Prices move in trends, but they do not generally rise and fall in a straight line as reactions to the prevailing trend develop. The same principle applies to volume.

On the left side of figure 11.1, for instance, the dashed line shows that the volume trend is up. By the same token, it is apparent that the level of activity does not expand every day. There are quiet days and there are active ones, but the general thrust is up. On the right side of the diagram the trend is down, but irregularly so. *When we talk of rising or contracting volume we are, therefore, referring to the trend.* Volume trends, like those of price, can be of a short-, intermediate-, or long-term duration.

Activity should always be measured in relation to the recent past; otherwise, it has little meaning. For example, the number of stocks listed on the NYSE in 1990 was much higher than the number of securities listed at the beginning of the century. The increase in volume due to an expansion in the number of listed companies, therefore, has no significance from a technical per-

Figure 11.1

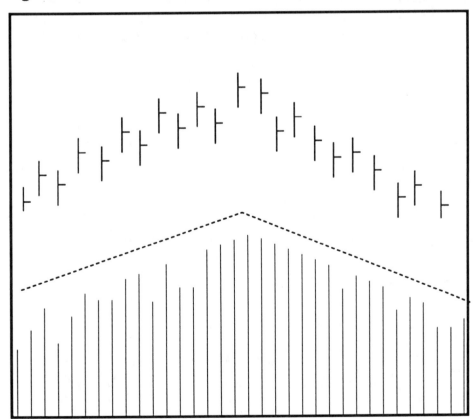

spective. Furthermore, NYSE trading activity expanded in the 1970s and 1980s because of the advent of options and futures. A substantial amount of this activity is associated with hedging and arbitrage. Thus, comparing volume before and after the introduction of these derivative products for the purpose of identifying trends becomes a meaningless exercise.

The same principle applies to a comparison of the volume in a newly launched contract on the futures exchange with the volume of that same contract several years later after the commodity gained widespread popularity. Volume-momentum indicators overcome these problems because *they express volume changes in relation to a trend or measure the ratio of volume over a limited period.*

Chart 11.1 for the Hang Seng Index indicates that through the 1989–92 period volume, as measured by the vertical bars, is in a gradually expanding uptrend. On the other hand, the 12-week rate-of-change of volume indicates that the climactic expansion in activity occurs, not in late 1992, when volume is heaviest, but in the summer of 1990 when the momentum indicator reaches its highest point. From that moment, the spiked peaks become lower and lower.

Chart 11.1   Hang Seng Index and 13-Day Volume Rate-of-Change

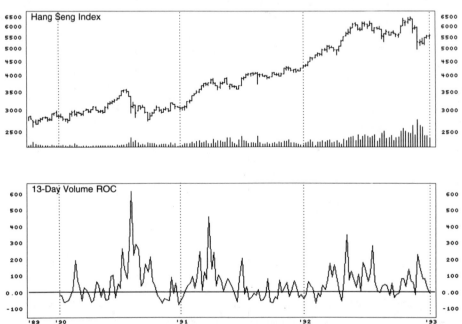

The following are some broad rules for volume interpretation. They relate both to the actual level of activity and volume as might be reflected in a momentum indicator:

1. Rising volume and price are a normal phenomenon. This combination indicates that the market is "in gear" and has no forecasting value, except that it is normal to expect the final top in prices to be *preceded* by a volume peak. Consequently, if the two are in gear it is reasonable to expect at least one more rally that reaches a new price high where they are not in gear.

2. Volume normally leads price. A new high in price that is not confirmed by volume should be regarded as a red flag and a warning that the prevailing trend may be about to reverse (figure 11.2).

3. Rising prices and falling volume are abnormal and indicate a weak and suspect rally (figure 11.3). Volume measures the

Figure 11.2

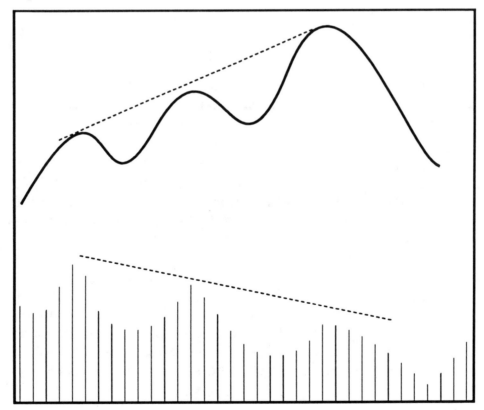

Figure 11.3

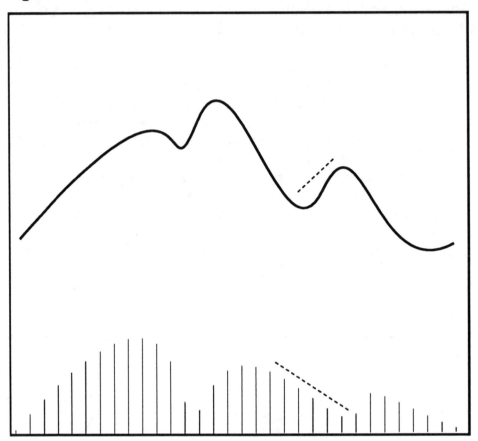

enthusiasm of buyers relative to sellers. Consequently, rising prices and declining volume indicate that the market is rallying because of a lack of selling pressure, not because buyers are enthusiastic. Sooner or later the market will reach a price level that stimulates selling. After this occurs prices will fall substantially.

4. A parabolic rise in prices and a sharp increase in volume are unsustainable and eventually will result in an exhaustion move (figure 11.4). Exhaustion is a characteristic of an important market turning point. Its significance will depend on the nature of the buying frenzy relative to its time span. A buying panic spread over four or five days will have far less significance than one that gradually builds up over, say, a period of six weeks.

Figure 11.4

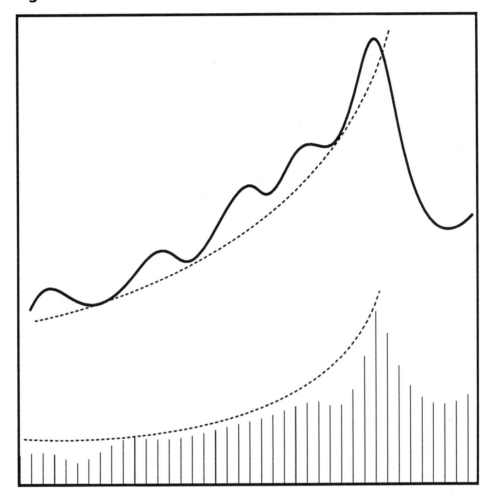

5. The reverse set of circumstances epitomizes a selling climax (figure 11.5a). The implications and principles for a buying panic hold for a selling climax, but in this case the trend reverses from down to up. Selling climaxes normally, but not always, represent the final low of a declining price trend (figure 11.5b). By definition, the rise in price following a selling climax is accompanied by *declining volume*. This is one of the few times that a volume and price divergence is normal. Having said that, I stress that it is still of paramount importance that

Figure 11.5a

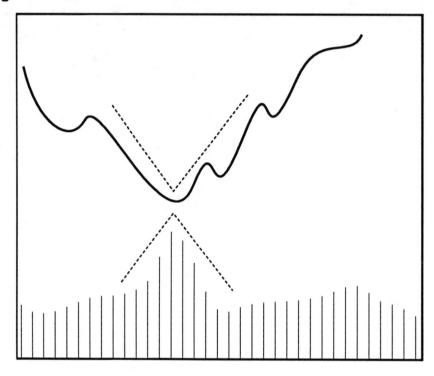

Figure 11.5b

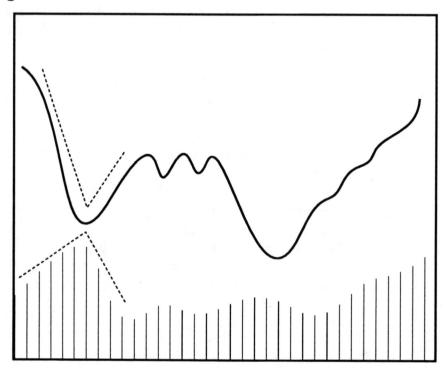

subsequent rallies be accompanied by expanding volume, even though the actual level will be below that experienced during the selling climax.

6. When a test of an important low is accompanied by lower volume, this is a bullish sign (figure 11.6). It is not important whether the first low is marginally violated by the second or whether the second low holds just above the first. There is an old saying on Wall Street, "Never short a dull market." It applies very much to this type of situation where a previous low is being tested. The almost nonexistent volume indicates a complete lack of selling interest.

7. An expansion of volume following a price peak—when the expansion occurs during a consolidation or accompanies a downward price-pattern completion—is a bearish sign because it indicates that volume *is not* going with the trend (figure 11.7).

8. Churning market activity is characterized by a price that has been in a rallying phase for "some time" and by additional increases that are anemic and accompanied by heavy volume.

Figure 11.6

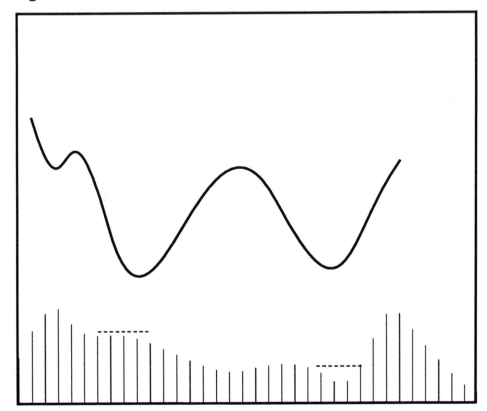

Figure 11.7

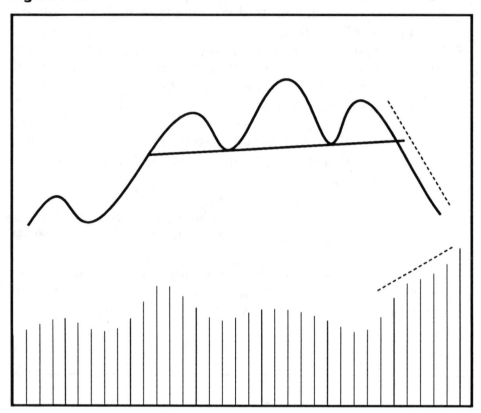

These are bearish signs as seen in figure 11.8. The definition
of "some time" depends on the nature of the price trend under
consideration.

9. If, after a lengthy decline, prices stabilize and volume expands
to abnormal proportions, the market is in an accumulation
phase. This is also a bullish sign. It is an extremely positive
sign if the price subsequently breaks out on the upside accompanied by even higher volume as in figure 11.9.

10. Record volume coming off a major low is generally an extremely reliable signal that a very significant bottom has been
seen. For instance, the 1982 U.S. stock market low was
accompanied by record volume, as was the 1987 bear market
low in Treasury Bond futures. This, by definition, is a very
unusual event. One confirming sign is a widespread disbelief
in the rally by traders, investors, and the media. Record volume
is a very reliable indicator and should *never* be overlooked.

Figure 11.8

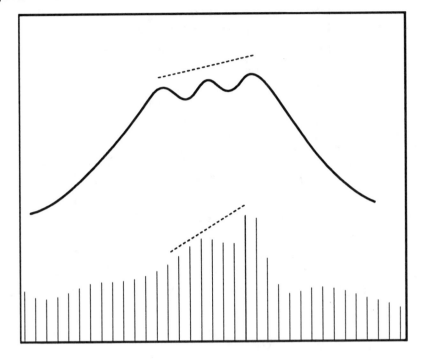

Figure 11.9

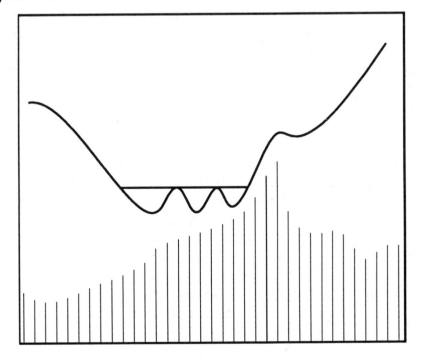

An important factor to remember is that volume reflects an exchange between buyers and sellers. By definition the amount of money flowing into the market must always equal the amount of money flowing out. This is true whether volume is heavy or light. It is the *relative enthusiasm* of buyers to sellers that determines the direction of prices. Heavy volume accompanied by rising prices implies that a substantial amount of potential selling is being absorbed. This means that there is likely to be less overhead resistance as prices climb further.

In a similar way, a selling climax involves liquidation by almost all the "weak" holders. As a result, any additional bad news will unlikely cause any significant selling. A market that can take bearish news in its stride indicates a strong technical position.

To be meaningful, volume should be expressed in relation to a previous period. There are two principal methods for doing this: volume expressed either as a rate-of-change or as a deviation from trend. First, let's consider volume from a rate-of-change aspect.

Rate-of-Change of Volume

Chart 11.2 shows volume expressed as a 10-day rate-of-change. This is a very jagged and misleading indicator. Occasionally, though, it is possible to construct trendlines and to observe divergences. In addition, the peaks at A, B, and C could guide traders with a very short-term time horizon, since they are all followed by a consolidation lasting at least two days; but by and large, the volatile nature of the indicator means that it is not very helpful. If the time span is extended to 30 days as in chart 11.3, different characteristics appear, but the overall effect still remains one of irregularity. One characteristic brought out is the cluster of declining peaks in the volume-momentum indicator that precedes the July and October peaks in the yen. Trendline and divergence analysis are also featured in the chart.

One solution to the problem of irregular movement of the raw numbers is to smooth the indicator with a moving average. Chart 11.4 features a 10-day rate-of-change smoothed with a 10-day simple moving average. Now we can see the contracting volume that precedes the July and October peaks much more clearly. In

Chart 11.2   Japanese Yen (Spot) and 10-Day Volume Rate-of-Change

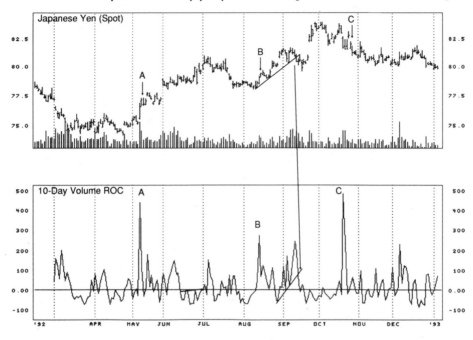

Chart 11.3   Japanese Yen (Spot) and 30-Day Volume Rate-of-Change

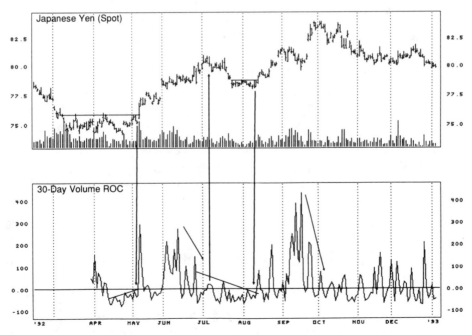

Chart 11.4   Japanese Yen (Spot) and a 10-Day Moving Average
of a 10-Day Rate-of-Change of Volume

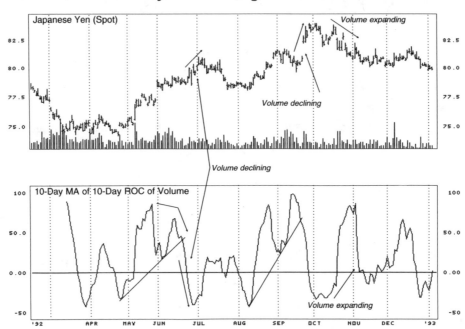

fact, chart 11.4 shows that at the time when both price peaks are being formed, volume on a smoothed rate-of-change basis is actually declining.

Chart 11.5 shows the same data, but this time the zero crossovers are highlighted. Normally, a positive crossover should be associated with a rising market and a negative crossover with a declining one. The solid arrows on the chart indicate when volume goes with the trend and the dashed line when it is going against it. In this example, expanding activity is defined as a volume-oscillator above zero and contracting volume defined as a volume-oscillator below zero. Consequently, a rising oscillator and declining volume are represented in the chart by a declining dashed arrow because the price and volume are in conflict. Solid declining arrows reflect periods when volume and price are in sync on the downside.

When the price breaks out of a trading pattern and this is accompanied by a positive-volume zero-crossover, the expanding volume strongly backs up the price action, indicating that the breakout will likely be a valid one. In this respect, the completion

Chart 11.5 Japanese Yen (Spot) and a 10-Day Moving Average
of a 10-Day Rate-of-Change of Volume

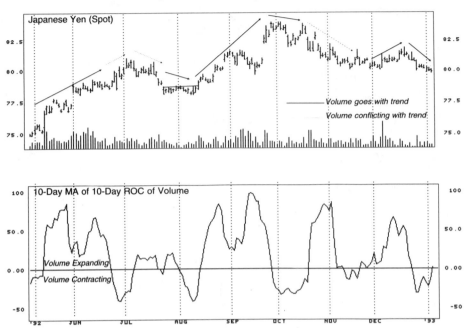

of a small base in mid-August 1992 is accompanied by a positive
zero-crossover in the volume oscillator.

At the other end of the scale, declining volume accompanying
rising prices is a bearish factor and throws considerable suspicion
on the rally. When this action is subsequently followed by an
expansion of volume and prices peak out and start to decline, that
is when we get what I call the "double-whammy volume effect." An
example of the double whammy at work is shown in chart 11.6,
which features the October 1992 top in the yen. It can be
represented symbolically with a letter "N" over the price and the
letter "V" above the volume. The double part of the whammy comes
because prices are rising but volume is bearishly declining. Then
when the price declines, volume expands, which is again an
abnormal and bearish characteristic.

Another important feature of volume interpretation is that *overbought readings in volume momentum indicators can occur around
tops or bottoms*. In chart 11.7, featuring the S & P Composite, the
first peak in the volume momentum indicates a selling climax; the
second and third, exhaustion moves. The September high also

Chart 11.6   Japanese Yen (Spot) and a 10-Day Moving Average
of a 10-Day Rate-of-Change of Volume

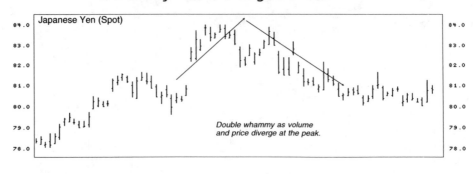

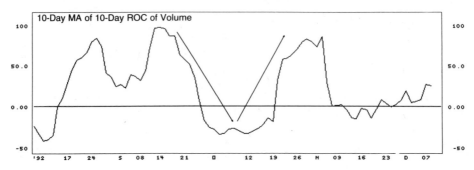

Chart 11.7   S&P Composite and a 10-Day Moving Average
of a 10-Day Rate-of-Change of Volume

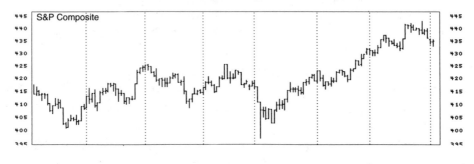

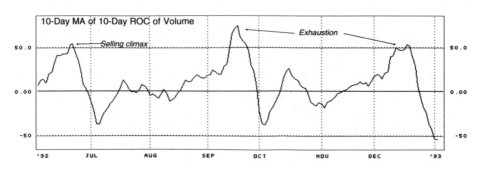

underscores the fact that *not all* price peaks are preceded by volume, for in this case both top out simultaneously.

Volume momentum can also be expressed in other time frames. Even with monthly data the raw figures are usually fairly jagged, so it is still a good idea to smooth it in order to obtain a better feel for the underlying trend. Chart 11.8 features a 9-month rate-of-change of monthly NYSE volume, smoothed by a 6-month moving average. A similar measure is overlaid for the S & P Composite Index. Most of the time volume and price momentum are moving in the same direction. This tells us very little except that the prevailing trend is intact. It is when they diverge that we really need to pay attention. In this respect the relationship between these two momentum series is consistent with the general principle that *volume momentum normally leads price momentum at market peaks.* (The evidence is more contradictory at bottoms.) As long as the price is in a positive trend (e.g., above a long-term moving average), and the volume oscillator is rising, a major decline is unlikely. Once the volume oscillator starts to decline, it is time to take a more cautious stance because the odds of a bear market have increased. When *both* series are declining simultaneously, this also has been associated, in most instances, with a bear market or sharp, intermediate correction.

Chart 11.8   S & P Composite

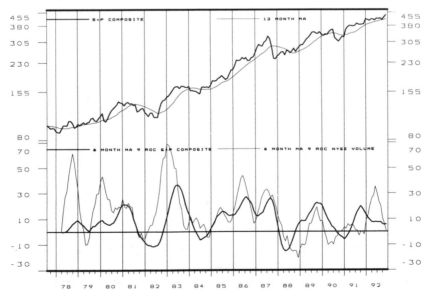

Technical analysis is far from perfect, and there are bound to be exceptions to every rule. In this respect the joint decline in price and volume momentum in 1985 and 1986 were not followed by a sell-off, as would normally be expected. This again underscores the point that weak momentum should always be confirmed by a break in price.

Volume Oscillator

A slightly better approach to interpreting volume is to express volume in an oscillator form, where two moving averages are related to each other. This is a trend-deviation method in which volume is substituted for price in the calculation. This technique also offers a way in which subtle changes in volume levels can be accentuated in a graphic way.

The simplest form of calculation involves the division of one period (moving average) of volume, such as a day or week, by a moving average constructed from a number of different periods. The result is a jagged curve, similar to those shown in charts 11.1 and 11.2. A superior method is featured in figure 11.10. The

Figure 11.10

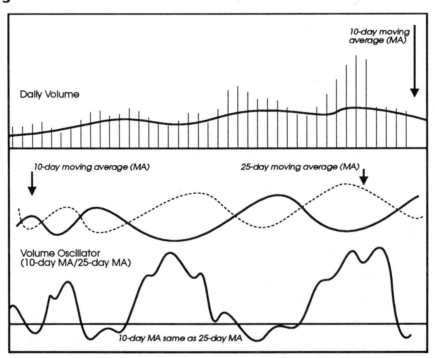

process involves the construction of two moving averages, the shorter being divided by the longer. The equilibrium line represents points when the two moving averages are at identical levels. Movements above and below this horizontal line indicate that the two averages are crossing each other. The time spans of the averages can be varied to reflect short-term, intermediate-, and long-term trends. For daily charts I favor the combination of a 10-day divided by a 25-day simple moving average. This may be too long a span for very short-term traders who may prefer a 5/20 EMA combination.

In a normal market environment volume and price should move in roughly the same direction. For instance, in the case of a rally the volume oscillator should rise. When it reverses from an overbought condition this would typically signal that a correction of some kind is in the cards. This type of condition occurred for the Nikkei in the August-September period of 1992 (see chart 11.9). On the other hand, when prices move sideways or decline, volume should contract. There are few instances of this phenomenon in chart 11.9, because the Nikkei is in a bear market. Such abnormal volume characteristics signal the probability of a declining primary trend environment.

Chart 11.9   Nikkei Stock Index and a 10 x 25-Day Volume Oscillator

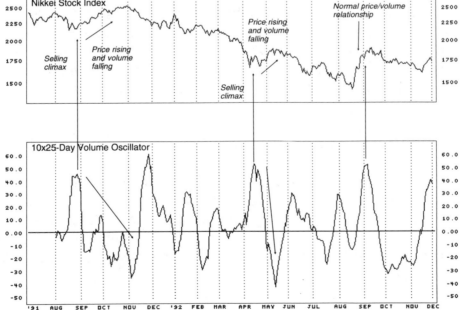

As discussed earlier, the major difference between volume and price oscillators is that an "overbought " volume reading can be, and often is, associated with an oversold market. This occurred in April 1992 for the Nikkei average (chart 11.9). Remember, we are measuring changes in volume, and volume expands during a selling climax. It is a well-known technical characteristic that an increase in price associated with declining volume is bearish. This means that we can also get an "oversold" volume reading at a market high. This occurred at the November 1991 and May 1992 peaks. Any interpretation of the volume oscillator should relate its *direction and level* to the prevailing trend in price.

Chart 11.10 also includes a price oscillator, constructed on the same lines as those used for volume but using price data. It shows a classic negative divergence between price and volume during the mid-April to mid-June 1992 periods. The arrows show that the volume oscillator is rallying in the face of a declining price oscillator. Typically, when the volume oscillator bottoms at around the same time that the price oscillator is peaking from an overbought condition, the market or security being monitored will move sideways as it did in December 1991 or, more often, experience a sharp decline. In mid-May, when the advance is virtually over, volume begins to expand. Rising volume and falling prices is not a normal phenomenon and is bearish. Not surprisingly this is later followed by a substantial price correction.

I have noticed that it is a useful exercise to construct trendlines for the volume oscillator. When a line is violated it should be confirmed by some kind of trend reversal in the price as well since these signals are usually followed by a strong price move. We can see this in practice from trendlines AB and CD in chart 11.11.

Upside/Downside Volume

Ideally, technicians would like to be able to dissect the volume numbers to see whether they are being initiated at the option of buyers or sellers. Some very sophisticated techniques based on the upticks and downticks of individual transactions have been calculated by individuals with access to computer power and large data bases.

Chart 11.10 Nikkei Stock Index, 10 x 25 Volume Oscillator
and a 10 x 25 Price Oscillator

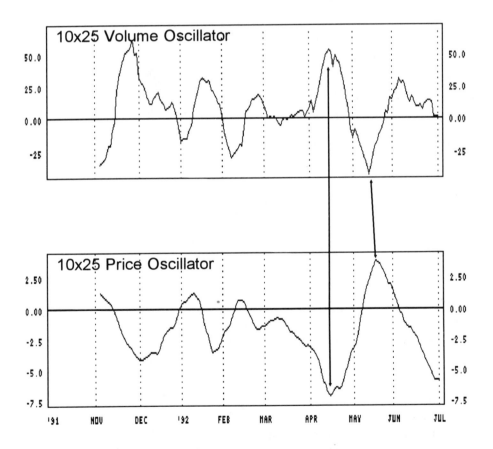

Chart 11.11   Financial Times Stock Exchange 100, 10 x 15 Volume
Oscillator and a 10 x 25 Price Oscillator

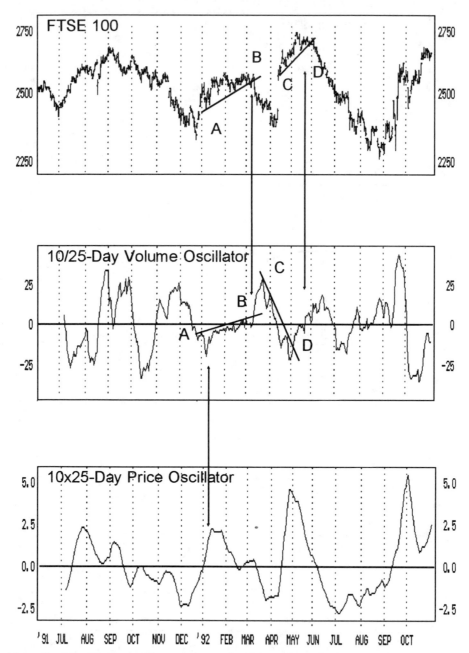

Here, the 10 × 25-day moving average ratio of the volume (volume oscillator) and
the 10 × 25-day moving average ratio of the price (price oscillator) are plotted.
Volume expansion and the price breakdown (trendline AB) are negative indications.
Contracting volume during a price rally (trendline CD) is also a negative indication.

Unfortunately, this kind of information is not available to the general public. It is possible, though, to break down volume information on the three principal U.S. stock exchanges (NYSE, NASDAQ, and Amex) into volume that is attributable to stocks that advance or decline on a particular day. This information is published in the financial press and is also available on several publicly accessible data bases, such as Compuserve or CSI Data. The concept is that if more volume is moving into rising stocks this should be a bullish sign, and if the activity is greater in declining stocks it is a bearish sign. In a general sense this is usually true. However, it is possible to have a substantial amount of volume moving into a declining stock where most of that volume occurs between the low and the close (i.e., when the stock is rising). In this instance the volume would be recorded as a negative, whereas the true picture is actually positive. We have to accept the fact that all indicators suffer from flaws, and this one is no exception.

The most common method of calculation is to divide a 10-day moving average of upside volume by a similar measure for downside volume as in the following formula.

$$\frac{\text{Upside Volume 10-Day MA}}{\text{Downside Volume 10-Day MA}}$$

Chart 11.12 shows such a measure for 1984. Since volume leads price, the most obvious characteristics to be on the lookout for are divergences between the oscillator and the price. We certainly see that between the April and May peaks and again between June and August 1989 in chart 11.13. Typically, when the index rallies to the 2.5 area, which indicates an unusually large increase in volume, this is almost always followed by higher prices within a few months.

The oscillator can sometimes be helpful during market bottoms, although its lead characteristics are less pronounced. At the October 1990 low, for example, we see that as the market is making its final bottom, the oscillator has already reversed to the upside, indicating that selling pressure had started to dry up.

Chart 11.14 shows the 1981–82 bear market. Note that the spring 1982 rally is preceded by a positive divergence between the oscillator and the S & P Composite Index, as was the final low in the summer. What is remarkable about this period is not that the

Chart 11.12   S&P Composite and a 10-Day
Upside/Downside Oscillator

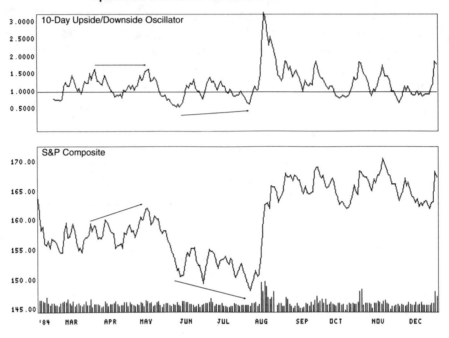

Chart 11.13   S&P Composite and a 10-Day
Upside/Downside Oscillator

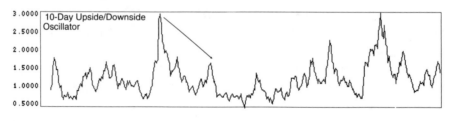

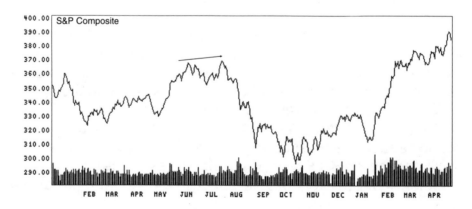

Chart 11.14   S&P Composite and a 10-Day
Upside/Downside Oscillator

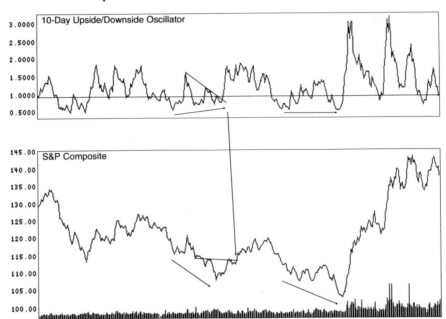

oscillator is able to rally above the 2.5 area, but that it does so on *two* occasions within the space of a month. This unprecedented action not only indicates that the market is headed higher, but also that a highly significant shift in the supply/demand equation has taken place.

Chart 11.14 portrays both bull and bear market environments, whereas the other charts depict a bull market. This illustrates that in normal circumstances the 2.0 level represents an overbought level and the 0.50 zone an oversold. In a bear market the indicator may linger in the 0.50 zone, but in a bull market the slightest touch on this sensitive point almost always triggers a major rally or signals that an intermediate-term consolidation-low has been reached. This can be seen from the June 1982 bottom when an oversold readily failed to trigger a rally of any significance.

Upside/downside volume oscillators can, of course, be calculated for any time span, as seen in chart 11.15 which shows a 30-day series. Note how the July 1990 peak is associated with an oscillator that is barely able to rally above the 1.0 equilibrium line. This is a classic signal of extreme technical weakness, which is

Chart 11.15   S&P Composite and a 30-Day
                  Upside/Downside Volume Oscillator

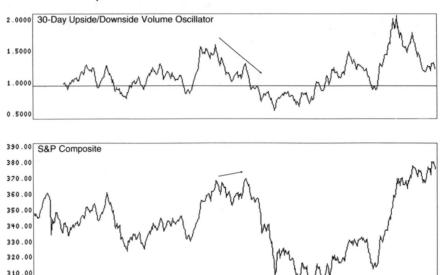

often followed by a precipitous decline. The market's "excuse" at the time was the invasion of Kuwait by Iraq. However, it is quite clear from the technical action that it was already in a vulnerable position.

Upside/downside data can also be expressed using weekly data. The formula for a 6-week time span is:

$$\text{Oscillator} = \left[\frac{6M \times UVOL}{6M \times DVOL} \right] - 1$$

Here the number 1 is subtracted from the formula to give the indicator a positive-negative feel. It does not change the direction and amplitude of the oscillator but merely lowers the equilibrium level to zero. There is no reason why this method of calculation should not be done for daily data. The interpretation of this oscillator is precisely the same as the 10- and 30-day varieties. The only difference is that the weekly arrangement makes it possible to compare the performance over a much longer period. It also reflects intermediate-term as opposed to short-term trends.

One final variation is to calculate separate oscillators for upside and downside data. In this case it is a good idea to include total volume (T) in the calculation. The formula for a 6-week oscillator based on upside volume is:

$$\text{Upside Volume Oscillator} = \frac{6M \times UVOL}{6M \times TVOL}$$

An example for both upside and downside volume is shown in chart 11.16. This arrangement allows us to compare the relative performance of the two series. When they both *converge* as they do at the 1987 low, it is a sign of a *selling climax*, where almost all the volume is associated with declining stocks and very little with advancing issues. On the other hand, a *divergence* such as the one that occurs in late 1985 is *positive.*

It is also possible to construct trendlines for both series and treat their joint violations as confirmation. In the summer of 1984, for instance, the downtrend in up volume and the uptrend in down volume were both simultaneously violated. This arrangement can also give more subtle signals of a potential trend reversal. You can see this happening at the time of the early 1986 peak when the upside volume indicator rallies up to its late 1985 high. Given the "volume-leads-price" rule discussed earlier, there would have been no warning that a consolidation or even price decline lay ahead. However, if we look at the downside oscillator we can see that it makes a higher low at the time of the price peak. This warns us that even though the market is rallying, volume moving into declining stocks is increasing.

Demand Index

The Demand Index was developed by Jim Sibbet, editor of the *Let's Talk Silver and Gold* market letter, as a method of simulating upside and downside volume for markets and stocks where such data is not generally available. This index combines price and volume into

Chart 11.16   Wilshire 5000 and NYSE Up Volume
                        and NYSE Down Volume

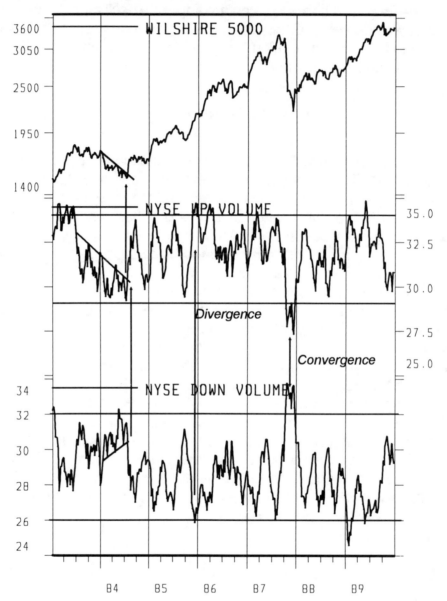

one indicator with the objective of leading market turning points.
The Demand Index is based on the premise that volume leads
price. It is included in many charting packages including MetaStock
and Computrac and is interpreted in the following ways:

1. Divergences between the indicator and the price indicate underlying strength or weakness, depending on whether it is a positive or negative divergence.
2. A long-term divergence between the Index and the price indicates a major top.
3. The Index sometimes forms price patterns, both at tops and bottoms. They normally represent a reliable *advance* warning of an impending price trend reversal.
4. A zero-crossover represents a change in trend. Normally, it will occur after the fact, so it serves as a confirming indicator.
5. Constant fluctuations around the zero line indicate a weak price trend that will soon reverse.
6. Overbought and oversold crossovers generate good buy and sell signals in some markets. What represents an overbought or oversold level will depend upon the volatility of the security in question. The ±25 level appears to be a good compromise for most markets.

Chart 11.17 shows a Demand Index for the Canadian dollar for 1991. A number of interesting points stand out. First, note the head-and-shoulders bottom in July; the breakout occurs simultaneously with the price. Prior to that, the price traces out a small top, which is completed in June. The Demand Index does not form a classifiable top but experiences an almost horizontal price movement during June. This indicates that the balance between demand and supply is extremely delicate. Consequently, when the Index does finally cross below the overbought zone it offers a reliable sell signal. Although this is not, strictly speaking, a distribution pattern, I have called it a "smooth top" on the chart because that is the role that it actually serves.

The November high is actually the top of the bull market. Quite often at such important junctures a momentum indicator will trace out a price pattern of unusual length and significance, sometimes in advance, at other times coincidentally. In this case the pattern's base occurs at the zero level. When it was finally completed the currency embarks on a precipitous decline. Note how zero crossovers confirm important changes in the direction of the short-term trend. Even so, this is not a perfect indicator as we can see from the January and February whipsaw.

Chart 11.17   Canadian Dollar (Spot) and Demand Index

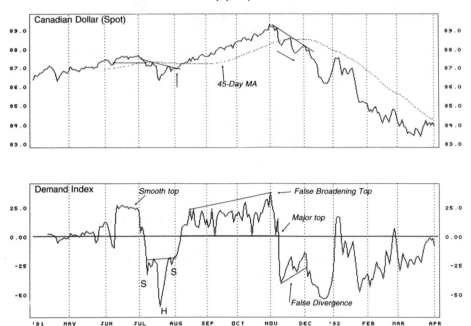

Chart 11.17 also shows why it is very important to make sure that positive momentum characteristics are confirmed by price. In this instance, the November price decline is associated with a positive divergence in the Demand Index. However, this proves to be a false dawn, since the currency is never able to rally above its 45-day moving average, i.e., the bear trendline. The signal that all is not well would have come when the uptrendline in the demand Index was violated in early December.

Chart 11.18 of the mark also brings out some useful points of interpretation. First, it shows that overbought/oversold crossovers are not always reliable. This can be seen not only from the indecisive action in July and August, but also from the action in October as well. The chart also brings out another very important point. Between July and September 1990 the Demand Index traces out a head-and-shoulders top. This looks pretty ominous, especially when the currency appears to be going through the same process. Tops in momentum indicators are quite rare but this particular one seems to have all the right ingredients. In this instance, though, the August/September top in the currency is

Chart 11.18   Deutsche Mark (Spot) and Demand Index

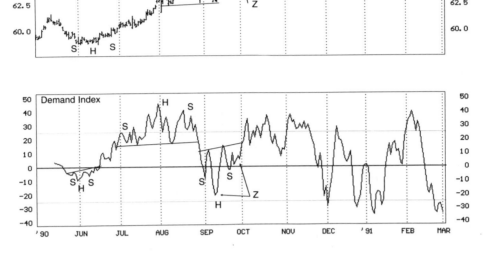

never actually completed. Indeed, what we see is an unusual case of a momentum head-and-shoulders top being immediately canceled or neutralized by a head-and-shoulders bottom. This misleading action is, unfortunately, a fact of life. One can never blindly assume that once a trend is set in motion it cannot reverse before its indicated potential has been realized.

In this example, the signal that the trend is up and not down would have been given at Point Z at the end of September. This is where both the Demand Index and the currency break out from a small base.

Finally, on the Demand Index we can see in chart 11.19 the power in the combination of a momentum index that experiences several positive divergences and an important trendbreak in price. The chart shows that the Nikkei makes a series of five lower lows between April and August 1992. At the same time the Demand Index is, slowly but surely, "walking up hill," as flagged by the rising dotted line. This improving momentum is like pouring gasoline on a fire; once the match has been lit the fire explodes. In this case the match is the violation of the downtrend. The strength of this type

Chart 11.19   Nikkei Stock Index and Demand Index

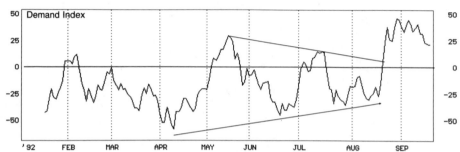

of situation is determined by the length of the trendline, the number of times it has been touched or approached, and the fact that the final low is accompanied by just a small decline in momentum.

This example should be compared to the December 1990-March 1991 period (chart 11.20) when it appears that a similarly strong technical position is building. The difference is that the bear market trendline in price is never violated. Furthermore, the

Chart 11.20   Nikkei Stock Index and Demand Index

uptrendline in the momentum index is broken in March at Point V. Often, when a potentially bullish momentum structure appears to be developing and then breaks down, it is followed by a nasty decline. It is almost as if the market is winding up a spring which at the right moment will be released to trigger explosively higher prices, but before the spring can be fully wound it breaks.

chapter 12

INTERNAL MARKET MOMENTUM

- **Introduction**
- **Types of Breadth Momentum**
    Advance/Decline Momentum Indicators
    McClellan Oscillator
    McClellan Summation Index
    McClellan and Weekly Data
- **Diffusion Indicators**
- **Momentum and Relative Strength**
- **Miscellaneous Momentum Indicators**
    Net New Highs
    The Arms (TRIN) Index

Introduction

All of the momentum indicators that we have examined so far are constructed from price or volume data related to a specific security. In some cases, though, a "market" comprises an aggregate measure of a number of different components. A stock market, for instance, consists of a universe of stocks. Similarly, a commodity index is calculated from the prices of a number of different commodities.

In these cases it is possible to extend our analysis of momentum indicators by studying some or all of the components within a particular momentum format. This concept is known as "breadth" momentum analysis because it measures a broad spectrum of the components of the specific market under consideration. In some ways breadth momentum is far more revealing than price momentum, since the index, or price, may be unduly influenced by a few highly weighted elements. On the other hand, a momentum indicator calculated from a "basket" of components can better reveal more of what is occurring below the surface of a particular market, since the indicator has more information to draw on. Generally, the fewer issues participating in an uptrend, the greater the probability that the trend is about to reverse. In a similar way, if fewer stocks are declining in the face of a new low in the market averages, the greater the possibility that the market is about to reverse to the upside. Breadth momentum thus serves as an additional tool for monitoring potential divergences.

Most of these types of analyses are undertaken with stock markets, since securities are the most widely followed markets and there is an abundance of extensively published data available. Furthermore, the components (i.e., the individual stocks) tend to be more homogeneous than, say, commodities. I have also experimented with breadth momentum series for currencies, gold, and other markets, but have found the indicators to be less reliable here than stock market indicators. The reason for this is fairly obvious. More data is available for the U.S. securities market than for any other type of market in terms of both historical depth and the range of data.

Nevertheless, breadth momentum analysis also works for other stock markets. It is even possible to expand this process by combining a number of markets from different countries to calculate global breadth momentum indicators. Since there is a close relationship between the individual countries and the global stock market cycle, such indicators work quite well.

Types of Breadth Momentum

Breadth momentum indicators fall into three general categories. The first and most widely used category is comprised of indicators that calculate the ratio of advancing issues to declining issues. The resulting number is an oscillator based on an equilibrium line. The calculation is identical to the one described for the upside-downside volume in the previous chapter except that the number of advancing and declining stocks are substituted for upside and downside volume. There are also variations of this concept, such as the relationship between two moving averages of the ratio or a smoothing of the ratio itself. Larger time spans result in more reliable and smoother indicators. The disadvantage of using longer spans, of course, is that the element of timeliness decreases in effectiveness over time. Short time spans, on the other hand, result in timely signals, but they also cause tremendous volatility and give a large number of misleading indications.

The second category comprises indicators for measuring the percentage of a basket of stocks in a positive trend. This form of calculation is known as a "diffusion" index. What actually constitutes as a trend in this context can be any measurable technical tool, such as the percentage of stocks above a specific moving average or the percentage of a basket of stocks with a positive rate-of-change (i.e., an ROC above zero). The possibilities are virtually endless.

The third form of internal breadth measurement I will call "miscellaneous," since none of the indicators fall conveniently into either of the above two categories. They include such things as high/low data; the Arms Index, which combines volume and advance/decline data; and several others. Let's begin the examination of breadth momentum indicators with the first category—indicators based on simple advance/decline data.

Advance/Decline Momentum Indicators

Advance/decline momentum indicators can take many different forms, but the most basic involves the calculation of a ratio of the number of stocks advancing to the number of those issues in decline. This calculation is made over a specific period such as a day or a week. This ratio is then smoothed with a moving average (the time span) and the result plotted as an oscillator. The calculation for the most commonly used period, a 10-day ratio, is shown in table 12.1. Since the result appears as a percentage, 100 is often deducted from the answer to give a positive/negative effect. The 100% or half-way level then becomes zero.

An alternative measurement of this data requires separately calculating a 10-day moving average of the advances and declines and then subtracting the latter from the former. An example is represented in chart 12.1 and the calculation is shown in table 12.2. In almost all cases the results will be very similar as a comparison of the two methods, but there will be some subtle changes.

Table 12.1   Calculation of 10-Day A/D Ratio

Date	Advancing	Declining	Ratio	10-Day Total of Ratio		Oscillator
Jan 2	300	1200	25			
3	500	800	62			
4	700	800	87			
5	900	600	150			
8	1000	500	200			
9	800	800	100			
10	850	950	113			
11	950	550	172			
12	800	500	160			
15	500	900	55	1124	+10	112
16	800	700	114	1213	+10	121
17	900	600	150	1301	+10	130
18	1200	300	400	1551	+10	155

Chart 12.1   S & P Composite and a 10-Day
              Advance/Decline Oscillator

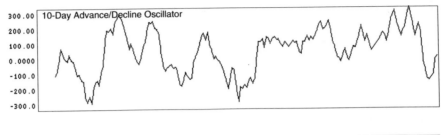

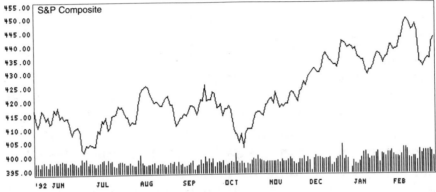

Table 12.2   Calculation of 10-Day A/D Ratio

Date	Advancing	Declining	10-Day Total Advancing	10-Day Total Declining	Ratio	Subtract 1.0 from the Ratio and × 100
Jan 2	300	1200				
3	500	800				
4	700	800				
5	900	600				
8	1000	500				
9	800	800				
10	850	750				
11	950	550				
12	800	500				
15	500	900	7300	7400	.99	−1
16	800	700	7800	6900	1.13	+13
17	900	600	8200	6700	1.22	+22
18	1200	300	8700	6400	1.36	+36

Some technicians prefer to include the number of issues that are unchanged in price. In this case the formula would be as follows:

$$\frac{A - D}{U}$$

where
A = advances
D = declines, and
U = unchanged.

The result is then smoothed by a moving average of some kind. There are two reasons for including stocks with unchanged prices. First, over long periods of time the number of issues on the exchange increases. The inclusion of all issues in the calculation means that long-term comparisons are consistent regardless of the number of issues listed. Using long-term time periods is more important for determining the calculation of a cumulative total of the data, known as an advance/decline line, than a short-term momentum indicator, where changes in the number of issues over the span of one or two months have little effect.

The second reason for including unchanged prices is that a market advance or decline loses momentum as it reaches maturity. Breadth data reflects this fact by showing an increase in the proportion of unchanged issues. Their inclusion in the formula makes it possible to asses a slowdown in breadth momentum at an earlier date.

In a strict sense, a breadth momentum indicator should be compared with a market average that includes all stocks in the basket such as the NYSE Composite Index, rather than the Dow Jones Industrial Average which consists of only thirty blue chip stocks. However, in practice it does not seem to matter too much. In any event, the original objective of the breadth indicator is to determine whether the overall environment for equities is favorable or unfavorable. After all, very few people limit themselves to the purchase of the thirty stocks that make up the Dow; therefore, traders should find the broad market trend more important for their decision making than the trend in the index. This will certainly be true for traders involved in individual stocks or stock options, but what of those who get involved in futures such as the XMI or S & P Contracts? In this case the breadth momentum series of the whole market can be substituted by special breadth measurements calculated purely from the components of the average. In the case of the Dow, or XMI, this would be represented by an A/D ratio of the thirty components that are included in the calculation.

Similar measures could be concocted for the five-hundred stocks that comprise the S & P Composite Index. Those of us who do not have access to the data or to the computing power with the number-crunching capability to calculate such measures will have to fall back on general breadth measurements. This is fine as long as we keep in mind that in a very minor way we are comparing apples and oranges.

Most of the examples discussed here have all been concerned with daily data, but it is also possible to construct these indicators from weekly or even monthly numbers. Such indicators will be useful for gaining perspective on market trends. A useful variation on the A/U – D/U formula is to take a weekly ratio calculated in this way and then compute the square root of the result. Since it is not possible to take a square root of a negative number, the ratios for down weeks are treated as a positive number and the result subtracted from the moving average calculation. An example is shown in table 12.3.

This approach first came to my attention through Hamilton Bolton, founder of the Bank Credit Analyst. He discovered that using the square root calculation enables the weekly advance/decline line to closely reflect unweighted indexes such as the Value Line Composite. Since breadth data all the way back to the 1930s is available and the data for the Value Line date from only the early 1960s, he was able to simulate the broad market in the 1930s, '40s,

Table 12.3

Date	Issues traded (1)	Advances (2)	Declines (3)	Unchanged (4)	Advances + unchanged (5)	Declines + unchanged (6)	Col. 5 – col. 6 (7)	√col. 7 (8)	Cumulative A/D line (9)
Jan. 7	2129	989	919	221	448	416	32	5.7	2475.6
14	2103	782	1073	248	315	433	–118	–10.9	2464.7
21	2120	966	901	253	382	356	26	5.1	2469.8
28	2103	835	1036	232	360	447	–87	–9.3	2460.5
Feb. 4	2089	910	905	274	332	330	2	1.4	2461.9
11	2090	702	1145	243	289	471	–18.2	–13.5	2448.4
18	2093	938	886	269	349	329	20	4.5	2452.9
25	2080	593	1227	260	228	472	244	–15.6	2437.3

Martin J. Pring, *Technical Analysis Explained*. 3rd edition, McGraw-Hill, New York, 1991.

and '50s. An example of a 10-week ratio using this formula with the S & P Composite is shown in chart 12.2.

The most active stocks on the exchange over a given period often reflect what "big money" is doing in the market. Data is published in the popular financial press on both a daily and weekly basis. This information is worth consideration not only because it reflects institutional activity, but also because it accounts for 20% to 25% of the total NYSE volume. Indicators based on the most active data, therefore, serve as a kind of rough benchmark of whether institutions' enthusiasm skews toward buying or selling.

Oscillators derived from this type of data are calculated by subtracting the number of declining issues from the number of advancing issues over a chosen period. For example, a 10-day most active indicator would involve the separate addition of the plurality of stocks that are advancing on a daily basis and those that are declining. If more active stocks are declining than advancing, this sum would be represented by a negative number. The individual ratios are then totaled for a 10-day period and the result plotted as a continuous oscillator. A 30-day most active indicator would involve a 30-day total; an 8-day indicator, an 8-day total, and so forth.

An alternative approach for a 10-day time span requires subtracting the total of all declining issues over a 10-day period from

Chart 12.2   The S & P Composite and a 10-Week Breadth Oscillator

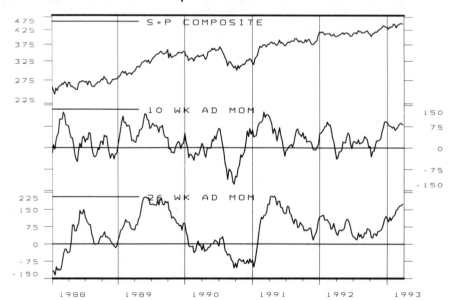

the number of advancing issues. Movements in the resulting oscillator would be more or less the same as the most active indicator. The indicator would then be interpreted in the same way as any other momentum series. Chart 12.3 shows how decisive zero-crossovers in the 30-day most active series offer reasonable buy and sell signals. Since the market was in a bear trend at the time, buy signals did not generally result in any worthwhile rallies.

McClellan Oscillator

A market indicator that has gained great popularity in recent years is the McClellan Oscillator. The McClellan Oscillator calculates the difference between two exponential moving averages using the daily advances minus the daily declines. The two averages are for 19- and 39-day time spans, which represent a 10% and 5% trend value respectively. The formula is:

McClellan Oscillator = [19 EMA of (A − D)] − [39 EMA of (A − D)]

An example of the McClellan Oscillator is shown in figure 12.1. Positive values are recorded when the short-term average moves above the longer-term one.

This 19–39 day calculation is the accepted default used by most traders and computer software programs, but there is absolutely no

Chart 12.3 The NYSE Composite Versus the
30-Day Most Active Indicator

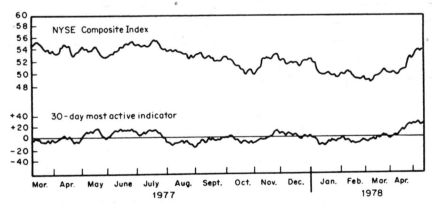

Martin J. Pring, *Technical Analysis Explained*, 3rd edition, McGraw-Hill, New York, 1991.

Figure 12.1

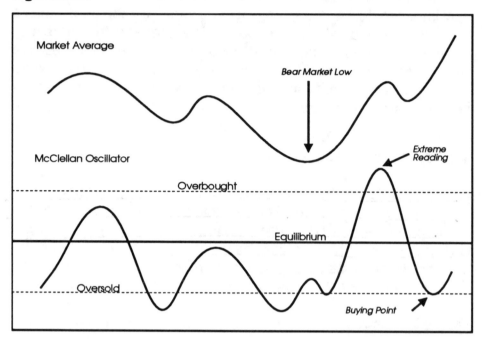

reason why you cannot experiment with other time periods. The oscillator is in effect the equivalent for breadth momentum of the MACD indicator discussed in chapter 4.

The McClellan Oscillator is generally regarded as overbought when it reaches the plus 70–100 range and oversold in the minus 70–100 range. Some analysts have extended this range to include the plus 60–100 and minus 60–100. It is common practice to use the overbought and oversold readings as entry and exit points. My view is that you should treat McClellan's interpretation as you would any other momentum indicator by using trendline violations, divergences, and so forth. This approach certainly seems to give smoother results and a better underlying feeling for the market than the straight 10-, 25-, or 30-day A/D breadth momentum ratios. Movements are far less volatile, while at the same time the subtle changes in the underlying technical picture are still evident. When using the 19- and 39-EMA default values, the McClellan is regarded as a short-to-intermediate-term indicator.

The McClellan Oscillator is certainly no exception to the rule that momentum leads price. Consequently, one of its characteristics is that major price peaks are typically preceded by several divergences. Quite often, actual confirmations of market turning points will be given as the oscillator crosses above and below zero.

Extreme readings in excess of ±130 reflect very strong underlying momentum. Logically, such action would appear to indicate an excellent buying or selling point, depending on whether the reading is overbought or oversold. However, such movement is usually a reliable sign that a new primary trend is underway. Under these conditions it is normally better to await the subsequent reaction and enter the market in the direction of the extreme reading on the next turning point in the oscillator (Figure 12.1 shows an example).

As I have said, it is always a good idea in any momentum analysis to compare at least two indicators to see whether they are in agreement. Chart 12.4 includes a McClellan Oscillator and a 12-day rate-of-change indicator. Most of the time, both indicators are "in gear," but at Points A, B, and C it is apparent that the McClellan Oscillator is acting much weaker than the ROC. These particular discrepancies are short-term in nature and are followed by a brief, but unpleasant, decline. The weaker action of the oscillator undoubtedly reflects the fact that the broad underlying market is not as strong as the averages would have us believe.

McClellan Summation Index

The Summation Index is a slower moving version of the McClellan Oscillator. It is calculated by accumulating the daily readings of the McClellan Oscillator. When it is above the zero level, the Summation Index rises; when it is below zero, it falls. This is shown graphically in figure 12.2. This means that changes in the direction of the Summation Index will occur as the "raw" oscillator crosses above and below zero. The slope of the Summation curve will depend on the reading of the raw oscillator. The more overbought it is (i.e., the greater the distance above zero), the steeper the slope will be. Conversely, if the oscillator is just above zero it will not add much to the Summation total so its angle of ascent will be very narrow. Overbought and oversold readings in the Summation Index will be determined by a combination of the length of time that the raw oscillator remains above and below zero and the level of the readings.

Chart 12.4   S & P Composite and McClellan Oscillator
Versus 12-Day Rate-of-Change

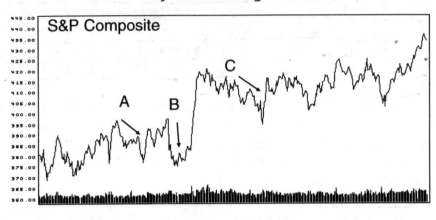

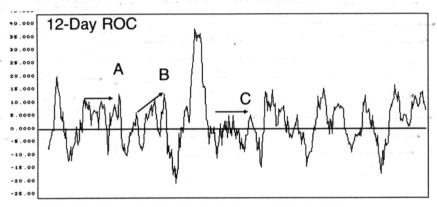

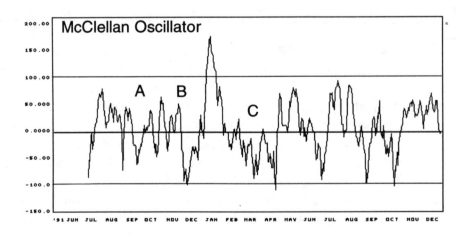

Figure 12.2

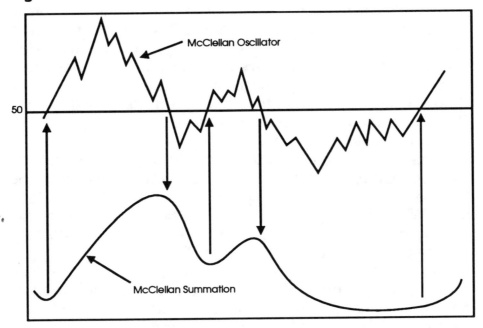

Normally, the Summation Index moves in a slow, deliberate manner, giving useful signals from the standpoint of intermediate-term timing. However, on those rare occasions when the raw oscillator vacillates around zero, the Summation Index will also give a number of indecisive signals.

It is fairly easy to see from the action of the Summation Index that a zero-based crossover system in the oscillator is not likely to lead to many trading profits. My view is that the Summation Index should be used primarily to gain some perspective about the nature of the current short-term technical condition. For example, if the Summation Index is at an extreme reading—above or below the +500 or –500 zone—it indicates that the intermediate trend is at a fairly mature stage. Therefore, it is dangerous to use short-term buy signals to take a position in the direction of that trend. In other words, if the trend is up, it is too late to go long. By the same token, if the Summation Index is still rising it is premature to go short or liquidate the position until a trend-reversal signal in the price is given. Sometimes this also occurs when the Summation Index reverses direction.

Quite often, when an intermediate-term, smoothed-momentum indicator reverses direction from an extreme, it does so long after the peak has come and gone, making its timeliness questionable. The great advantage of the Summation Index is that it reverses direction when the McClellan Oscillator crosses zero. This means that a Summation buy or sell signal is never given when the market is short-term overbought or oversold. Of course, this timeliness does not come without a price and that is whipsaw signals. However, if you pay close attention to directional changes in the Summation Index only when it is overbought, many of these whipsaw signals will be filtered out.

Under such circumstances you can also use what I call the "domino" approach. That is, look for an extreme reading in the Summation Index *and* some signs of a reversal in the short-term trend. When the short-term trend gives a signal, chances are that it will have a domino effect on the overextended intermediate-trend and the Summation Index.

Occasionally, the Summation Index sounds an extremely loud signal by failing to reach a very high level despite a long and sharp rally in the market. A classic example is shown in chart 12.5 where the summer high at point A is associated with a Summation reading that is barely above zero despite a rally in the S & P Composite from around 320 to 370. Rarely are such signals given, but when they

Chart 12.5 S & P Composite and McClellan Summation

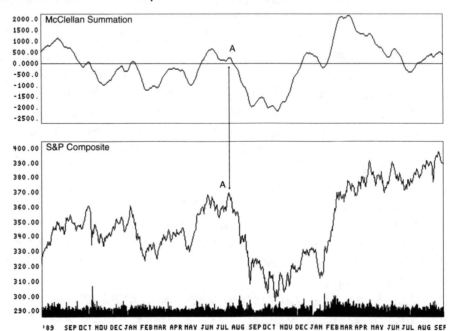

are it pays to give them your attention because they are usually followed by a memorable decline.

The Summation Index can also be used in conjunction with moving-average crossovers. Trial and error has shown that a 35-day simple moving-average crossover offered very good results in the 1980s (see chart 12.6). However, as with all purely mechanical approaches there were some years when it did not operate well at all.[1] (See *Technical Analysis Explained*, 3rd Edition, pages 396-399.)

Another feature of the Summation Index is that it can be used to show divergences and occasionally lend itself to trendline construction. As with all smoothed indicators, this is quite a rare phenomenon. When a line is violated and the violation can be related in a timely fashion to a reversal in direction of a market average, such combinations offer very reliable and often powerful signals as shown in chart 12.7.

McClellan and Weekly Data

In an article in the September 1990 issue of *Stocks and Commodities*, Arthur Merrill tested the Oscillator using weekly data. Since the short-term EMA roughly corresponds to four weeks and the long-term average to eight weeks, he used these periods as his testing base. The EMA factors were 0.4% and 0.22%, respectively. He found that the best forecasting results were achieved not from zero-crossovers but from extreme overbought and oversold readings. They occurred over a five-week forecasting period using a full standard deviation above and below zero. The benchmarks were plus and minus 280. In other words, when the oscillator reached a +280 overbought zone it was forecasting that the market would be down five weeks later. The opposite would be true for a negative 280 reading. Chart 12.8 is reproduced from the article.

Diffusion Indicators

Diffusion indicators measure a basket of items within a specific universe that are in a positive trend. The trend measurement could be anything from a moving average, a positive rate-of-change,

[1] Martin J. Pring, *Technical Analysis Explained*, 3rd edition, McGraw-Hill, New York, 1991, pp. 396-399.

Chart 12.6 McClellan Summation Index Versus a 35-Day MA

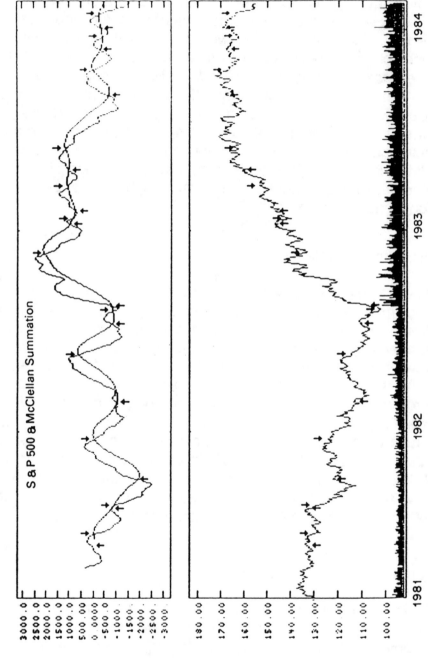

Martin J. Pring, *Technical Analysis Explained*, 3rd edition, McGraw-Hill, New York, 1991.

Chart 12.7 S & P Composite, McClellan Summation and Trendlines

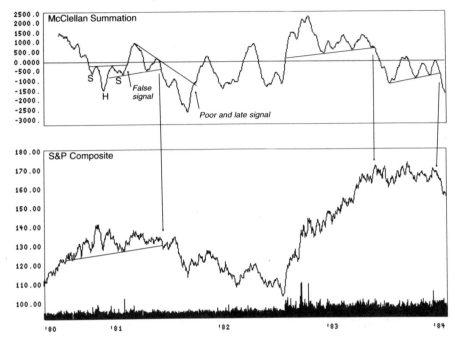

positive stochastics characteristics, and so forth. The concept behind these indicators is simply to try to characterize the momentum of the broad market as opposed to a market average or index. Logically, one would expect the best buying points to occur when all the items are in a positive trend, but in actuality the exact opposite is normally the case. It turns out that when most or all of the items are in a positive trend things are about as bullish as they can get. This means that the next step is certain to be a deterioration in some of the components and a subsequent decline in the market as more and more issues follow suit.

In this regard it is important to remember that these comments refer to a specific time frame. Just as a short-term indicator reflects, say, a short-term overbought condition, it is still possible to have intermediate- and long-term trends in an early stage of development. Similarly, a 100% reading in the percentage of stocks above a 10-day moving average tells us only about the short-term condition of the market. For a longer-term view we would need to look at stocks in relation to such traits as their 12-month moving average, to choose one example.

Chart 12.8   Weekly McClellan Oscillator

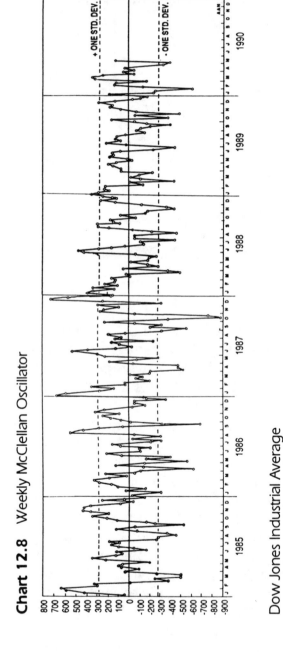

Dow Jones Industrial Average

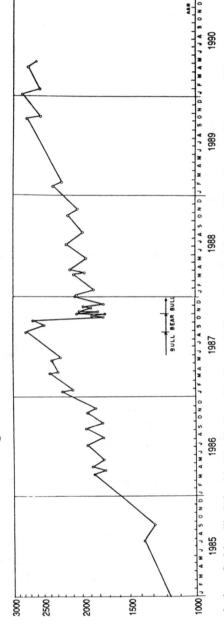

Arthur C. Merrill, "Weekly McClellan Oscillator," *Technical Analysis of Stocks and Commodities,*
Sept. 1990.

Diffusion indicators are subject to the same vagaries as other momentum series and should be interpreted using the principles outlined in chapters 1 and 2.

The most common form of diffusion indicator measures the percentage of stocks that have risen above a specific moving average. Just as short-term time spans in a rate-of-change calculation show more volatility than longer-term ones, a diffusion indicator based on a 10-day moving average will be much more volatile than one based on a 60-day average.

There is a natural tendency to include as many parts of a universe as possible (e.g., all the stocks on the NYSE etc). I have found that as long as the universe is carefully selected to reflect key industrial segments there is not much difference in the results. This was not important in the past, since such calculations required maintaining a huge data base and some serious number crunching. Today, this task can be achieved much more easily with a combination of automatic data collection and spreadsheet analysis. It is now possible for the individual investor to maintain these indicators without much trouble once the system has been set up.

Some of this data is also available publicly. *Investors Intelligence* publishes the percentage of NYSE stocks that are above their 10- and 30-week moving averages. These stocks are shown in chart 12.9.

Chart 12.9   S & P Composite and Three Breadth Indicators

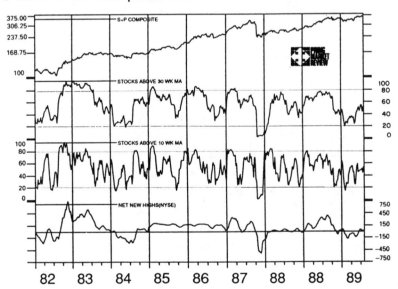

Martin J. Pring, *Pring Market Review.*

As you would expect, the 10-week series is much more volatile than its 30-week counterpart. It is used to identify short-term selling points. The indicator is said to be oversold when less than 20% of NYSE issues are above their 10-week moving averages and overbought when the number is greater than 80%. This diffusion series is subject to the principles of divergences, trendline construction, and so forth.

The 30-week series operates in a similar fashion but obviously on a longer time frame with commensurately greater significance at turning points. The chart also shows how the two series can be compared. For instance, just after the 1984 low both indicators broke above downtrendlines. Note also in the 10-week series how the best buy signals from an oversold condition have a *tendency* to occur when the 30-week series is also close to an oversold reading. Such an event occurred at the 1982 low. Sometimes, though, major bottoms are confusing and volatile affairs, which means that not all "double-oversold" conditions are immediately followed by a rally. The premature signal from early 1984 is a fine example. In such instances it is usually better to await a double-trendline violation similar to the one that occurred later in 1984. It is even better still to wait for a trend-reversal signal in the average being monitored.

It is also important to note that 10-week oversold conditions do not usually translate into much of a rally when the 30-week series is in an overbought condition. Examples of this phenomenon occurred in mid-1983, the spring of 1987, and the spring of 1988.

Momentum and Relative Strength

Relative strength (RS) measures the performance of one item in relation to another. It should not be confused in any way with the RSI, or Relative Strength Indicator, discussed in chapter 4. The most common approach for using RS is to divide a stock price by a popular market average such as the S & P Composite Index. When the line plotted on the chart is rising, the stock is outperforming the market, and vice versa. The RS does not reflect the actual performance of the security (i.e., whether the stock itself is rising or falling). Usually, a rising RS line is associated with a rising price, but it is still possible to have a rising RS line at a time when both the stock and the market are declining. All that the RS line would be telling us in this instance is that the stock is declining at a slower rate than the market. Clearly, if a trader is optimistic about the market he is better off to focus on a stock showing positive RS.

Since relative strength moves in trends, it follows that it is subject to the same trend-identification techniques as the price. This means that it is appropriate to construct momentum indicators to determine when a particular stock is oversold or overbought on a *relative* basis. Ideally, one would wish to enter a stock when both its RS and its price are oversold and the trends for both the absolute and relative price are showing a reversal to the upside. In my experience it is very difficult to find such "perfect" situations, but this does not mean that the RS momentum concept is useless. It can certainly warn you of an overbought condition where the stock is becoming overly popular. Also as charts 12.10 and 12.11 indicate, RS momentum and trendline violations in the RS can be very helpful at certain junctures. One problem with the RS line is that it tends to be far more volatile than the actual price of the stock. This is why you must be careful in drawing conclusions based solely on RS data.

Chart 12.10   The Relative Strength of Texas Instruments and a 39-Week Rate-of-Change of Relative Strength

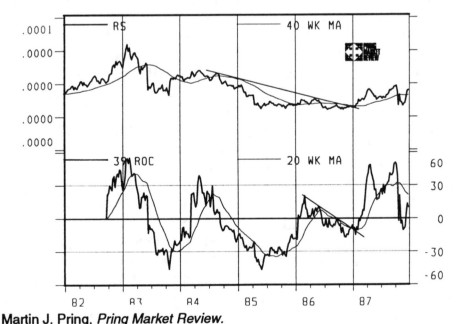

Martin J. Pring, *Pring Market Review.*

Chart 12.11   S & P Financial Index and Three Indicators

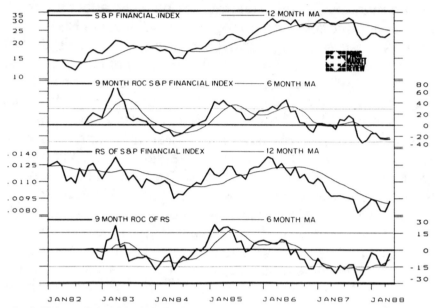

Martin J. Pring, *Pring Market Review.*

It is also possible to develop a diffusion indicator based on RS relationships. We could develop such an indicator for the most common form of RS relationship: the strength of a stock vis-à-vis the market, for instance. However, we could also create an RS line between stocks A and B and see whether the RS line charts above a specific moving average. Then we could compare A to C in a similar way. This process could be continued for a whole basket of stocks and the percentage of positive RS relationships could be totaled in the same way as the percentage of NYSE stocks above their 10- and 30-week moving averages. The result would be an RS Diffusion Indicator.

If properly constructed with the correct basket of stocks, the RS Diffusion Indicator would tell us when a stock is out of favor (i.e., below its RS moving average in relation to most of the other stocks) or when it is in. An example of this possibility is shown in chart 12.12. In this case the diffusion indicator measures the RS relationship between the S & P Oil Composite and twenty other S & P Industry group series. The demarcation point for determining a positive and negative trend is the 12-month moving average. Thus, when the Index is at 100% the RS of the Oil Composite, vis-à-vis

Chart 12.12 Relative Strength of Oil Composite Versus S&P Composite and Relative Strength Diffusion Index of Oil

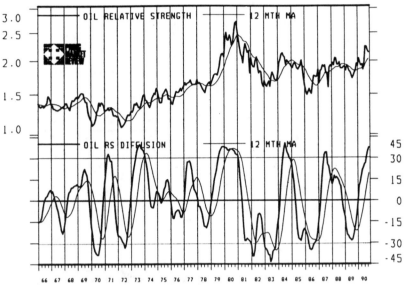

Martin J. Pring, *Pring Market Review.*

the other nineteen industry groups, is above its 12-month moving average. The actual results are quite volatile, so the thin line in chart 12.12 is actually a 6-month moving average of the raw data. Note that this series is being measured against the RS of the Oil Index to the S & P Composite and not the Oil Index itself.

This last example has taken us some distance from our basic momentum explanation, but it is nevertheless useful from the point of view of deciding *what* to buy as opposed to *when*.

The concept of RS and RS momentum can be just as easily applied to the relationship between two markets. In chart 12.13, the second panel shows the RS of Treasury Bonds to crude oil. Above it is the 25-day rate-of-change for this relationship. Between late October 1991 and January of 1992 this line is rising, indicating that bonds were outperforming oil. Then, in early January, both the RS line and the ROC break below important trendlines, indicating that oil will now likely do better than bond prices. In one sense these RS relationships are useful because they often give us some clear indications of *which* futures contract to buy or sell.

Such relationships can also be helpful in a broader sense. For example, following the January reversal favoring oil over bonds it

Chart 12.13   Bond/Oil Ratio and 25-Price ROC and
Treasury Bonds and 30-Price ROC

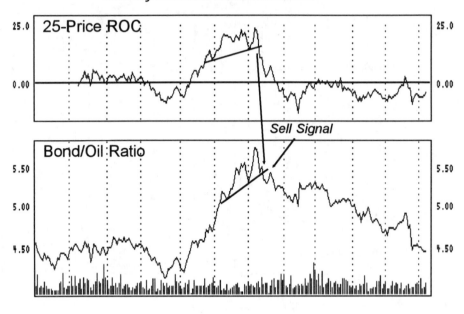

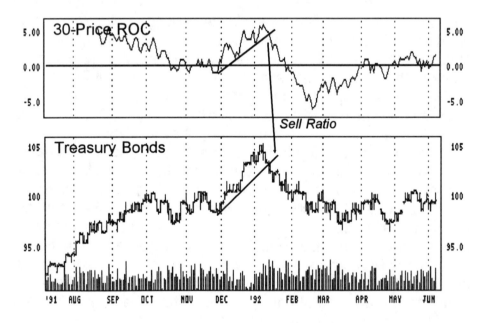

would have also made sense to short bonds and buy an equivalent amount of oil against it. After all, this signal does not tell us that the bonds themselves are going to rally or even that oil prices will decline. The only information provided by the RS relationship is that the *relative* trend of bonds vs. oil has reversed in favor of oil. The bottom two panels, on the other hand, indicate that taking a short position in bonds would have made sense, since the price and the momentum both break out on the downside.

Bond and oil prices are symbolic of deflationary and inflationary pressures. A bond rally and a decline in oil characterize a deflationary environment, while the converse is typical of an inflationary environment. Changes in the trend of a relationship of this nature can provide a valuable clue as to whether inflation-sensitive assets are going to outperform deflation-sensitive ones. Inflation-sensitive assets include commodity prices as well as mining and energy stocks. Deflationary assets apart from bonds involve utility stocks as well as insurance and financial issues. For example, if you are considering the purchase of an electric utility stock because its technical position is improving, your chances of success will be that much greater if the bond-oil or bond-gold relationship has recently reversed in favor of bonds. Over very short-term trends these inflation-deflation relationships are not as important as a general influence, but over an intermediate- or long-term horizon they can sometimes be very powerful.

In summary, the RS relationship can be helpful in four ways:

1. When you are considering buying or shorting two items, it indicates which one will outperform or underperform the other.
2. The relationship can be used as a benchmark for spread trading (i.e., buying one item and shorting an equivalent amount against it). In this way the trader is actually buying or shorting the RS line.
3. Using certain RS relationships can confirm signals in an absolute-price trend. For example, bond and oil prices usually move in opposite directions. Confirmation of a trend reversal in the absolute price of bonds by a bond/oil ratio reversal offers additional technical evidence that can be used for a more reliable indication of the momentum movement.
4. Using some relative relationships helps to establish whether an environment favors inflation or deflationary assets.

Miscellaneous Momentum Indicators

Net New Highs

Historically, the press has reported the number of stocks on the NYSE that have recorded new highs and lows for the year. This meant that the numbers were distorted at the beginning of the year and so it became the practice to begin the new year in March. In recent years the data has been calculated on a 52-week basis, obviating the need for such an adjustment. The 52-week span is a useful one, since it covers a complete calendar year and is not subject to seasonal distortions. However, there is no reason why other time spans can not be considered.

The concept behind examining new high data is that a consistent number of stocks making new highs implies that a substantial number of stocks are breaking out from price patterns. The more stocks breaking out, the greater the chances that the market averages will move higher as well. Most times this idea works pretty well, but occasionally extremely high or low numbers do occur at major turning points. This approach has a tendency to develop more at market bottoms than at tops. *In almost all instances we find that net new high data leads market peaks.* This will be represented in the charts by at least one divergence.

Normally, a net new high indicator is expressed as the number of stocks making new highs over a specific period, such as one day or one week, less those making a new low. From that point it is a matter of personal preference whether the data is smoothed, and if so, by what factor. I have found that smoothing daily data with a 10-day moving average is very helpful, as is using a 6-week average for weekly data. Occasionally, technicians like to display both the highs and lows on the same chart. This is because subtle indications of weakness can be given in a rising or topping market if the number of *new* lows begins to increase noticeably. At market bottoms this would be represented by a slow but deliberate expansion in new highs.

Interpretation of high-low data can take many forms, but the most valuable appear to be divergences and zero-crossovers. It is also possible to spot moving average crossovers and trendline violations from time to time, but price-pattern formation is very rare indeed.

Chart 12.14 shows a weekly 6-week moving average of net new
high data. Almost all bull market peaks are preceded by at least one
divergence in this indicator. This is true of nearly every market peak
since the 1960s. This means that as long as a new high in the
average is accompanied with a higher high in the net new high
indicator there is little danger that this represents the bull market
peak. This does not mean that a correction won't take place; it most
likely will. In fact, when this indicator peaks it is actually a signal of
slowing momentum, and the peak is almost invariably followed by
a sell-off or consolidation. For example, in chart 12.14 we can see
that the new high index reaches an important high in the beginning
of 1987, a small consolidation follows, and the market goes on to
make a new high in the summer. Since the net new high indicator
does not confirm this, it represents the kind of *major* warning sign
that was not present earlier in the year.

We see the same kind of effect at the end of 1982, where the
index reaches an extremely overbought level. The fact that it had
been able to attain such heights is in itself a testimony that a major
new uptrend is underway. Compare this to late 1983 when the
market reaches a marginal new high, but the new high index is

Chart 12.14   S & P Composite and a 6-Week Moving Average
of the Net New High/Low Ratio

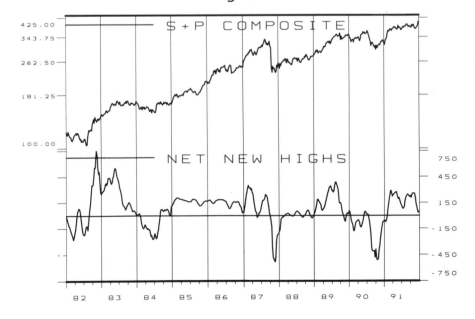

barely able to rally above the zero line. Not only does the index
deviate from the S & P Composite, but the divergence is also a
blatant one to boot!

At the beginning of 1984 the new high indicator falls below the
zero level. This means that the number of new lows has begun to
outpace new highs on a six-week basis. Quite often this drop into
negative territory is associated with a major top in the market
averages, and vice versa. In the 1982–91 period there were very
few major setbacks apart from the 1987 crash, which meant that a
decline below zero more often than not represented a false signal
of weakness. However, in more normal times such crossovers
have proven to be timely indicators of a major intermediate setback. I believe that they are likely to resume this role in the mid to
late 1990s.

These same principles of divergence and zero crossovers can
be applied to daily data. Chart 12.15 shows a chart of the S & P
Composite and a 10-day average of net new high data. Note the
head-and-shoulders top that is completed in May 1986. It is not
followed, as one might expect, by a serious decline but by a
consolidation instead. There are several false breakdowns below

Chart 12.15   S & P Composite and 10-Day Net New High

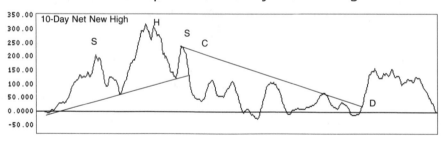

the zero level in the next few months, but there is no mistaking the break above trendline CD after the indicator just crosses above zero for the third time in three months. Note that by the time the market makes its high in the summer of 1987 the new high indicator has already diverged with the average. This is shown in chart 12.16.

I have concentrated here on new highs and lows experienced over the period of a year, but other time spans are equally valid. Charts 12.17 and 12.18 show examples in the Italian market where 26-week and 30-day smoothed net new high data work quite well. The charts also demonstrate that the kind of data used in the U.S. market can also be applied to other markets around the world.

The Arms (TRIN) Index

This indicator was developed by Richard Arms and is regularly featured on the CNBC network's market tape. Some quote services refer to it as TRIN or MKDS. It is a combination of breadth and

Chart 12.16   S & P Composite and a 10-Day Moving Average of Net New High/Low Ratio

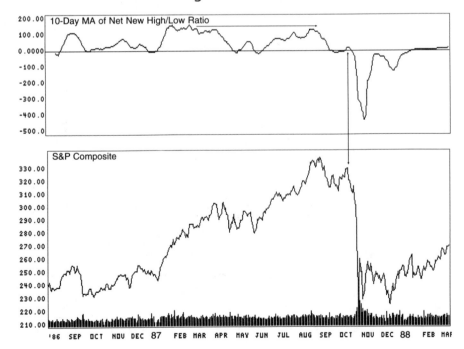

Chart 12.17   Indice Comit Index (Italy) and a 30-Day Net New High

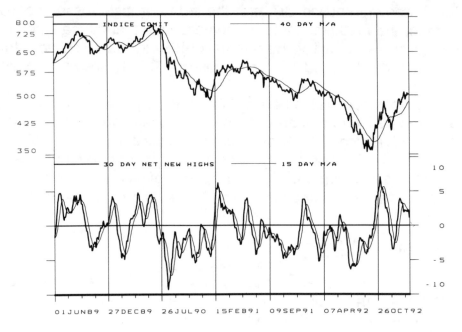

Chart 12.18   Indice Comit Index (Italy) and a 26-Week Net New High

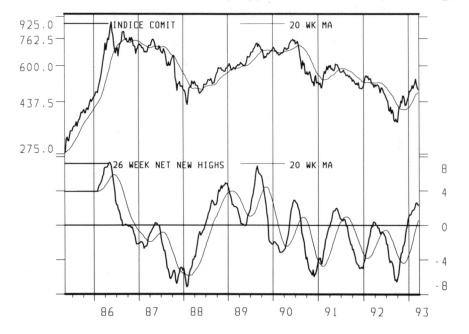

volume measurements because it requires both in its construction. It is calculated by dividing the ratio of advancing and declining stocks by the ratio of volume in advancing issues over volume in declining issues. In almost all cases, daily data is used but there is no reason why a weekly or even monthly series could not be constructed. Normally, the Arms Index is used in conjunction with NYSE data, but its principles can be applied to any market situation where upside-downside volume and breadth data are available. There is one important thing to note and that is that movements in the Arms Index run contrary to those of the market. This means that oversold conditions appear as peaks and overbought conditions as valleys. This is contrary to virtually all other indicators described in this book, so the charts for these examples are presented inversely to their normal format in order to be consistent with the other indicators as seen in charts 12.19 and 12.20.

The concept behind this indicator is to monitor the power of the volume associated with advancing issues in relation to that of

Chart 12.19   S & P Composite Versus a 10-Day Arms Index (Inverted)

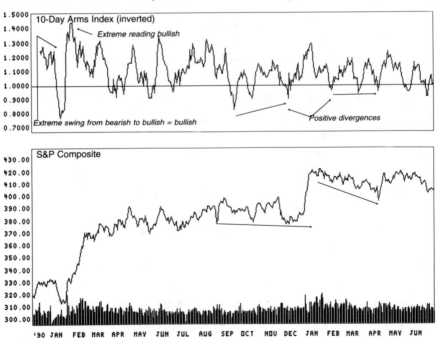

Chart 12.20   S & P Composite Versus a 30-Day Arms Index (Inverted)

declining ones. Ideally, you want to see a healthy amount of volume moving into rising issues relative to the volume associated with declining stocks. If this is not the case the indicator will diverge negatively with the market average, and vice versa.

This momentum series can be calculated for any period. For example, the quote services and the number appearing on the CNBC ticker represent an instant in time and are based on the volume and number of issues experiencing an uptick or a downtick. Unless you are fortunate enough to be able to chart this indicator on a continuous basis through a "real time service," isolated quotes of this nature are limited to gauging whether the market is *intraday* overbought or oversold. In this respect 120 or higher is regarded as oversold and 50 or below, overbought. (Remember that these numbers are inverse to the numbers in the other momentum indicators we have discussed.)

The Arms Index can also be used with a moving average where the 10-day (open TRIN) time span is the most widely followed. It is interpreted in much the same way as the 10-day A/D ratio discussed earlier in this chapter. Most of the time these two series move in a consistent manner, but from time to time the Arms Index gives some subtle indications that the prevailing trend is about to reverse.

In an October 1991 article in *Stocks and Commodities* Jack Rusin asserted that the open TRIN is better calculated by using a moving average of its components than by using a moving average of the daily ratio. His rationale is a somewhat complex one based on statistical theory, but there can be no denying that "day-weighted" open TRIN, as he calls it, gives more timely signals than the "issue-volume weighted" series. The two are compared in charts 12.21 and 12.22, both of which are reproduced from the article. When either series moves above 1, more volume is said to be moving into declining issues, and vice versa. Note, though, that in the period under scrutiny the issue-volume series offers more timely buy signals than crossovers below the 1 level as indicated by the arrows.

Chart 12.21   S & P Composite and a 21-Day
Moving Average Arms Index

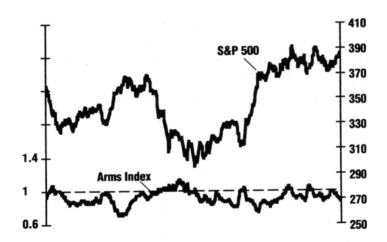

Readings above 1 indicate that more volume is occuring in declining stocks, while readings below 1 indicate the advancing stocks are receiving more volume. The above chart uses a 21-day moving average of the daily Arms Index. This smoothing of the daily Arms Index can produce late buy signals. Jack Rusin, "An Issue/Volume Weighted Long-Term Arms Index," *Technical Analysis of Stocks & Commodities*, Oct. 1991.

Chart 12.22   S & P Composite and a 21-Day
Issue/Volume-Weighted Arms Index

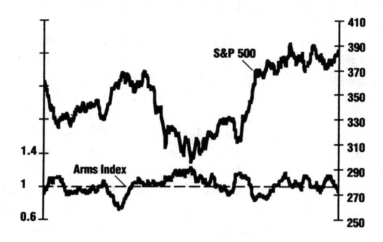

Using 21-day averages of each of the components of the Arms Index to form
a 21-day average issue/volume weighted index will indicate if advancing stocks
or declining stocks are receiving the most volume.

Summary

1. There are a wide variety of momentum indicators that are
   available for analyzing individual stock markets. In addition to
   the regular indicators based on price and aggregate volume,
   others can be constructed from volume and breadth data.
2. The same principles of interpretation outlined in chapters 2
   and 3 apply to these market indicators.

RESOURCES

Books

Appel, G.: *Winning Stock Market Systems*, Signalert Corp., Great Neck, N.Y., 1974.

Bernstein, J.: *The Handbook of Commodity Cycles: A Window on Time*, John Wiley and Sons, Inc., New York, 1982.

Bressert, Walter: *The Power of Oscillator/Cycle Combinations*, Bressert and Associates, Tucson, 1991.

Colby, Robert W., and Thomas A. Meyers: *The Encyclopedia of Technical Market Indicators*, Dow Jones-Irwin, Homewood, Il., 1988.

Dewey, E. R.: *Cycles: The Mysterious Forces That Trigger Events*, Hawthorne Books, New York, 1971.

__ and E. F. Dakin: *Cycles: The Science of Prediction*, Henry Holt, New York, 1947.

Elder, Alexander: *Trading For A Living*, John Wiley and Sons, Inc., New York, 1993.

Granville, J.: *Strategy of Daily Stock Market Timing*, Prentice-Hall, Englewood Cliffs, N.J., 1960.

Hurst, J. M.: *The Profit Magic of Stock Transaction Timing*, Prentice-Hall, Englewood Cliffs, N.J., 1970.

Kaufmann, Perry: *New Commodity Trading Systems*, John Wiley and Sons, Inc., New York, 1987.

Murphy, John J.: *Intermarket Technical Analysis*, John Wiley and Sons, Inc., New York, 1991.

___: *Technical Analysis of the Futures Market*, New York Institute of Finance, New York, 1986.

Pring, Martin J.: *Technical Analysis Explained*, 3rd ed., McGraw-Hill, New York, 1991.

Wilder, J. Welles: *New Concepts in Technical Trading*, Trend Research, Greensboro, N.C., 1978.

Dealers in Financial Books

Edward Dobson
Traders Press, Inc.
P.O. Box 6206
Greenville, SC 29606
(803) 298-0222

Dr. Alexander Elder
Financial Trading Seminars
74-09 37th Avenue, Room 422
Jackson Heights, NY 11372
(718) 507-1033

James Fraser
Fraser Publishing
P.O. Box 494
Burlington, VT 05402
(802) 658-0322

Chris Myers
Expert Trading
5060 Symphony Woods Road, Suite 206
Columbia, MD 21044
(410) 964-0026

Charting Software

Computrac
1017 Pleasant Street
New Orleans, LA 70115
1-800-535-7990
(504) 895-1474

Downloader (data collection program)
MetaStock (technical analysis software)
The Technician (stock market analysis software)

The above three programs are available from:

International Institute for Economic Research
P.O. Box 624
Gloucester, VA 23061-0624
1-800-221-7514
(804) 694-0415
(804) 694-0028 (fax)

Audio and Video Courses

Financial Trading Seminars
74-09 37th Avenue, Room 422
Jackson Heights, NY 11372
1-800-458-0939
(718) 507-1033

Featuring Dr. Alexander Elder:

1. MACD and MACD-Histogram
2. Relative Strength Index
3. Stochastics
4. Triple-Screen Trading System

Featuring Gerald Appel: Day-Trading

International Institute for Economic Research
P.O. Box 624
Gloucester, VA 23061-0624
1-800-221-7514
(804) 694-0415
(804) 694-0028 (fax)

Featuring Martin J. Pring:

1. Video Course on Technical Analysis (5-tape course)
   Lesson I   The Basic Principles of Technical Analysis
   Lesson II Price Patterns
   Lesson III Support, Resistance, Trendlines, and
              Moving Averages
   Lesson IV Momentum, Relative Strength, and Volume
   Lesson V   Mechanical Trading Systems and Correct
              Investment Attitudes
2. Video Course on Momentum
   1) Basic Principles
   2) Individual Indicators I (ROC, RSI Stochastics)
   3) Individual Indicators II (MACD, Directional Movement,
      Demand Index, Direct Payoff)
3. KST Audio Tape and Explanatory Booklet

Data Vendors

Commodity Systems, Inc.
200 West Palmetto Park Road
Boca Raton, FL 33432-3788
(407) 392-8663

CompuServe
1-800-848-8199
(614) 457-8650

Dow Jones News/Retrieval
P.O. Box 300
Princeton, NJ 08543-0300
(609) 452-1511

Magazines

Technical Analysis of Stocks & Commodities
3517 S.W. Alaska Street
P.O. Box 46518
Seattle, WA 98146-0518
(206) 938-0570

INDEX

Why Fight the Trend?

Let the Pring Market Review's long-term perspective work for you!

The **Pring Market Review** is a 48-page monthly overview of the long-term technical position of the world's financial markets, offering primary emphasis on the U.S. The **Pring Market Review** includes unique global indicators, U.S. stocks, bonds, commodity indexes, currencies and precious metals. The **Pring Market Review** integrates all of this into a complete picture for more informed trading and investment decisions.

1. KST Market Cycle Model

The KST is an original momentum indicator designed to identify turning points in the markets and securities. In each edition, Martin's three KST's (short-, intermediate-, and long-term time frames) are arranged all in one chart for each of the world's principle markets giving you a bird's eye view of the maturity of the prevailing trends and the latest market turning points!

2. Asset Allocation

The 4-year business cycle has recurred consistently in the U.S. economy in the last 200 years. The Pring Market Review recognizes that different phases of the business cycle are suited to different portfolio mixes of stocks, bonds, cash and inflation hedge assets. With the aid the its proprietary models, which recognize positive and negative environments for these assets, the **Pring Market Review** is able to categorize the six stages that virtually every business cycle undergoes recommending an appropriate asset mix for each stage.

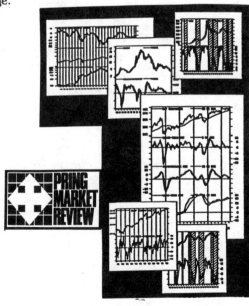

The All-Season Investor: Investment Strategies
For Every Stage in the Business Cycle
John Wiley & Sons, Inc.
hardcover, 352 pages
$29.95

   Each business cycle progresses through six different stages in a similar manner to the four seasons of the calendar year. Each one favoring a different asset class. **The All-Season Investor** describes these stages, why they repeat and how they can be recognized.
   Based on research covering over forty years of data, **The All-Season Investor** recommends which assets (bonds, stocks, cash, or inflation hedge) should be emphasized as the cycle unfolds.
   Chapters describing the available investment vehicles and their characteristics, risk management, the power of compounding and diversification round out this useful down-to-earth practicum.

Investment Psychology Explained
John Wiley & Sons, Inc.
hardcover, 273 pages
$24.95

   Investment Psychology Explained puts the emphasis back on the basics of sound investment philosophy.
   It's full of the wisdom from history's most respected investment minds and Martin's own vast experience. **Investment Psychology Explained** shows you when to "go contrarian" or not, how to follow objective analysis rather than your emotions and how to deal more effectively with your broker and money manager.
   Learn to use and understand the classic trading rules that have been proven effective over time, and how to create an investment plan and stick to it, avoiding fads and quick-fix "experts".
   The appendix lists the rules followed by nine of the greatest market practitioners - from Bernard Baruch to W.D. Gann. This wisdom alone is worth the price!

Technical Analysis Explained 3rd Edition
Mc-Graw-Hill
hardcover, 521 pages
$49.95

   Since the first edition of this unique book on technical analysis appeared in 1979, it has established itself as the number one guide of its kind. While it is describes many original concepts that will be of interest to professionals, its clear, concise style makes it suitable for the serious investor wishing to learn about technical analysis for the first time. It has also been recommended by the Market Technicians Association for their professional (CMT) certification.
   Technical Analysis Explained covers in detail such topics as Dow Theory, price patterns, , moving averages, momentum cycles, sentiment, speculation, interest rates, the stock market, breadth, volume and technical analysis of international stock markets.
   The third edition also includes a chapter covering candlestick charting, automated trading systems, and includes descriptions of popular oscillators such as the RSI, stochastics, and Martin's own KST system.

ORDER FORM

BOOKS

Technical Analysis Explained	$49.95
The All Season Investor	$29.95
Investment Psychology Explained	$24.95

Pring Market Review
    Introductory Rates: 3 Months $ 45.00
                        6 Months $210.00
                        1 Year $295.00
    Includes Free KST Audio Course

Book of Your Choice_____

Metastock Software	$349.00
Special Shipping & Handling:	10.00
Total:	$359.00

VIDEOS

Market Momentum – Set	$245.00
Tape I –	$ 95.00
Tape II –	$ 95.00
Tape III –	$ 95.00

Technical Analysis - 5 Tape Course
w/Technical Analysis Explained	$395.00
w/o the Book	$375.00
Tape I	$ 95.00
Tape II	$ 95.00
Tape III	$ 95.00
Tape IV	$115.00
Tape V	$95.00

How to Forecast Interest Rates	$ 95.00
Asset Allocation in the Business Cycle	$ 95.00

QTY.	PRODUCT	DISK SIZE	PRICE
_____	_____	_____	$_____
_____	_____		$_____
_____	_____		$_____
_____	_____		$_____
_____	_____		$_____
_____	_____		$_____
		MERCHANDISE TOTAL	_____
		CT. SALES TAX 6%	_____
		SHIPPING & HANDLING	_____
		TOTAL COST	$ _____

Overseas Shipping & Handling Rates
$ 8.00	per book
$12.00	for 1 tape
$15.00	for 2 tapes
$18.00	for 3-10 tapes
$25.00	Int'l Pring Market Review Subscriptions - 1 year
$12.50	Int'l Pring Market Review Subscriptions - 6 months
$ 7.00	Int'l Pring Market Review Subscriptions - 3 months

MAIL ORDERS TO:
THE INTERNATIONAL INSTITUTE
FOR
ECONOMIC RESEARCH, INC.
P.O. BOX 624
GLOUCESTER, VA 23061-0624

ORDER FORM

CALL TODAY
1-800-221-7514
or 804-694-0415; FAX 804-694-0028

BOOKS

Technical Analysis Explained	$49.95
The All Season Investor	$29.95
Investment Psychology Explained	$24.95

Pring Market Review
  Introductory Rates: 3 Months $ 45.00
                        6 Months $210.00
                        1 Year $295.00
  Includes Free KST Audio Course

Book of Your Choice_____

Metastock Software	$349.00
Special Shipping & Handling:	10.00
Total:	$359.00

VIDEOS

Market Momentum	- Set	$245.00
Tape I	-	$ 95.00
Tape II	-	$ 95.00
Tape III	-	$ 95.00

Technical Analysis - 5 Tape Course	
w/Technical Analysis Explained	$395.00
w/o the Book	$375.00
Tape I	$ 95.00
Tape II	$ 95.00
Tape III	$ 95.00
Tape IV	$115.00
Tape V	$95.00

How to Forecast Interest Rates	$ 95.00
Asset Allocation in the Business Cycle	$ 95.00

QTY.	PRODUCT	DISK SIZE	PRICE
_____	_____		$_____
_____	_____		$_____
_____	_____		$_____
_____	_____		$_____
_____	_____		$_____
_____	_____		$_____
		MERCHANDISE TOTAL	_____
		CT. SALES TAX 6%	_____
		SHIPPING & HANDLING	_____
		TOTAL COST	$ _____

Overseas Shipping & Handling Rates

$ 8.00	per book
$12.00	for 1 tape
$15.00	for 2 tapes
$18.00	for 3-10 tapes
$25.00	Int'l Pring Market Review Subscriptions - 1 year
$12.50	Int'l Pring Market Review Subscriptions - 6 months
$ 7.00	Int'l Pring Market Review Subscriptions - 3 months

MAIL ORDERS TO:
THE INTERNATIONAL INSTITUTE
FOR
ECONOMIC RESEARCH, INC.
P.O. BOX 624
GLOUCESTER, VA 23061-0624